GEORGIA LEGISLA

MW00892303

GEORGIA CODE

TITLE 9

CIVIL PRACTICE

2024 EDITION

Table of Contents

Chapter 1 - [RESERVED]

Section 9-1-1 et seq - [Reserved]

Chapter 2 - ACTIONS GENERALLY

Article 1 - GENERAL PROVISIONS

Section 9-2-1 - Definitions

As used in this title, the term:

(1) "Action" means the judicial means of enforcing a right.

(2) "Civil action" means an action founded on private rights, arising either from contract or tort.

(3) "Penal action" means an action allowed in pursuance of public justice under particular laws.

Section 9-2-2 - Actions in personam; actions in rem

(a) An action may be against the person, or against property, or both.

(b) Generally, a proceeding against the person shall bind the property also. A proceeding against property without service on the person shall bind only the particular property.

Section 9-2-3 - Remedy for every right

For every right there shall be a remedy; every court having jurisdiction of the one may, if necessary, frame the other.

Section 9-2-4 - Pursuit of consistent or inconsistent remedies

A plaintiff may pursue any number of consistent or inconsistent remedies against the same person or different persons until he shall obtain a satisfaction from some of them.

Section 9-2-5 - Prosecution of two simultaneous actions for same cause against same party prohibited; election; pendency of former action as defense; exception

(a) No plaintiff may prosecute two actions in the courts at the same time for the same cause of action and against the same party. If two such actions are commenced simultaneously, the defendant may require the plaintiff to elect which he will prosecute. If two such actions are commenced at different times, the pendency of the former shall be a good defense to the latter.

(b) The rule requiring a plaintiff to elect shall not apply to a prior attachment against property where the defendant is subsequently served personally nor to an attachment obtained during the pendency of an action. However, the judgment in the case against the person shall set out the fact of its identity with the proceedings against the property.

Section 9-2-6 - Demand prior to action not necessary

No demand shall be necessary before the commencement of an action, except in such cases as the law or the contract prescribes.

Section 9-2-7 - Implied promise to pay for services or property

Ordinarily, when one renders service or transfers property which is valuable to another, which the latter accepts, a promise is implied to pay the reasonable value thereof. However, this presumption does not usually arise in cases between very near relatives.

Section 9-2-8 - Private rights of action not created unless expressly stated

(a) No private right of action shall arise from any Act enacted after July 1, 2010, unless such right is expressly provided therein.

(b) Nothing in subsection (a) of this Code section shall be construed to prevent the breach of any duty imposed by law from being used as the basis for a cause of action under any theory of recovery otherwise recognized by law, including, but not limited to, theories of recovery under the law of torts or contract or for breach of legal or private duties as set forth in Code Sections 51-1-6 and 51-1-8 or in Title 13.

Added by 2010 Ga. Laws 543, § 2, eff. 7/1/2010.

Article 2 - PARTIES

Section 9-2-20 - Parties to actions on contracts; action by beneficiary

(a) As a general rule, an action on a contract, whether the contract is expressed, implied, by parol, under seal, or of record, shall be brought in the name of the party in whom the legal interest in the contract is vested, and against the party who made it in person or by agent.

(b) The beneficiary of a contract made between other parties for his benefit may maintain an action against the promisor on the contract.

Section 9-2-21 - Parties to actions for torts; notice to Department of Community Health for a party who has received medical assistance benefits

(a) An action for a tort shall, in general, be brought in the name of the person whose legal right has been affected. In the case of an injury to property, a tort action shall be brought in the name of the person who was legally interested in the property at the time the injury thereto was committed or in the name of his assignee.

(b) An action for a tort shall be brought against the party committing the injury, either by himself, his servant, or an agent in his employ.

(c) If the person whose legal right has been affected has received medical assistance benefits pursuant to Chapter 4 of Title 49, prior to initiating recovery action, the representative or attorney who has actual knowledge of the receipt of said benefits shall notify the Department of Community Health of the claim. Mailing and deposit in a United States post office or public mail box of said notice addressed to the Department of Community Health with adequate postage affixed is adequate legal notice of the claim. Notice as provided in this subsection shall not be a condition precedent to the filing of any action for tort. Initiating recovery action shall include any communication with a party who may be liable or someone financially responsible for that liability with regard to recovery of a claim including but not limited to the filing of an action in court.

Section 9-2-22 - Joinder of defendants in action for deficiencies in construction

In any action arising out of alleged deficiencies in the construction of improvements on real property, the party plaintiff may join in one action, as parties defendants, all parties who allegedly contributed in the construction of the improvements as well as all bonding companies who bonded the performance of the parties defendant.

Section 9-2-23 - Separate action by tenant in common

A tenant in common may bring an action separately for his own interest, and the judgment in such case shall affect only himself.

Section 9-2-24 - Action by unincorporated association

An action may be maintained by and in the name of any unincorporated organization or association.

Section 9-2-25 - Action against unincorporated association; service of process; venue; what property bound by judgment

(a) Actions may be maintained against and in the name of any unincorporated organization or association for any cause of action for or upon which the plaintiff therein may maintain such an action against the members of the organization or association.

(b) Service of process in the action against the organization or association shall be had by service upon any officer or official member of such organization or association, or upon any officer or official member of any branch or local of the organization or association, provided that any such organization or association may file with the Secretary of State a designated officer or agent upon whom service shall be had and his residence address within the state. If the designation is made and filed, service of process shall be had only on the officer or agent designated, if he can be found within the state.

(c) The organization or association shall be suable in any cause of action. The action may be maintained in any county where the organization or association does business or has in existence a branch or local organization.

(d) Where a judgment in such actions is rendered in favor of the plaintiff against the organizations or associations, the property of the organization or association shall be liable to the satisfaction of the judgment. No such judgment shall be enforced against the individual property of any member of an unincorporated association, unless the member has personally participated in the transaction for which the action was instituted and has been served with process as provided by law.

Section 9-2-26 - Prosecution of action against less than all joint contractors or copartners

When two or more joint contractors, joint and several contractors, or copartners are defendants in the same action and service is perfected on one or more of the contractors or copartners and the officer serving the writ or process returns that the rest are not to be found, the plaintiff may proceed to judgment and execution against the defendants served with process in the same manner as if they were the sole defendants. If any of the defendants die pending the action, his representative may be made a party and the case may proceed to judgment and execution as in other cases against the representatives of deceased persons.

Section 9-2-27 - Action against representative of joint obligor

Where any person is in possession, in his own right or in any other capacity, of any note, bill, bond, or other obligation in writing, signed by two or more persons, and one or more of the persons whose names are so signed dies before the payment of the money or the compliance with the conditions of such bond or obligation in writing, the person holding the bill, bond, note, or other obligation in writing shall not be compelled to bring an action against the survivors alone, but may at his discretion bring an action against (1) the survivor or survivors, (2) the representative or representatives of the deceased person or persons, or (3) the survivor or survivors and the representative or representatives of the deceased person or persons in the same action. However, nothing contained in this Code section shall authorize the bringing of an action against the representative of any estate until six months after the probate of the will or the granting of letters of administration on the estate or estates. This Code section shall be so construed as to embrace debts against copartners as well as debts against joint or joint and several contractors.

Section 9-2-28 - Effect of action by minor alone

An action commenced and prosecuted by an infant alone shall not be void. Although the action may be defective in wanting a guardian or next friend, the defect shall be amendable before verdict and cured by verdict.

Section 9-2-29 - Plaintiff in penal action

If no special officer is authorized to be the plaintiff in a penal action, the state, the Governor, the Attorney General, or a prosecuting attorney may be the plaintiff.

Section 9-2-30 - Substitution of plaintiff's spouse or others in action on chose in action assigned as year's support

When a party plaintiff dies during litigation concerning any chose in action and the chose in action is assigned to the surviving spouse, the surviving spouse and children, or the children only of the decedent as any part of a year's support, the surviving spouse personally or for the use of the surviving spouse and the children, or, in the event of children only, a next friend for the children may be made a party plaintiff upon the same terms and in the same manner that administrators are made parties plaintiff to actions in favor of their intestate, upon the submission by the person to the court of a certified copy of the assignment; and the action shall proceed in the name of the parties so made.

Article 3 - ABATEMENT

Section 9-2-40 - No abatement on death of party where cause survives

No action shall abate by the death of either party, where the cause of action shall in any case survive to or against the legal representatives of the deceased party, either in the same or any other form of action.

Section 9-2-41 - Nonabatement of tort actions; survival of cause; no punitive damages against representative

No action for a tort shall abate by the death of either party, where the wrongdoer received any benefit from the tort complained of; nor shall any action or cause of action for the recovery of damages for homicide, injury to the person, or injury to property abate by the death of either party. The cause of action, in case of the death of the plaintiff and in the event there is no right of survivorship in any other person, shall survive to the personal representative of the deceased plaintiff. In case of the death of the defendant, the cause of action shall survive against said defendant's personal representative. However, in the event of the death of the wrongdoer before an action has been brought against him, the personal representative of the wrongdoer in such capacity shall be subject to the action just as the wrongdoer himself would have been during his life, provided that there shall be no punitive damages against the personal representative.

Section 9-2-42 - Death of one or more codefendants; suggestion of record

In all actions against two or more defendants, one or more of whom have died or may die pending the action, the plaintiff may suggest the death of record and proceed against the surviving defendants to the extent of their respective liabilities.

Section 9-2-43 - No abatement where some defendants not liable

An action against several persons shall not abate where it appears that some of the defendants are not liable but may proceed against those who are liable.

Section 9-2-44 - Effect of former recovery; pendency of former action

(a) A former recovery or the pendency of a former action for the same cause of action between the same parties in the same or any other court having jurisdiction shall be a good cause of abatement. However, if the first action is so defective that no recovery can possibly be had, the pendency of a former action shall not abate the latter.

(b) Parol evidence shall be admissible to show that a matter apparently covered by the judgment was not passed upon by the court.

Section 9-2-45 - No abatement for pendency of action in another state

The pendency of a prior action in another state shall not abate an action between the same parties for the same cause in this state.

Section 9-2-46 - Institution of action on same cause in other state; setting case in this state; postponement limited

(a) Whenever it is made to appear to the judge of any court that any party to a case pending in the court, after the case has been commenced, has instituted proceedings in any court of any other state involving the same controversy or cause of action, or in which the judgment which might be rendered in the other state might be pleadable in the case in this state as affecting the relief sought, it shall be the duty of the judge of the court in which the case is pending to set the case specially and ahead of all other business for trial as the first case at the next ensuing term of the court, except for other cases having precedence for the same reason.

(b) No case so assigned for trial shall be continued or postponed for more than 30 days for any cause whatsoever at the instance of the party who has instituted the case or proceedings in the foreign state. The case may be postponed from day to day for good cause for not exceeding 30 days at the instance of such party, but after being postponed for the 30 days it shall not be further postponed at his instance. If the term of court ends within the 30 days and the case has not been continued for the term, it shall stand for trial as the first case at the next ensuing term. This Code section shall not be applied so as to set any case for trial before proper times have elapsed for notice, the filing of defensive pleadings, and discovery. Proper time limits for discovery shall be in the discretion of the judge.

Section 9-2-47 - Precedence of first filed informer's action; abatement of others

In the case of actions by informers to recover any fine, forfeiture, or penalty, the first filed in the clerk's office shall have precedence for the same cause of action and the latter filed actions shall abate.

Article 4 - DISMISSAL AND RENEWAL

Section 9-2-60 - Dismissal for want of prosecution; costs; recommencement within six months

(a) For the purposes of this Code section, an order of continuance will be deemed an order and the word "proceedings" shall be held to include, but shall not be limited to, an appeal from an award of assessors or a special master in a condemnation proceeding.

(b) Any action or other proceeding filed in any of the courts of this state in which no written order is taken for a period of five years shall automatically stand dismissed with costs to be taxed against the party plaintiff.

(c) When an action is dismissed under this Code section, if the plaintiff recommences the action within six months following the dismissal then the renewed action shall stand upon the same footing, as to limitation, with the original action.

Section 9-2-61 - Renewal of case after dismissal

(a) When any case has been commenced in either a state or federal court within the applicable statute of limitations and the plaintiff discontinues or dismisses the same, it may be recommenced in a court of this state or in a federal court either within the original applicable period of limitations or within six months after the discontinuance or dismissal, whichever is later, subject to the requirement of payment of costs in the original action as required by subsection (d) of Code Section 9-11-41; provided, however, if the dismissal or discontinuance occurs after the expiration of the applicable period of limitation, this privilege of renewal shall be exercised only once.

(b) This Code section shall not apply to contracts for the sale of goods covered by Article 2 of Title 11.

(c) The provisions of subsection (a) of this Code section granting a privilege of renewal shall apply if an action is discontinued or dismissed without prejudice for lack of subject matter jurisdiction in either a court of this state or a federal court in this state.

Section 9-2-62 - Retraxit and dismissal or discontinuance distinguished

A retraxit differs from a dismissal or discontinuance in that a retraxit is the open, public, and voluntary renunciation by the plaintiff in open court of his action or cause of action. It is positive and conclusive of the plaintiff's right of action. Where a retraxit is entered by the plaintiff and a judgment is entered thereon by the defendant, the plaintiff's right of action shall be forever gone. A dismissal or discontinuance is negative, and the plaintiff may recommence his action on the payment of costs.

Section 9-2-63 - Affidavit of indigence for renewal of action

When any action is dismissed or discontinued and the plaintiff desires to recommence his action, if he will make and file with his complaint, summons, or other proceedings an affidavit in writing stating that he is advised and believes that he has good cause for recommencing his action and that because of his indigence he is unable to pay the costs that have accrued in the case, he shall have the right to renew the action without payment of the cost as aforesaid.

Chapter 3 - LIMITATIONS OF ACTIONS
Article 1 - GENERAL PROVISIONS

Section 9-3-1 - Limitations against the state

Except as otherwise provided by law, the state shall be barred from bringing an action if, under the same circumstances, a private person would be barred.

Section 9-3-2 - Limitations against municipalities

Any claim or demand held by any municipality not in the nature of a special contract or not reduced to execution shall be barred by the general statutes of limitation of force, and all executions issued by any municipality shall be subject to the same laws relating to the statutes of limitation governing other executions.

Section 9-3-3 - Applicability of limitation statutes; equitable bar

Unless otherwise provided by law, limitation statutes shall apply equally to all courts. In addition, courts of equity may interpose an equitable bar whenever, from the lapse of time and laches of the complainant, it would be inequitable to allow a party to enforce his legal rights.

Section 9-3-4 - [Repealed] Limitations as to trusts

Reserved. Repealed by Ga. L. 1991, p. 810, § 3, effective July 1, 1991.

Section 9-3-5 - Beneficiaries barred along with trustee

Where a trustee is barred, the beneficiaries of the estate represented by him shall also be barred.

Section 9-3-6 - Applicability of limitations to setoffs

The statute of limitations applies to the subject matter of setoff as well as to the plaintiff's demand.

Section 9-3-7 - When mutual accounts postpone running of limitations

The statute of limitations for a mutual account begins to run on the date of the last item thereof. A mutual account must include an indebtedness on both sides. Mere entries of credits of partial payments shall not be sufficient.

Article 2 - SPECIFIC PERIODS OF LIMITATION

Section 9-3-20 - Actions on foreign judgments

All actions upon judgments obtained outside this state, except judgments for child support or spousal support, or both, shall be brought within five years after such judgments have been obtained.

Section 9-3-21 - [Repealed] Proceedings to set aside judgments

Reserved. Repealed by Ga. L. 1986, p. 294, § 2, effective July 1, 1986.

Section 9-3-22 - Enforcement of rights under statutes, acts of incorporation; recovery of wages, overtime, and damages

All actions for the enforcement of rights accruing to individuals under statutes or acts of incorporation or by operation of law shall be brought within 20 years after the right of action has accrued; provided, however, that all actions for the recovery of wages, overtime, or damages and penalties accruing under laws respecting the payment of wages and overtime shall be brought within two years after the right of action has accrued.

Section 9-3-23 - Sealed instruments

Actions upon bonds or other instruments under seal shall be brought within 20 years after the right of action has accrued. No instrument shall be considered under seal unless so recited in the body of the instrument.

Section 9-3-24 - Actions on simple written contracts; exceptions

All actions upon simple contracts in writing shall be brought within six years after the same become due and payable. However, this Code section shall not apply to actions for the breach of contracts for the sale of goods under Article 2 of Title 11 or to negotiable instruments under Article 3 of Title 11.

Section 9-3-25 - Open accounts; breach of certain contracts; implied promise; exception

All actions upon open account, or for the breach of any contract not under the hand of the party sought to be charged, or upon any implied promise or undertaking shall be brought within four years after the right of action accrues. However, this Code section shall not apply to actions for the breach of contracts for the sale of goods under Article 2 of Title 11.

Section 9-3-26 - Other actions on contracts; exception

All other actions upon contracts express or implied not otherwise provided for shall be brought within four years from the accrual of the right of action. However, this Code section shall not apply to actions for the breach of contracts for the sale of goods under Article 2 of Title 11.

Section 9-3-27 - Actions against fiduciaries

All actions against executors, administrators, or guardians, except on their bonds, shall be brought within ten years after the right of action accrues.

Section 9-3-28 - Actions by informers

All actions by informers to recover any fine, forfeiture, or penalty shall be commenced within one year from the time the defendant's liability thereto is discovered or by reasonable diligence could have been discovered.

Section 9-3-29 - Breach of restrictive covenant

(a) All actions for breach of any covenant restricting lands to certain uses shall be brought within two years after the right of action accrues, excepting violations for failure to pay assessments or fees, which shall be governed by subsection (b) of this Code section. This Code section shall apply to rights of action which may accrue as a result of the violation of a building set-back line.

(b) In actions for breach of covenant which accrue as a result of the failure to pay assessments or fees, the action shall be brought within four years after the right of action accrues.

(c) For the purpose of this Code section, the right of action shall accrue immediately upon the erection of a permanent fixture which results in a violation of the covenant restricting lands to certain uses or the violation of a set-back line provision. When an alleged violation or complaint is based upon a continuous violation of the covenant resulting from an act or omission, the right of action shall accrue each time such act or omission occurs. This Code section shall not be construed so as to extend any applicable statute of limitations affecting actions in equity.

Amended by 2017 Ga. Laws 173,§ 1, eff. 7/1/2017.

Section 9-3-30 - Trespass or damage to realty

(a) All actions for trespass upon or damage to realty shall be brought within four years after the right of action accrues.

(b)

(1) The causes of action specified in Code Section 51-1-11 and subsection (a) of Code Section 9-3-51 for recovery of damages to a dwelling due to the manufacture of or the negligent design or installation of synthetic exterior siding shall accrue when the damage to the dwelling is discovered or, in the exercise of reasonable diligence, should have been discovered, whichever first occurs. In any event, such cause of action shall be brought within the time limits provided in Code Sections 51-1-11 and 9-3-51, respectively.

(2) This subsection shall apply to causes of action which had not expired under the former law before March 28, 2000. This subsection shall not revive any cause of action which was barred by former law before March 28, 2000.

Section 9-3-30.1 - Actions against manufacturers or suppliers of asbestos or material containing asbestos

(a) Notwithstanding the provisions of Code Section 9-3-30 or any other law, every action against a manufacturer or supplier of asbestos or material containing asbestos brought by or on behalf of any person or entity, public or private; or brought by or on behalf of this state or any agency, department, political subdivision, authority, board, district, or commission of the state; or brought by or on behalf of any municipality, county, or any state or local school board or local school district to recover for:

(1) Removal of asbestos or materials containing asbestos from any building owned or used by such entity;

(2) Other measures taken to correct or ameliorate any problem related to asbestos in such building;

(3) Reimbursement for such removal, correction, or amelioration related to asbestos in such building; or

(4) Any other claim for damage to real property allowed by law relating to asbestos in such building which might otherwise be barred prior to July 1, 1990, as a result of expiration of the applicable period of limitation, is revived or extended. Any action thereon shall be commenced no later than July 1, 1990.

(b) The enactment of this Code section shall not be construed to imply that any action against a manufacturer or supplier of asbestos or material containing asbestos is now barred by an existing limitations period.

(c) Nothing in this Code section shall be construed to revive, extend, change, or otherwise affect the applicable period of limitation for persons or entities not set forth and provided for in subsection (a) of this Code section.

(d) Nothing contained in this Code section shall be construed to have any effect on actions for personal injury or any other claim except as specifically provided in this Code section.

Section 9-3-30.2 - Actions against persons engaged in land surveying

(a) As used in this Code section, the term "land surveying" shall have the same meaning as provided by paragraph (6) of Code Section 43-15-2.

(b) No action to recover damages for any deficiency, defect, omission, error, or miscalculation in a survey or plat shall be brought against registered surveyors or their employees engaged in the practice of land surveying who performed or furnished such survey or plat more than six years from the date of the survey or plat. The cause of action in such cases shall accrue when such services are rendered as shown from the date on the survey or plat. Any such action not instituted within the six-year period provided by this subsection shall be forever barred.

Section 9-3-31 - Injuries to personalty

Actions for injuries to personalty shall be brought within four years after the right of action accrues.

Section 9-3-32 - Accrual of actions for recovery of personal property or loss of timber; damages for conversion or destruction

Actions for the recovery of personal property, or for damages for the conversion or destruction of the same, shall be brought within four years after the right of action accrues, and actions involving the unauthorized cutting or cutting and carrying away of timber from the property of another shall be brought within four years after the cutting or cutting and carrying away of timber.

Amended by 2014 Ga. Laws 619,§ 1, eff. 7/1/2014.

Section 9-3-33 - Injuries to the person; injuries to reputation; loss of consortium; exception

Except as otherwise provided in this article, actions for injuries to the person shall be brought within two years after the right of action accrues, except for injuries to the reputation, which shall be brought within one year after the right of action accrues, and except for actions for injuries to the person involving loss of consortium, which shall be brought within four years after the right of action accrues.

Amended by 2015 Ga. Laws 95,§ 2-1, eff. 7/1/2015.

Section 9-3-33.1 - Actions for childhood sexual abuse

(a)

(1) As used in this subsection, the term "childhood sexual abuse" means any act committed by the defendant against the plaintiff which occurred when the plaintiff was under 18 years of age and which would be in violation of:

(A) Rape, as prohibited in Code Section 16-6-1;

(B) Sodomy or aggravated sodomy, as prohibited in Code Section 16-6-2;

(C) Statutory rape, as prohibited in Code Section 16-6-3;

(D) Child molestation or aggravated child molestation, as prohibited in Code Section 16-6-4;

(E) Enticing a child for indecent purposes, as prohibited in Code Section 16-6-5;

(F) Pandering, as prohibited in Code Section 16-6-12;

(G) Reserved;

(H) Solicitation of sodomy, as prohibited in Code Section 16-6-15;

(I) Incest, as prohibited in Code Section 16-6-22;

(J) Sexual battery, as prohibited in Code Section 16-6-22.1; or

(K) Aggravated sexual battery, as prohibited in Code Section 16-6-22.2.

(2) Notwithstanding Code Section 9-3-33 and except as provided in subsection (d) of this Code section as it existed on June 30, 2017, any civil action for recovery of damages suffered as a result of childhood sexual abuse committed before July 1, 2015, shall be commenced on or before the date the plaintiff attains the age of 23 years.

(b)

(1) As used in this subsection, the term "childhood sexual abuse" means any act committed by the defendant against the plaintiff which occurred when the plaintiff was under 18 years of age and which would be in violation of:

(A) Trafficking a person for sexual servitude, as prohibited in Code Section 16-5-46;

(B) Rape, as prohibited in Code Section 16-6-1;

(C) Statutory rape, as prohibited in Code Section 16-6-3, if the defendant was 21 years of age or older at the time of the act;

(D) Aggravated sodomy, as prohibited in Code Section 16-6-2;

(E) Child molestation or aggravated child molestation, as prohibited in Code Section 16-6-4, unless the violation would be subject to punishment as provided in paragraph (2) of subsection (b) of Code Section 16-6-4 or paragraph (2) of subsection (d) of Code Section 16-6-4;

(F) Enticing a child for indecent purposes, as prohibited in Code Section 16-6-5, unless the violation would be subject to punishment as provided in subsection (c) of Code Section 16-6-5;

(G) Incest, as prohibited in Code Section 16-6-22;

(H) Aggravated sexual battery, as prohibited in Code Section 16-6-22.2; or

(I) Part 2 of Article 3 of Chapter 12 of Title 16.

(2)

(A) Notwithstanding Code Section 9-3-33, any civil action for recovery of damages suffered as a result of childhood sexual abuse committed on or after July 1, 2015, shall be commenced:

(i) On or before the date the plaintiff attains the age of 23 years; or

(ii) Within two years from the date that the plaintiff knew or had reason to know of such abuse and that such abuse resulted in injury to the plaintiff as established by competent medical or psychological evidence.

(B) When a plaintiff's civil action is filed after the plaintiff attains the age of 23 years but within two years from the date that the plaintiff knew or had reason to know of such abuse and that such abuse resulted in injury to the plaintiff, the court shall determine from admissible evidence in a pretrial finding when the discovery of the alleged childhood sexual abuse occurred. The pretrial finding required under this subparagraph shall be made within six months of the filing of the civil action.

(c)

(1) As used in this subsection, the term:

(A) "Entity" means an institution, agency, firm, business, corporation, or other public or private legal entity.

(B) "Person" means the individual alleged to have committed the act of childhood sexual abuse.

(2) If a civil action for recovery of damages suffered as a result of childhood sexual abuse is commenced pursuant to division (b)(2)(A)(i) of this Code section and if the person was a volunteer or employee of an entity that owed a duty of care to the plaintiff, or the person and the plaintiff were engaged in some activity over which such entity had control, damages against such entity shall be awarded under this Code section only if by a preponderance of the evidence there is a finding of negligence on the part of such entity.

(3) If a civil action for recovery of damages suffered as a result of childhood sexual abuse is commenced pursuant to division (b)(2)(A)(ii) of this Code section and if the person was a volunteer or employee of an entity that owed a duty of care to the plaintiff, or the person and the plaintiff were engaged in some activity over which such entity had control, damages against such entity shall be awarded under this Code section only if by a preponderance of the evidence there is a finding that there was gross negligence on the part of such entity, that the entity knew or should have known of the alleged conduct giving rise to the civil action and such entity failed to take remedial action.

Amended by 2019 Ga. Laws 30,§ 2-1, eff. 7/1/2019.

Amended by 2018 Ga. Laws 562,§ 9, eff. 5/8/2018.

Amended by 2015 Ga. Laws 97,§ 2, eff. 7/1/2015.

Amended by 2015 Ga. Laws 95,§ 2-2, eff. 7/1/2015.

Section 9-3-34 - Article not applicable to malpractice

This article shall not apply to actions for medical malpractice as defined in Code Section 9-3-70.

Section 9-3-35 - Actions by creditor seeking relief under Uniform Voidable Transactions Act

An action by a creditor seeking relief under the provisions of Article 4 of Chapter 2 of Title 18, known as the "Uniform Voidable Transactions Act," shall be brought within the applicable period set out in Code Section 18-2-79.

Amended by 2015 Ga. Laws 167,§ 4B-1, eff. 7/1/2015.

Added by 2002 Ga. Laws 427, § 1, eff. 7/1/2002.

Section 9-3-36 - Limitations on claims arising before decedent's death

(a) In no event may claims against a decedent's estate that arose before the death of the decedent be brought more than six years after the date of the decedent's death.

(b) Subsection (a) of this Code section is intended to create a six-year statute of ultimate repose and abrogation.

(c) Nothing in this Code section shall be construed as placing a limitation on the time for commencing a proceeding to enforce any mortgage, pledge, or other lien upon property owned by a decedent immediately prior to the decedent's death.
Added by 2020 Ga. Laws 508,§ 2-3, eff. 1/1/2021.

Article 3 - LIMITATIONS ON RECOVERY FOR DEFICIENCIES CONNECTED WITH IMPROVEMENTS TO REALTY AND RESULTING INJURIES

Section 9-3-50 - Definitions

As used in this article, the term:

(1) "Person" means an individual, corporation, partnership, business trust, unincorporated organization, association, or joint-stock company.

(2) "Substantial completion" means the date when construction was sufficiently completed, in accordance with the contract as modified by any change order agreed to by the parties, so that the owner could occupy the project for the use for which it was intended.

Section 9-3-51 - Limitations on recovery for deficiency in planning, supervising, or constructing improvement to realty or for resulting injuries to property or person

(a) No action to recover damages:

(1) For any deficiency in the survey or plat, planning, design, specifications, supervision or observation of construction, or construction of an improvement to real property;

(2) For injury to property, real or personal, arising out of any such deficiency; or

(3) For injury to the person or for wrongful death arising out of any such deficiency shall be brought against any person performing or furnishing the survey or plat, design, planning, supervision or observation of construction, or construction of such an improvement more than eight years after substantial completion of such an improvement.

(b) Notwithstanding subsection (a) of this Code section, in the case of such an injury to property or the person or such an injury causing wrongful death, which injury occurred during the seventh or eighth year after such substantial completion, an action in tort to recover damages for such an injury or wrongful death may be brought within two years after the date on which such injury occurred, irrespective of the date of death, but in no event may such an action be brought more than ten years after the substantial completion of construction of such an improvement.

(c) This Code section shall not apply to actions for breach of contract, including, but not limited to, actions for breach of express contractual warranties.
Amended by 2020 Ga. Laws 380,§ 1, eff. 7/1/2020.
See 2020 Ga. Laws 380, § 2.

Section 9-3-52 - Limitation not available to owner or tenant

The limitation prescribed by this article shall not be asserted as a defense by any person who would otherwise be entitled to its benefits but who is in actual possession or control, as owner, tenant, or otherwise, of such an improvement at the time any deficiency of such an improvement constitutes the proximate cause of the injury or death for which it is proposed to bring an action.

Section 9-3-53 - Period of limitations not extended

Nothing in this article shall extend the period of limitations prescribed by the law of this state for the bringing of any action or shall postpone the time as of which a cause of action accrues.

Article 4 - LIMITATIONS FOR MALPRACTICE ACTIONS

Section 9-3-70 - "Action for medical malpractice" defined

As used in this article, the term "action for medical malpractice" means any claim for damages resulting from the death of or injury to any person arising out of:

(1) Health, medical, dental, or surgical service, diagnosis, prescription, treatment, or care rendered by a person authorized by law to perform such service or by any person acting under the supervision and control of the lawfully authorized person; or

(2) Care or service rendered by any public or private hospital, nursing home, clinic, hospital authority, facility, or institution, or by any officer, agent, or employee thereof acting within the scope of his employment.

Section 9-3-71 - General limitation

(a) Except as otherwise provided in this article, an action for medical malpractice shall be brought within two years after the date on which an injury or death arising from a negligent or wrongful act or omission occurred.

(b) Notwithstanding subsection (a) of this Code section, in no event may an action for medical malpractice be brought more than five years after the date on which the negligent or wrongful act or omission occurred.

(c) Subsection (a) of this Code section is intended to create a two-year statute of limitations. Subsection (b) of this Code section is intended to create a five-year statute of ultimate repose and abrogation.

(d) Nothing contained in subsection (a) or (b) of this Code section shall be construed to repeal Code Section 9-3-73, which shall be deemed to apply either to the applicable statutes of limitation or repose.

Section 9-3-72 - Foreign objects left in body

The limitations of Code Section 9-3-71 shall not apply where a foreign object has been left in a patient's body, but in such a case an action shall be brought within one year after the negligent or wrongful act or omission is discovered. For the purposes of this Code section, the term "foreign object" shall not include a chemical compound, fixation device, or prosthetic aid or device.

Section 9-3-73 - Certain disabilities and exceptions applicable

(a) Except as provided in this Code section, the disabilities and exceptions prescribed in Article 5 of this chapter in limiting actions on contracts shall be allowed and held applicable to actions, whether in tort or contract, for medical malpractice.

(b) Notwithstanding Article 5 of this chapter, all persons who are legally incompetent because of intellectual disability or mental illness and all minors who have attained the age of five years shall be subject to the periods of limitation for actions for medical malpractice provided in this article. A minor who has not attained the age of five years shall have two years from the date of such minor's fifth birthday within which to bring a medical malpractice action if the cause of action arose before such minor attained the age of five years.

(c) Notwithstanding subsections (a) and (b) of this Code section, in no event may an action for medical malpractice be brought by or on behalf of:

(1) A person who is legally incompetent because of intellectual disability or mental illness more than five years after the date on which the negligent or wrongful act or omission occurred; or

(2) A minor:

(A) After the tenth birthday of the minor if such minor was under the age of five years on the date on which the negligent or wrongful act or omission occurred; or

(B) After five years from the date on which the negligent or wrongful act or omission occurred if such minor was age five or older on the date of such act or omission.

(d) Subsection (b) of this Code section is intended to create a statute of limitations and subsection (c) of this Code section is intended to create a statute of repose.

(e) The limitations of subsections (b) and (c) of this Code section shall not apply where a foreign object has been left in a patient's body. Such cases shall be governed by Code Section 9-3-72.

(f) The findings of the General Assembly under this Code section include, without limitation, that a reasonable relationship exists between the provisions, goals, and classifications of this Code section and the rational, legitimate state objectives of providing quality health care, assuring the availability of physicians, preventing the curtailment of medical services, stabilizing insurance and medical costs, preventing stale medical malpractice claims, and providing for the public safety, health, and welfare as a whole.

(g) No action which, prior to July 1, 1987, has been barred by provisions relating to limitations of actions shall be revived by this article, as amended. No action which would be barred before July 1, 1987, by the provisions of this article, as amended, but which would not be so barred by the provisions of this article and Article 5 of this chapter in force immediately prior to July 1, 1987, shall be barred until July 1, 1989.

Amended by 2015 Ga. Laws 70,§ 4-15, eff. 7/1/2015.

Section 9-3-74 - Barred actions not revived

No action for medical malpractice which, prior to July 1, 1976, has been barred by the provisions of this chapter relating to actions shall be revived by this article.

Article 5 - TOLLING OF LIMITATIONS

Section 9-3-90 - Individuals under disability or imprisoned when cause of action accrues

(a) Individuals who are legally incompetent because of intellectual disability or mental illness, who are such when the cause of action accrues, shall be entitled to the same time after their disability is removed to bring an action as is prescribed for other persons.

(b) Except as otherwise provided in Code Section 9-3-33.1, individuals who are less than 18 years of age when a cause of action accrues shall be entitled to the same time after he or she reaches the age of 18 years to bring an action as is prescribed for other persons.

(c) No action accruing to an individual imprisoned at the time of its accrual which:

(1) Prior to July 1, 1984, has been barred by the provisions of this chapter shall be revived by this chapter, as amended; or

(2) Would be barred before July 1, 1984, by the provisions of this chapter, as amended, but which would not be so barred by the provisions of this chapter in force immediately prior to July 1, 1984, shall be barred until July 1, 1985.

Amended by 2015 Ga. Laws 97,§ 3, eff. 7/1/2015.

Amended by 2015 Ga. Laws 95,§ 2-3, eff. 7/1/2015.

Amended by 2015 Ga. Laws 70,§ 4-15, eff. 7/1/2015.

Section 9-3-91 - Disabilities suffered after accrual of cause

If any person suffers a disability specified in Code Section 9-3-90 after his right of action has accrued and the disability is not voluntarily caused or undertaken by the person claiming the benefit thereof, the limitation applicable to his cause of action shall cease to operate during the continuance of the disability.

Section 9-3-92 - Five-year tolling for unrepresented estate - In favor of estate

The time between the death of a person and the commencement of representation upon his estate or between the termination of one administration and the commencement of another shall not be counted against his estate in calculating any limitation applicable to the bringing of an action, provided that such time shall not exceed five years. At the expiration of the five years the limitation shall commence, even if the cause of action accrued after the person's death.

Section 9-3-93 - Five-year tolling for unrepresented estate - In favor of creditors

The time between the death of a person and the commencement of representation upon his estate or between the termination of one administration and the commencement of another shall not be counted against creditors of his estate, provided that such time does not exceed five years. At the expiration of the five years the limitation shall commence.

Section 9-3-94 - Removal of defendant from state

Unless otherwise provided by law, if a defendant removes from this state, the time of his absence from the state until he returns to reside shall not be counted or estimated in his favor.

Section 9-3-95 - Disability of one or more with joint right of action; effect of severability

Where there is a joint right of action and one or more of the persons having the right is under any of the disabilities specified in Code Section 9-3-90, the terms of limitation shall not be computed against the joint action until all the disabilities are removed. However, if the action is severable so that each person may bring an action for his own share, those free from disability shall be barred after the running of the applicable statute of limitations, and only the rights of those under disability shall be protected.

Section 9-3-96 - Tolling of limitations for fraud of defendant

If the defendant or those under whom he claims are guilty of a fraud by which the plaintiff has been debarred or deterred from bringing an action, the period of limitation shall run only from the time of the plaintiff's discovery of the fraud.

Section 9-3-97 - Limitations extended for counterclaims and cross-claims

The limitations of time within which various actions may be commenced and pursued within this state to enforce the rights of the parties are extended, only insofar as the enforcement of rights which may be instituted by way of counterclaim and cross-claim, so as to allow parties, up to and including the last day upon which the answer or other defensive pleadings should have been filed, to commence the prosecution and enforcement of rights by way of counterclaim and cross-claim, provided that the final date allowed by such limitations for the commencement of such actions shall not have expired prior to filing of the main action.

Section 9-3-97.1 - Tolling of limitations for medical malpractice

(a) The periods of limitation for bringing an action for medical malpractice as provided in Code Sections 9-3-71 and 9-3-72 shall be tolled if:

(1) The injured person or his duly appointed attorney makes a request by certified or registered mail or statutory overnight delivery, return receipt requested, upon any physician, hospital, or other health care provider for medical records in their custody or control relating to such injured person's health or medical treatment which medical records the injured person is entitled by law to receive;

(2) The request, if made by an injured person's duly appointed attorney, has enclosed therewith a properly executed medical authorization authorizing release of the requested information to said attorney;

(3) Such request expressly requests that the medical records be mailed to the injured person or his attorney by certified or registered mail or statutory overnight delivery, return receipt requested and states therein that the requested records are needed by the injured person for possible use in a medical malpractice action;

(4) The injured person or his attorney has promptly paid all fees and costs charged by such physician, hospital, or other health care provider for compiling, copying, and mailing such medical records; and

(5) Such medical records or a letter of response stating that the provider does not have custody or control of the medical records has not been received by the injured person or his attorney within 21 days of the date of receiving such request. Such periods of limitation shall cease to run on the twenty-second day following the day such request was received and shall resume on the day following the date such medical records, or response stating that the provider does not have custody or control of the medical records, are actually received by such injured person or his attorney; provided, however, that such periods of limitation shall be tolled only once for any cause of action.

(b) Any action filed in reliance upon a tolling of the statute of limitations as authorized by this Code section shall contain in the complaint as first filed allegations showing that the plaintiff is entitled to rely upon the provisions of this Code section, and said complaint as first filed shall have attached thereto as exhibits copies of the request, medical release, and evidence of mailing and receipt by certified or registered mail or statutory overnight delivery.

(c) Notwithstanding any other provision of this Code section, no period of limitation shall be tolled for a period exceeding 90 days except as provided in this subsection. In the event the procedure set forth in subsection (a) of this Code section has been followed by an injured person but the requested records or a letter of response stating that the provider does not have custody or control of the medical records have not been received within 85 days, the injured person shall have the right to petition the court for an order tolling the period of limitation beyond the 90 days and requiring the delivery of the medical records originally requested or a letter of response stating that the provider does not have custody or control of the medical records.

(d) It is intended that the provisions of this Code section tolling the statute of limitations for medical malpractice under certain circumstances be strictly complied with and strictly construed.

Section 9-3-98 - Applicability of article

This article shall apply to tort actions as well as actions on contracts.

Section 9-3-99 - Tolling of limitations for tort actions while criminal prosecution is pending

The running of the period of limitations with respect to any cause of action in tort that may be brought by the victim of an alleged crime which arises out of the facts and circumstances relating to the commission of such alleged crime committed in this state shall be tolled from the date of the commission of the alleged crime or the act giving rise to such action in tort until the prosecution of such crime or act has become final or otherwise terminated, provided that such time does not exceed six years, except as otherwise provided in Code Section 9-3-33.1.

Amended by 2015 Ga. Laws 97,§ 4, eff. 7/1/2015.

Amended by 2015 Ga. Laws 95,§ 2-4, eff. 7/1/2015.

Added by 2005 Ga. Laws 20,§ 2, eff. 7/1/2005.

Article 6 - REVIVAL

Section 9-3-110 - New promise to be in writing

A new promise, in order to renew a right of action already barred or to constitute a point from which the limitation shall commence running on a right of action not yet barred, shall be in writing, either in the party's own handwriting or subscribed by him or someone authorized by him.

Section 9-3-111 - Written promise following discharge in bankruptcy

No promise made after discharge in bankruptcy to pay a debt provable in bankruptcy from the liability of which the debtor has been discharged shall be valid or binding upon the debtor or promisor unless the same is made in writing and signed by the party making the same or to be charged therewith, or by someone duly authorized by him.

Section 9-3-112 - Payment or written acknowledgment equivalent to new promise

A payment entered upon a written evidence of debt by the debtor or upon any other written acknowledgment of the existing liability shall be equivalent to a new promise to pay.

Section 9-3-113 - Effect of new promise

A new promise shall revive or extend the original liability; it shall not create a new one.

Section 9-3-114 - Whom new promise by joint contractor binds

In cases of joint or joint and several contracts, a new promise by one of the contractors shall operate only against the promisor.

Section 9-3-115 - Effect of new promise by partner

After the dissolution of a partnership, a new promise by one partner shall revive or extend a partnership debt only as to the promisor and not as to his copartner or copartners.

Chapter 4 - DECLARATORY JUDGMENTS

Section 9-4-1 - Purpose and construction of chapter

The purpose of this chapter is to settle and afford relief from uncertainty and insecurity with respect to rights, status, and other legal relations; and this chapter is to be liberally construed and administered.

Section 9-4-2 - Declaratory judgments authorized; force and effect

(a) In cases of actual controversy, the respective superior courts of this state and the Georgia State-wide Business Court shall have power, upon petition or other appropriate pleading, to declare rights and other legal relations of any interested party petitioning for such declaration, whether or not further relief is or could be prayed; and the declaration shall have the force and effect of a final judgment or decree and be reviewable as such.

(b) In addition to the cases specified in subsection (a) of this Code section, the respective superior courts of this state and the Georgia State-wide Business Court shall have power, upon petition or other appropriate pleading, to declare rights and other legal relations of any interested party petitioning for the declaration, whether or not further relief is or could be prayed, in any civil case in which it appears to the court that the ends of justice require that the declaration should be made; and the declaration shall have the force and effect of a final judgment or decree and be reviewable as such.

(c) Relief by declaratory judgment shall be available, notwithstanding the fact that the complaining party has any other adequate legal or equitable remedy or remedies.

Amended by 2019 Ga. Laws 271,§ 3-1, eff. 5/7/2019.

Section 9-4-3 - Further relief; interlocutory extraordinary relief to preserve status quo

(a) Further plenary relief, legal or equitable, including but not limited to damages, injunction, mandamus, or quo warranto, may be sought in a petition seeking declaratory judgment, and in such case, the action shall be governed as to process, service, and procedure by Code Section 9-4-5. In all such cases, the court shall award to the petitioning party such relief as the pleadings and evidence may show him to be entitled; and the failure of the petition to state a cause of action for declaratory relief shall not affect the right of the party to any other relief, legal or equitable, to which he may be entitled.

(b) The court, in order to maintain the status quo pending the adjudication of the questions or to preserve equitable rights, may grant injunction and other interlocutory extraordinary relief in substantially the manner and under the same rules applicable in equity cases.

Section 9-4-4 - Declaratory judgments involving fiduciaries

(a) Without limiting the generality of Code Sections 9-4-2, 9-4-3, 9-4-5 through 9-4-7, and 9-4-9, any person interested as or through an executor, administrator, personal representative, trustee, guardian, conservator, or other fiduciary, creditor, devisee, distributee, legatee, heir, next of kin, or beneficiary in the administration of a trust or of the estate of a decedent, a minor, a ward, an incapacitated person, a protected person, a person who is otherwise legally incompetent because of mental illness or intellectual disability, or an insolvent may have a declaration of rights or legal relations in respect thereto and a declaratory judgment:

(1) To ascertain any class of creditors, devisees, legatees, heirs, next of kin, beneficiaries, or others;

(2) To direct the executor, administrator, trustee, or other fiduciary to do or abstain from doing any particular act in his or her fiduciary capacity;

(3) To determine title to property in which the trust or estate has or is purported to have an ownership or other interest; or

(4) To determine any question arising in the administration of the estate or trust, including questions of construction of wills, trust instruments, and other writings.

(b) The enumeration in subsection (a) of this Code section does not limit or restrict the exercise of general powers conferred in Code Section 9-4-2 in any proceeding covered thereby where declaratory relief is sought in which a judgment or decree will terminate the controversy or remove the uncertainty.

Amended by 2020 Ga. Laws 508,§ 2-4, eff. 1/1/2021.

Amended by 2015 Ga. Laws 70,§ 4-15, eff. 7/1/2015.

Section 9-4-5 - Filing and service; time of trial; drawing of jury

A proceeding instituted under this chapter shall be filed and served as are other cases in the superior courts of this state or in the Georgia State-wide Business Court; provided, however, that a proceeding instituted in the probate court pursuant to paragraph (1) of subsection (a) of Code Section 15-9-127 shall be filed and served in the manner provided for proceedings in the probate courts of this state in Chapter 11 of Title 53. A proceeding instituted under this chapter may be tried at any time designated by the court not earlier than 20 days after the service thereof, unless the parties consent in writing to an earlier trial. If there is an issue of fact that requires a submission to a jury, the jury may be drawn, summoned, and sworn either in regular term or specially for the pending case.

Amended by 2020 Ga. Laws 508,§ 2-5, eff. 1/1/2021.

Amended by 2019 Ga. Laws 271,§ 3-2, eff. 5/7/2019.

Section 9-4-6 - Submission of fact issues to jury

When a declaration of right or the granting of further relief based thereon involves the determination of issues of fact triable by a jury and jury trial is not waived, the issues shall be submitted to a jury of 12 in the form of interrogatories, with proper instructions by the court, whether a general verdict is required or not. The instructions by the court shall in all respects be governed by the laws of this state relating to instructions or charges by a court to a jury.

Section 9-4-7 - Only parties affected; when municipality made party; when Attorney General served and heard

(a) No declaration shall prejudice the rights of persons not parties to the proceeding.

(b) In any proceeding involving the validity of a municipal ordinance or franchise, the municipality shall be made a party and shall be entitled to be heard as a party.

(c) If an Act of the General Assembly, a statute of the state, any order or regulation of any administrative body of the state, or any franchise granted by the state is alleged in an action for declaratory judgment or as a part of any other action to be unconstitutional or otherwise invalid, the Attorney General of the state shall be served with a copy of the proceeding and shall be entitled to be heard in defense of said Act, statute, order, regulation, or franchise, which may include appearing as a party as of right as he or she determines is appropriate.

Amended by 2022 Ga. Laws 564,§ 1, eff. 3/4/2022.

Section 9-4-8 - When court may refuse declaratory judgment

The court may refuse to render or enter a declaratory judgment or decree where the judgment or decree, if rendered or entered, would not terminate the uncertainty or controversy giving rise to the proceeding.

Section 9-4-9 - Costs

In any proceeding under this chapter the court may make such award or division of costs as may seem equitable and just.

Section 9-4-10 - Equity jurisdiction not impaired

Nothing in this chapter is intended to impair the equity jurisdiction of the superior courts of the state or of the Georgia State-wide Business Court.

Amended by 2019 Ga. Laws 271,§ 3-3, eff. 5/7/2019.

Section 9-4-11 - Combining proceedings in probate court

A declaratory judgment proceeding brought in the probate court as provided in paragraph (1) of subsection (a) of Code Section 15-9-127 may be combined with or made a part of any proceeding properly before the probate court to the greatest extent that does not infringe the exclusive jurisdiction of the superior courts pursuant to Article VI, Section IV, Paragraph I of the Constitution of this state.

Added by 2020 Ga. Laws 508,§ 2-6, eff. 1/1/2021.

Chapter 5 - INJUNCTIONS

Section 9-5-1 - For what purposes injunctions may be issued

Equity, by a writ of injunction, may restrain proceedings in another or the same court, a threatened or existing tort, or any other act of a private individual or corporation which is illegal or contrary to equity and good conscience and for which no adequate remedy is provided at law.

Section 9-5-2 - No interference by equity in administration of criminal laws

Equity will take no part in the administration of the criminal law. It will neither aid criminal courts in the exercise of their jurisdiction, nor will it restrain or obstruct them.

Section 9-5-3 - When court proceedings enjoined; injunctions against sheriffs' sales

(a) Equity will not enjoin the proceedings and processes of a court of law, absent some intervening equity or other proper defense of which a party, without fault on his part, cannot avail himself at law.

(b) Writs of injunction may be issued by judges of the superior courts to enjoin sales by sheriffs, at any time before a sale takes place, in any proper case made by application for injunction.

Section 9-5-4 - Grounds for restraint of trespass

Equity will not interfere to restrain a trespass, unless the injury is irreparable in damages, or the trespasser is insolvent, or other circumstances exist which, in the discretion of the court, render the interposition of the writ necessary and proper, among which shall be the avoidance of circuity and multiplicity of actions.

Section 9-5-5 - When waste enjoined

Equity will not interfere by injunction to restrain waste when the petitioner's title is not clear. Such relief shall be granted only when the title is free from dispute.

Section 9-5-6 - Injunction against debtors not generally available to creditors

Creditors without liens may not, as a general rule, enjoin their debtors from disposing of property nor obtain injunctions or other extraordinary relief in equity.

Section 9-5-7 - When breach of contract for personal services enjoined

Generally an injunction will not issue to restrain the breach of a contract for personal services unless the services are of a peculiar merit or character and cannot be performed by others.

Section 9-5-8 - Grant of injunctions in discretion of court; power to be exercised cautiously

The granting and continuing of injunctions shall always rest in the sound discretion of the judge, according to the circumstances of each case. This power shall be prudently and cautiously exercised and, except in clear and urgent cases, should not be resorted to.

Section 9-5-9 - Second injunction in court's discretion

A second injunction may be granted in the discretion of the judge.

Section 9-5-10 - Perpetual injunction after hearing

A perpetual injunction shall be granted only after hearing and upon a final decree.

Section 9-5-11 - Injunctions against certain transactions outside state

Equity may enjoin the defendant as to transactions involving fraud, trust, or contracts beyond the limits of this state.

Chapter 6 - EXTRAORDINARY WRITS

Article 1 - GENERAL PROVISIONS

Section 9-6-1 - Final judgment prerequisite to appeal; grant of new trial subject to review

No appeal as to any ruling or decision in a mandamus or quo warranto proceeding or in a case involving a writ of prohibition may be taken until there has been a final judgment in the trial court. The grant of a new trial shall be treated as a final judgment in these cases and subject to review as in other cases.

Amended by 2016 Ga. Laws 626,§ 3-4, eff. 1/1/2017.

Article 2 - MANDAMUS

Section 9-6-20 - When mandamus may issue

All official duties should be faithfully performed, and whenever, from any cause, a defect of legal justice would ensue from a failure to perform or from improper performance, the writ of mandamus may issue to compel a due performance if there is no other specific legal remedy for the legal rights; provided, however, that no writ of mandamus to compel the removal of a judge shall issue where no motion to recuse has been filed, if such motion is available, or where a motion to recuse has been denied after assignment to a separate judge for hearing.

Amended by 2009 Ga. Laws 121,§ 1, eff. 7/1/2009.

Section 9-6-21 - Not a private remedy; enforcement of officer's discretionary acts

(a) Mandamus shall not lie as a private remedy between individuals to enforce private rights nor to a public officer who has an absolute discretion to act or not to act unless there is a gross abuse of such discretion. However, mandamus shall not be confined to the enforcement of mere ministerial duties.

(b) On the application of one or more citizens of any county against the county board of commissioners where by law supervision and jurisdiction is vested in such commissioners over the public roads of such counties and the overseers of the public roads complained of; or against the judge of the probate court where by law supervision, control, and jurisdiction over such public roads is vested in the judge and the overseers of the public roads that may be complained of; or against either, both, or all of the named parties, as the facts and methods of working the public roads in the respective counties may justify, which application or action for mandamus shall show that one or more of the public roads of the county of the plaintiff's residence are out of repair; do not measure up to the standards and do not conform to the legal requirements as prescribed by law; and are in such condition that ordinary loads, with ordinary ease, cannot be hauled over such public roads, the judges of the superior courts are authorized and given jurisdiction and it is made their duty, upon such showing being made, to issue the writ of mandamus against the parties having charge of and supervision over the public roads of the county; and to compel by such proceedings the building, repairing, and working of the public roads as are complained of, up to the standard required by law, so that ordinary loads, with ordinary ease and facility, can be continuously hauled over such public roads. The judges of the superior courts shall, by proper order, in the same proceedings compel the work done necessary to build, repair, and maintain such public roads up to the standard so prescribed.

Section 9-6-22 - Enforcement of officer's duties under Title 5

If any sheriff, clerk, or other officer fails to discharge any duty required of him by any provision of Title 5, upon petition the appellate court or the superior, state, or city court, as the case may be, may compel the performance of such duty by mandamus. No party shall lose any right by reason of the failure of the officer to discharge his duties when the party has been guilty of no fault himself and has exercised ordinary diligence to secure the discharge of such duties.

Section 9-6-23 - Enforcement of corporation's public duty

A private person may by mandamus enforce the performance by a corporation of a public duty as to matters in which he has a special interest.

Section 9-6-24 - What interest required to enforce public right

Where the question is one of public right and the object is to procure the enforcement of a public duty, no legal or special interest need be shown, but it shall be sufficient that a plaintiff is interested in having the laws executed and the duty in question enforced.

Section 9-6-25 - Loss prerequisite to enforcing private right

In order for a plaintiff to enforce a private right by mandamus he must show pecuniary loss for which he cannot be compensated in damages.

Section 9-6-26 - Mandamus not granted where fruitless, nor on suspicion

Mandamus will not be granted when it is manifest that the writ would, for any cause, be nugatory or fruitless, nor will it be granted on a mere suspicion or fear, before a refusal to act or the doing of a wrongful act.

Section 9-6-27 - Time of hearing; notice; how and when issues of fact determined

(a) Upon the presentation of an application for mandamus, if the mandamus nisi is granted the judge shall cause the same to be returned for trial not less than ten nor more than 30 days from such date. The defendant shall be served at least five days before the time fixed for the hearing.

(b) If no issue of fact is raised by the application and answer, the case shall be heard and determined by the court without the intervention of a jury.

(c) If an issue of fact is involved, it may be heard by the judge upon the consent of all parties. Otherwise, the case shall be set for trial upon the first day of the next term of the superior court as other jury cases are tried. However, if the court has a scheduled session for jury trials which will occur before the next term, the case shall stand for trial at the present term.

Section 9-6-28 - Appeal

(a) Upon refusal of the court to grant the mandamus nisi, the applicant may appeal as in other cases. Either party dissatisfied with the judgment on the hearing of the answer to the mandamus nisi may likewise appeal.

(b) Mandamus cases shall be heard on appeal under the same laws and rules as apply to injunction cases.

Amended by 2016 Ga. Laws 626,§ 3-5, eff. 1/1/2017.

Article 3 - PROHIBITION

Section 9-6-40 - Prohibition counterpart of mandamus

The writ of prohibition is the counterpart of mandamus, to restrain subordinate courts and inferior judicial tribunals from exceeding their jurisdiction where no other legal remedy or relief is given. The granting or refusal thereof is governed by the same principles of right, necessity, and justice as apply to mandamus; provided, however, that no writ of prohibition to compel the removal of a judge shall issue where no motion to recuse has been filed, if such motion is available, or where a motion to recuse has been denied after assignment to a separate judge for hearing.

Amended by 2009 Ga. Laws 121,§ 2, eff. 7/1/2009.

Section 9-6-41 - When writ granted; time for return; trial of fact issues

The writ of prohibition may be granted at any time, on proper showing made. The return must be in term. Any issue of fact made thereon must be tried as in equity cases.

Section 9-6-42 - Prohibition against executive and military officers; Governor exempt

The writ of prohibition will not lie to the duly inaugurated Governor, but it lies to all other executive or military officers when acting as a judicial or quasi-judicial tribunal.

Article 4 - QUO WARRANTO

Section 9-6-60 - For what purpose quo warranto may issue; who may bring action

The writ of quo warranto may issue to inquire into the right of any person to any public office the duties of which he is in fact discharging. It may be granted only after the application by some person either claiming the office or interested therein.

Section 9-6-61 - Writ lies against civil and military officers; Governor exempt

The question of who is the lawful Governor of this state may not be tried by quo warranto, but the writ of quo warranto will lie to all other civil or military officers.

Section 9-6-62 - When granted; how issues of fact tried

The writ of quo warranto may be granted at any time, on proper showing made. Any issue of fact made thereon must be tried as in equity cases.

Section 9-6-63 - Service of writ and process

(a) As used in this Code section, the term "personal service" means service by placing a copy of the writ and process in the quo warranto proceeding in the hands of the defendant.

(b) The writ and process in a quo warranto proceeding shall be served on the defendant personally.

(c) Service of the writ and process in such proceeding upon a resident of this state who is temporarily residing or sojourning outside this state may be perfected in the same manner as is provided for service of process by publication as set forth in paragraph (1) of subsection (f) of Code Section 9-11-4 or personal service outside the state as set forth in paragraph (2) of subsection (f) of Code Section 9-11-4. When service is perfected upon any such person as provided for in the aforesaid Code section, then the person shall be bound by the final decision of the proceedings as fully as though the person had been personally served within this state.

Section 9-6-64 - How issues of law determined; time for final determination; appeal; application to issues of fact

(a) In all applications for writs of quo warranto, of informations in the nature of quo warranto, or of proceedings by such writs to determine the right to hold office, where the case presented by the applicant involves only questions of law, the same may be determined, as are equitable proceedings, by the judge of the superior court before whom the case was begun; and the judge shall so order all the proceedings connected with and usual in such cases that the final determination shall be had by him within ten days from the commencement of the action, application, or proceeding. If either party to the application or proceeding desires to except to the final decision of the judge of the superior court, he shall file an appeal as in other cases, and the duties of the clerk shall be the same as in other cases.

(b) All the provisions of subsection (a) of this Code section are extended to proceedings quo warranto, or writs of that nature, involving issues of fact to be tried by a jury, when the same can be applied; but nothing in the subsection shall be construed to affect any rights or remedies in this class of cases which are not covered thereby.

Section 9-6-65 - Jury trial where facts at issue; time of trial; continuances

In cases where the facts alleged are denied by the defendant or defendants on oath, the judge shall forthwith, in the usual manner, draw a jury of 12 to try the issue of fact, and the judge shall have the power to fix a day for trial of the issue of fact with an order that the sheriff shall notify the parties of the time and place of trial. The date fixed for the trial shall not be less than ten nor more than 30 days from the date of the order. The judge shall have the discretion to continue the hearing from day to day, as provided for in other cases.

Section 9-6-66 - Disposition of books and papers by judgment

Whenever the right to any office is decided, the judgment fixing the right shall further provide for the delivery to the person held to be entitled to the office of all the books and papers of every sort belonging to the office, which judgment shall be enforced as decrees in equity are enforced.

Chapter 7 - AUDITORS

Section 9-7-1 - Duties of auditor

The duties heretofore performed by a master in the superior court shall be performed by an auditor.

Section 9-7-2 - When facts referred to auditor; on application and notice; on court's own motion

Upon application of either party, after notice to the opposite party, the judge of the superior court, in equitable proceedings if the case shall require it, may refer any part of the facts to an auditor to investigate and report the result to the court. Furthermore, the judge may, upon his own motion, when in his judgment the facts and circumstances of any such case require it, refer the same to an auditor.

Section 9-7-3 - Appointment of auditor in matters of account; on application and notice; on court's own motion

In all cases in the superior, state, or city courts involving matters of account, if the case shall require it, the judge may appoint an auditor to investigate the matters of account and report the result to the court upon the application of either party and after notice to the opposite party, or upon his own motion when in his judgment the facts and circumstances of any such case require it.
Amended by 2007 Ga. Laws 18,§ 9, eff. 5/11/2007.

Section 9-7-4 - Appointment of person agreed on

In all cases where the parties agree upon the person to be appointed as auditor, the court shall appoint such person.

Section 9-7-5 - Where hearing held; notice of hearing; auditor's oath

Except by the written consent of all parties, the auditor shall not hear evidence or argument outside the county in which the case is proceeding. He shall give both parties or their counsel reasonable notice of the time and place of hearing and shall be sworn to render a true report according to the law and the evidence without favor or affection to either party.

Section 9-7-6 - Powers of auditor generally

In all cases, unless modified by the order of appointment, in addition to the matter specially referred, the auditor shall have power to hear motions, allow amendments, and pass upon all questions of law and fact. He shall have power to subpoena and swear witnesses and compel the production of papers.

Section 9-7-7 - Contempt referred to superior court

In cases of contempt by either party, a witness, or other persons, upon application to the court making the appointment, the judge thereof shall take such proceedings and impose such penalty as the facts authorize or require.

Section 9-7-8 - Contents of report - Rulings, findings, and conclusions

After hearing the evidence and argument, the auditor shall file the evidence and a report in which he shall clearly and separately state all rulings made by him, classify and state his findings, and report his conclusions upon the law and facts.

Section 9-7-9 - Contents of report - Motions and rulings; transcript; documentary evidence

The auditor shall make an accurate report of all motions made before him and of his rulings thereon, and either the auditor or a party shall have the evidence and proceedings recorded by a court reporter. Any original document introduced in evidence shall be properly identified and attached to the report.

Section 9-7-10 - Contents of report - Evidence deemed inadmissible

All evidence offered but deemed inadmissible by the auditor shall nevertheless be reported by the auditor; and if, upon exception filed to his ruling thereon, the evidence is adjudged to be admissible, the same may be considered upon the trial of exceptions of fact.

Section 9-7-11 - Written notice of filing report

Upon filing his report, the auditor shall give both parties or their counsel written notice thereof.

Section 9-7-12 - Report prima facie true

The report of the auditor shall be prima facie the truth, either party having the liberty to except thereto.

Section 9-7-13 - When report recommitted

(a) For indefiniteness, omissions, errors of calculation, failure to report evidence, errors of law, or other proper cause, the judge may recommit the report for such further action as may be proper.

(b) In such cases, the evidence shall be confined to such issues as the judge, in the order of recommitment, may indicate. If ordered to be taken de novo, the parties may agree as to what portion of the original report shall be retained in lieu of reintroduction.

Section 9-7-14 - Time for filing exceptions; classification; extension on application; what exceptions to specify

(a) Within 20 days after the report is filed and notice is given to the parties, either party may file exceptions to be classified separately as "exceptions of law" and "exceptions of fact."

(b) The trial judge may, in his discretion, on application of any party and without notice to the other party or parties, grant and issue an order extending the time for filing exceptions to an auditor's report. Extensions shall be freely granted in cases involving complicated facts or accounts, complicated issues of law, or lengthy records, so as to allow adequate time for preparation of exceptions thereto. All applications for extensions of time must be made before the expiration of the period of time for filing exceptions as originally prescribed or as extended by previous order of the court. The order granting any extension of time shall be promptly filed with the clerk of the trial court who shall promptly give notice thereof to all other parties involved in the case.

(c) Exceptions to auditors' reports need not set out therein portions of the record in the original case, nor of the auditor's report, nor of the evidence reported by the auditor. It shall not be necessary that the grounds of any exceptions be complete in themselves. It shall be sufficient, for purposes of this Code section, if the exceptions point out by title and paragraph number such part of the pleadings, and by page number such part of the auditor's report, and such parts of the evidence reported by the auditor as are necessary to an understanding of the errors complained of.

Section 9-7-15 - Exceptions to matters outside record; certification by auditor or return with objections; application for mandamus; notice and hearing; effect of mandamus absolute

(a) Exceptions as to any matter not appearing on the face of the record, in the transcript of the evidence and proceedings, or in the report itself, shall be certified to be true by the auditor within 40 days after the report is filed. If the auditor determines that any such exception is not true or does not contain all of the necessary facts, he shall return the same within ten days to the party or his attorney with his objections in writing. If these objections are met and removed within ten days, he may then certify the same, specifying the cause of delay.

(b) If for any cause the exceptions are not certified by the auditor, without fault of the party or his attorney, the party or his attorney may apply to the judge of the superior court within 30 days from the tendering of the exceptions and on petition obtain a mandamus nisi directed to the auditor.

(c) The petition for a mandamus nisi shall set out a substantial copy of the exceptions, and shall be verified by the party or his counsel, or supported by other proof as to the truth of the facts stated therein. The mandamus nisi shall be served upon the auditor within ten days after the same is signed by the judge and shall be made returnable not more than 30 days after signing. The opposite party shall have notice of the time and place of hearing the mandamus nisi and may resist the application for a mandamus absolute. If there is a traverse filed to the answer, the same shall be determined by a jury. If the mandamus is made absolute, the order shall have the effect, to that extent, of amending the report of the auditor.

Section 9-7-16 - Exceptions of law for judge

Exceptions of law shall be for the exclusive consideration of the judge.

Section 9-7-17 - When exceptions of fact tried by jury; burden of proof; right to open and conclude

In all law cases where an auditor is appointed, exceptions of fact to his report shall be passed upon by the jury as in other issues of fact, and in equity cases by the jury when approved by the judge. The burden of proving error in the report of the auditor shall be upon the party making the exceptions, who shall have the right to open and conclude the argument. In all cases where both parties file exceptions of fact, the party against whom judgment would be rendered if the report were approved shall be entitled to open and conclude the argument.

Section 9-7-18 - Trial on the record; what additional evidence introduced; what evidence excluded

In all cases where exceptions of fact are submitted to the jury, the same shall be determined upon the testimony reported by the auditor. Only so much of the evidence as is material and pertinent to the issue then on trial shall be read to the jury. Admissible material evidence introduced and not reported and evidence improperly excluded shall also be submitted to the jury and all inadmissible evidence shall be excluded from their consideration.

Section 9-7-19 - When new testimony considered; application; notice; rights of opposite party

(a) No new testimony shall be considered, except in those cases where, according to the principles of law, a new trial would be granted for newly discovered evidence.

(b) Application to introduce such original and newly discovered evidence shall be made to the judge before the argument on the exceptions, if the same is then known, with a statement of the party and his attorney setting out the expected testimony and facts authorizing it to be admitted as newly discovered evidence.

(c) The opposite party shall be served with notice of the application. If the same is admitted, the opposite party shall be entitled to a continuance. On the trial he shall be entitled to introduce original testimony in rebuttal of the newly discovered evidence.

Section 9-7-20 - Form of jury's verdict

In all cases the jury shall find for or against each exception submitted, seriatim.

Section 9-7-21 - Court to frame judgment or decree

(a) If the auditor's report is not excepted to, the court shall frame a judgment or decree thereon as may be proper.

(b) If exceptions are filed, after the same have been considered and passed upon by the court or the jury, or both, as the case may be, the court shall order a judgment or a decree in accordance with the report and the changes made by the court or the jury, unless the same shall require a recommitment.

Section 9-7-22 - Auditor's fees

(a) The fees of an auditor to whom a case, whether legal or equitable, has been referred shall be determined and fixed by the trial judge making the referral or by any other judge having jurisdiction of the case and serving in the place and stead of the trial judge. The fees so determined and fixed may be apportioned between and among the parties at the discretion of the judge.

(b) The court with consent of the parties may fix the fees of the auditor in advance and incorporate the same in the order making the appointment.

(c) The fees of an auditor, as determined and fixed by the judge, shall be included in and made a part of the judgment of the court. The fees of the auditor shall be assessed as court costs and shall be paid prior to the filing of any appeal from the judgment of the court; provided, however, that if such fees have not been determined and assessed at the time of filing any such appeal, the same shall be paid within 30 days from the date of assessment.

Section 9-7-23 - Compensation of reporter; by whom paid

(a) The compensation of the court reporter for recording the evidence and proceedings in all cases before an auditor shall be as provided by law for civil cases.

(b) The court reporter shall be compensated as provided by law for furnishing transcripts of the evidence and proceedings. The compensation shall be paid by the parties to the case. The reporter, for additional transcripts of evidence and proceedings furnished by him, shall be paid by the party requesting the same as agreed between the parties and, in the event of a disagreement, shall be paid as provided by law.

Chapter 8 - RECEIVERS

Section 9-8-1 - Appointment of receiver - Grounds generally

When any fund or property is in litigation and the rights of either or both parties cannot otherwise be fully protected or when there is a fund or property having no one to manage it, a receiver of the same may be appointed by the judge of the superior court having jurisdiction thereof.

Section 9-8-2 - Appointment of receiver - To protect trust or joint property

Equity may appoint receivers to take possession of and protect trust or joint property and funds whenever the danger of destruction and loss shall require such interference.

Section 9-8-3 - Appointment of receiver - To hold assets liable for debt; appointment without notice; terms

Equity may appoint a receiver to take possession of and hold, subject to the direction of the court, any assets charged with the payment of debts where there is manifest danger of loss, destruction, or material injury to those interested. Under extraordinary circumstances, a receiver may be appointed before and without notice to the trustee or other person having charge of the assets. The terms on which a receiver is appointed shall be in the discretion of the court.

Section 9-8-4 - Caution to be exercised in appointing receiver

The power of appointing receivers should be prudently and cautiously exercised and except in clear and urgent cases should not be resorted to.

Section 9-8-5 - Intervention of persons asserting equitable remedies

Where property has been placed in the hands of a receiver, all persons properly seeking to assert equitable remedies against such assets shall become parties to the case by intervention and shall prosecute their remedies therein.

Section 9-8-6 - Lienholders made parties; divestment by receiver's sale

Persons holding liens on property in the hands of a receiver may be made parties to the case at any time. Unless otherwise provided in the order, liens upon the property held by any parties to the record, shall be dissolved by the receiver's sale and transferred to the funds arising from the sale of the property.

Section 9-8-7 - Investment of funds in receivership

The presiding judge, in his discretion under the law, may order any funds, in the hands of a receiver or any other officer of court, while awaiting the termination of protracted litigation, to be invested as provided in the case of executors and administrators.

Section 9-8-8 - Receiver an officer of court; subject to court's orders or removal

(a) The receiver is an officer and servant of the court appointing him, is responsible to no other tribunal than the court, and must in all things obey its direction.

(b) The receiver shall discharge his trust according to the orders or decrees of the court appointing him. He is at all times subject to its orders and may be brought to account and removed at its pleasure.

Section 9-8-9 - To which court receivers of corporations amenable

Receivers of corporations shall be amenable to and shall make their returns to the superior court of the county where they reside at the time of the appointment.

Section 9-8-10 - Receiver's bond

The judge of the superior court, in his discretion, may require a receiver to give bond conditioned for the faithful discharge of the trust reposed. If bond is so required, the judge shall fix the amount thereof and shall determine the sufficiency of the security. The judge shall also regulate the compensation paid to the receiver.

Section 9-8-11 - Liability of receiver where bank fails

Where funds are in the hands of a receiver pending a final disposition, the receiver may deposit the funds into a bank or trust company which is insured by the Federal Deposit Insurance Corporation, Federal Savings and Loan Insurance Corporation, or successor entities. If the receiver fails to utilize such an insured bank or trust company, he shall be personally liable for any resulting loss.

Section 9-8-12 - Garnishment not available against receiver

A receiver shall not be subject to the process of garnishment.

Section 9-8-13 - Award of attorneys' and receivers' fees; how determined

(a) In all cases where a receiver is appointed under the laws of this state to take charge of the assets of any person, firm, or corporation and a fund is brought into court for distribution, the court having jurisdiction thereof shall award to counsel filing the petition and representing the moving creditor or creditors, out of the fund, no greater sum as fees for services rendered in filing the petition and bringing the fund into court than the services are actually worth, taking as a basis therefor the amount represented by the counsel in the original petition and the assets brought into the hands of the receiver by the services of counsel not including the assets turned over to the receiver by defendants under order of the court.

(b) In all cases where a receiver is appointed to take charge of the assets of any person, firm, or corporation, the court having jurisdiction thereof shall award to the receiver as full compensation for his services, out of the fund coming into his hands, not more than 8 percent of the first $1,000.00, 4 percent of the excess up to $5,000.00, 3 percent of the amount above $5,000.00 and not exceeding $10,000.00, and 2 percent of all sums over $10,000.00. Where the business of an insolvent person, firm, or corporation is continued and conducted by a receiver, the judge may allow such compensation as may be reasonable for such services in lieu of commissions, not exceeding the compensation paid by persons in the usual and regular conduct of such business.

(c) In all cases, the presiding judge or other competent tribunal shall allow such compensation to the attorney or attorneys filing the original petition and to the receiver or receivers appointed thereunder as their services are reasonably worth.

Section 9-8-14 - Expenses of giving bond allowable as cost of administration

(a) Receivers who are required by law to give bond as such who have given as security on such bonds one or more guaranty companies, surety companies, fidelity insurance companies, or fidelity and deposit companies, as authorized by law, may include as part of their lawful expenses or costs of administration such reasonable sum or sums paid to the company or companies for the suretyship not exceeding 1 percent per annum on the amount of the bond as the court, judge, or other officer by whom they were appointed allows.

(b) Any court, judge, or other officer whose duty it is to pass upon the account of any person or corporation required to execute a bond with surety or sureties, whenever the person or corporation has given any such company or companies as security as provided in subsection (a) of this Code section, shall allow in the settlement of the account a reasonable sum for the expenses and premiums incurred in securing the surety, not exceeding the amounts specified in the subsection.

Chapter 9 - ARBITRATION
Article 1 - GENERAL PROVISIONS
Part 1 - ARBITRATION CODE

Section 9-9-1 - Short title

This part shall be known and may be cited as the "Georgia Arbitration Code."

Section 9-9-2 - Applicability; exclusive method

(a) Part 3 of Article 2 of this chapter, as it existed prior to July 1, 1988, applies to agreements specified in subsection (b) of this Code section made between July 1, 1978, and July 1, 1988. This part applies to agreements specified in subsection (b) of this Code section made on or after July 1, 1988, and to disputes arising on or after July 1, 1988, in agreements specified in subsection (c) of this Code section.

(b) Part 3 of Article 2 of this chapter, as it existed prior to July 1, 1988, shall apply to construction contracts, contracts of warranty on construction, and contracts involving the architectural or engineering design of any building or the design of alterations or additions thereto made between July 1, 1978, and July 1, 1988, and on and after July 1, 1988, this part shall apply as provided in subsection (a) of this Code section and shall provide the exclusive means by which agreements to arbitrate disputes arising under such contracts can be enforced.

(c) This part shall apply to all disputes in which the parties thereto have agreed in writing to arbitrate and shall provide the exclusive means by which agreements to arbitrate disputes can be enforced, except the following, to which this part shall not apply:

(1) Agreements coming within the purview of Article 2 of this chapter, relating to arbitration of medical malpractice claims;

(2) Any collective bargaining agreements between employers and labor unions representing employees of such employers;

(3) Any contract of insurance, as defined in Code Section 33-1-2; provided, however, that nothing in this paragraph shall impair or prohibit the enforcement of or in any way invalidate an arbitration clause or provision in a contract between insurance companies;

(4) Any other subject matters currently covered by an arbitration statute;

(5) Any loan agreement or consumer financing agreement in which the amount of indebtedness is $25,000.00 or less at the time of execution;

(6) Any contract for the purchase of consumer goods, as defined in Title 11, the "Uniform Commercial Code," under subsection (1) of Code Section 11-2-105 and subsection (a) of Code Section 11-9-102;

(7) Any contract involving consumer acts or practices or involving consumer transactions as such terms are defined in subsection (a) of Code Section 10-1-392, relating to definitions in the "Fair Business Practices Act of 1975";

(8) Any sales agreement or loan agreement for the purchase or financing of residential real estate unless the clause agreeing to arbitrate is initialed by all signatories at the time of the execution of the agreement. This exception shall not restrict agreements between or among real estate brokers or agents;

(9) Any contract relating to terms and conditions of employment unless the clause agreeing to arbitrate is initialed by all signatories at the time of the execution of the agreement; or

(10) Any agreement to arbitrate future claims arising out of personal bodily injury or wrongful death based on tort.

Amended by 2019 Ga. Laws 139,§ 1-94, eff. 7/1/2019.

Amended by 2013 Ga. Laws 33,§ 9, eff. 4/24/2013.

Amended by 2009 Ga. Laws 344,§ 1, eff. 7/1/2009.

Amended by 2001 Ga. Laws 191, § 25, eff. 7/1/2001.

Section 9-9-3 - Effect of arbitration agreement

A written agreement to submit any existing controversy to arbitration or a provision in a written contract to submit any controversy thereafter arising to arbitration is enforceable without regard to the justiciable character of the controversy and confers jurisdiction on the courts of the state to enforce it and to enter judgment on an award.

Section 9-9-4 - Application to court; venue; service of papers; scope of court's consideration; application for order of attachment or preliminary injunction

(a)

(1) Any application to the court under this part shall be made to the superior court of the county where venue lies, unless the application is made in a pending court action, in which case it shall be made to the court hearing that action. Subsequent applications shall be made to the court hearing the initial application unless the court otherwise directs.

(2) All applications shall be by motion and shall be heard in the manner provided by law and rule of court for the making or hearing of motions, provided that the motion shall be filed in the same manner as a complaint in a civil action.

(b) Venue for applications to the court shall lie:

(1) In the county where the agreement provides for the arbitration hearing to be held; or

(2) If the hearing has already been held, in the county where it was held; or

(3) In the county where any party resides or does business; or

(4) If there is no county as described in paragraph (1), (2), or (3) of this subsection, in any county.

(c)

(1) A demand for arbitration shall be served on the other parties by registered or certified mail or statutory overnight delivery, return receipt requested.

(2) The initial application to the court shall be served on the other parties in the same manner as a complaint under Chapter 11 of this title.

(3) All other papers required to be served by this part shall be served in the same manner as pleadings subsequent to the original complaint and other papers are served under Chapter 11 of this title.

(d) In determining any matter arising under this part, the court shall not consider whether the claim with respect to which arbitration is sought is tenable nor otherwise pass upon the merits of the dispute.

(e) The superior court in the county in which an arbitration is pending, or, if not yet commenced, in a county specified in subsection (b) of this Code section, may entertain an application for an order of attachment or for a preliminary injunction in connection with an arbitrable controversy, but only upon the ground that the award to which the applicant may be entitled may be rendered ineffectual without such provisional relief.

Section 9-9-5 - Limitation of time as bar to arbitration

(a) If a claim sought to be arbitrated would be barred by limitation of time had the claim sought to be arbitrated been asserted in court, a party may apply to the court to stay arbitration or to vacate the award, as provided in this part. The court has discretion in deciding whether to apply the bar. A party waives the right to raise limitation of time as a bar to arbitration in an application to stay arbitration by that party's participation in the arbitration.

(b) Failure to make this application to the court shall not preclude a party from asserting before the arbitrators limitation of time as a bar to the arbitration. The arbitrators, in their sole discretion, shall decide whether to apply the bar. This exercise of discretion shall not be subject to review of the court on an application to confirm, vacate, or modify the award except upon the grounds hereafter specified in this part for vacating or modifying an award.

Section 9-9-6 - Application to compel or stay arbitration; demand for arbitration; consolidation of proceedings

(a) A party aggrieved by the failure of another to arbitrate may apply for an order compelling arbitration. If the court determines there is no substantial issue concerning the validity of the agreement to submit to arbitration or compliance therewith and the claim sought to be arbitrated is not barred by limitation of time, the court shall order the parties to arbitrate. If a substantial issue is raised or the claim is barred by limitation of time, the court shall summarily hear and determine that issue and, accordingly, grant or deny the application for an order to arbitrate. If an issue claimed to be arbitrable is involved in an action pending in a court having jurisdiction to hear a motion to compel arbitration, the application shall be made by motion in that action. If the application is granted, the order shall operate to stay a pending or subsequent action, or so much of it as is referable to arbitration.

(b) Subject to subsections (c) and (d) of this Code section, a party who has not participated in the arbitration and who has not made an application to compel arbitration may apply to stay arbitration on the grounds that:

    (1) No valid agreement to submit to arbitration was made;

    (2) The agreement to arbitrate was not complied with; or

    (3) The arbitration is barred by limitation of time.

(c) A party may serve upon another party a demand for arbitration. This demand shall specify:

    (1) The agreement pursuant to which arbitration is sought;

    (2) The name and address of the party serving the demand;

    (3) That the party served with the demand shall be precluded from denying the validity of the agreement or compliance therewith or from asserting limitation of time as a bar in court unless he makes application to the court within 30 days for an order to stay arbitration; and

    (4) The nature of the dispute or controversy sought to be arbitrated; provided, however, that the demand for arbitration may be amended by either party to include disputes arising under the same agreement after the original demand is served.

(d) After service of the demand, or any amendment thereof, the party served must make application within 30 days to the court for a stay of arbitration or he will thereafter be precluded from denying the validity of the agreement or compliance therewith or from asserting limitation of time as a bar in court. Notice of this application shall be served on the other parties. The right to apply for a stay of arbitration may not be waived, except as provided in this Code section.

(e) Unless otherwise provided in the arbitration agreement, a party to an arbitration agreement may petition the court to consolidate separate arbitration proceedings, and the court may order consolidation of separate arbitration proceedings when:

    (1) Separate arbitration agreements or proceedings exist between the same parties or one party is a party to a separate arbitration agreement or proceeding with a third party;

    (2) The disputes arise from the same transactions or series of related transactions; and

    (3) There is a common issue or issues of law or fact creating the possibility of conflicting rulings by more than one arbitrator or panel of arbitrators.

(f) If all the applicable arbitration agreements name the same arbitrator, arbitration panel, or arbitration tribunal, the court, if it orders consolidation under subsection (e) of this Code section, shall order all matters to be heard before the arbitrator, panel, or tribunal agreed to by the parties. If the applicable arbitration agreements name separate arbitrators, panels, or tribunals, the court, if it orders consolidation under subsection (e) of this Code section, shall, in the absence of an agreed method of selection by all parties to the consolidated arbitration, appoint an arbitrator.

(g) In the event that the arbitration agreements in proceedings consolidated under subsection (e) of this Code section contain inconsistent provisions, the court shall resolve such conflicts and determine the rights and duties of various parties.

(h) If the court orders consolidation under subsection (e) of this Code section, the court may exercise its discretion to deny consolidation of separate arbitration proceedings only as to certain issues, leaving other issues to be resolved in separate proceedings.

Section 9-9-7 - Appointment of arbitrators

(a) If the arbitration agreement provides for a method of appointment of arbitrators, that method shall be followed. If there is only one arbitrator, the term "arbitrators" shall apply to him.

(b) The court shall appoint one or more arbitrators on application of a party if:

    (1) The agreement does not provide for a method of appointment;

    (2) The agreed method fails;

    (3) The agreed method is not followed for any reason; or

    (4) The arbitrators fail to act and no successors have been appointed.

(c) An arbitrator appointed pursuant to subsection (b) of this Code section shall have all the powers of one specifically named in the agreement.

Section 9-9-8 - Time and place for hearing; notice; application for prompt hearing; conduct of hearing; right to counsel; record; waiver

(a) The arbitrators, in their discretion, shall appoint a time and place for the hearing notwithstanding the fact that the arbitration agreement designates the county in which the arbitration hearing is to be held and shall notify the parties in writing, personally or by registered or certified mail or statutory overnight delivery, not less than ten days before the hearing. The arbitrators may adjourn or postpone the hearing. The court, upon application of any party, may direct the arbitrators to proceed promptly with the hearing and determination of the controversy.

(b) The parties are entitled to be heard; to present pleadings, documents, testimony, and other matters; and to cross-examine witnesses. The arbitrators may hear and determine the controversy upon the pleadings, documents, testimony, and other matters produced notwithstanding the failure of a party duly notified to appear.

(c) A party has the right to be represented by an attorney and may claim such right at any time as to any part of the arbitration or hearings which have not taken place. This right may not be waived. If a party is represented by an attorney, papers to be served on the party may be served on the attorney.

(d) The hearing shall be conducted by all the arbitrators unless the parties otherwise agree; but a majority may determine any question and render and change an award, as provided in this part. If during the course of the hearing, an arbitrator for any reason ceases to act, the remaining arbitrator or arbitrators appointed to act as neutrals may continue with the hearing and determination of the controversy.

(e) The arbitrators shall maintain a record of all pleadings, documents, testimony, and other matters introduced at the hearing. The arbitrators or any party to the proceeding may have the proceedings transcribed by a court reporter.

(f) Except as provided in subsection (c) of this Code section, a requirement of this Code section may be waived by written consent of the parties or by continuing with the arbitration without objection.

Section 9-9-9 - Power of subpoena; enforcement; use of discovery; opportunity to examine documents; compensation of witnesses

(a) The arbitrators may issue subpoenas for the attendance of witnesses and for the production of books, records, documents, and other evidence. These subpoenas shall be served and, upon application to the court by a party or the arbitrators, enforced in the same manner provided by law for the service and enforcement of subpoenas in a civil action.

(b) Notices to produce books, writings, and other documents or tangible things; depositions; and other discovery may be used in the arbitration according to procedures established by the arbitrators.

(c) A party shall have the opportunity to obtain a list of witnesses and to examine and copy documents relevant to the arbitration.

(d) Witnesses shall be compensated in the same amount and manner as witnesses in the superior courts.

Section 9-9-10 - Award to be in writing; copies furnished; time of making award; waiver

(a) The award shall be in writing and signed by the arbitrators joining in the award. The arbitrators shall deliver a copy of the award to each party personally or by registered or certified mail or statutory overnight delivery, return receipt requested, or as provided in the agreement.

(b) An award shall be made within the time fixed therefor by the agreement or, if not so fixed, within 30 days following the close of the hearing or within such time as the court orders. The parties may extend in writing the time either before or after its expiration. A party waives the objection that an award was not made within the time required unless he notifies in writing the arbitrators of his objection prior to the delivery of the award to him.

Section 9-9-11 - When award changed; application for change; objection thereto; time for disposition of application

(a) Pursuant to the procedure described in subsection (b) of this Code section, the arbitrators may change the award upon the following grounds:

    (1) There was a miscalculation of figures or a mistake in the description of any person, thing, or property referred to in the award;

    (2) The arbitrators have awarded upon a matter not submitted to them and the award may be corrected without affecting the merits of the decision upon the issues submitted; or

    (3) The award is imperfect in a matter of form, not affecting the merits of the controversy.

(b)

    (1) An application to the arbitrators for a change in the award shall be made by a party within 20 days after delivery of the award to the applicant. Written notice of this application shall be served upon the other parties.

    (2) Objection to a change in the award by the arbitrators must be made in writing to the arbitrators within ten days of service of the application to change. Written notice of this objection shall be served upon the other parties.

    (3) The arbitrators shall dispose of any application made under this Code section in a written, signed order within 30 days after service upon them of objection to change or upon the expiration of the time for service of this objection. The parties may extend, in writing, the time for this disposition by the arbitrators either before or after its expiration.

    (4) An award changed under this Code section shall be subject to the provisions of this part concerning the confirmation, vacation, and modification of awards by the court.

Section 9-9-12 - Confirmation of award by court

The court shall confirm an award upon application of a party made within one year after its delivery to him, unless the award is vacated or modified by the court as provided in this part.

Section 9-9-13 - Vacation of award by court; application; grounds; rehearing; appeal of order

(a) An application to vacate an award shall be made to the court within three months after delivery of a copy of the award to the applicant.

(b) The award shall be vacated on the application of a party who either participated in the arbitration or was served with a demand for arbitration if the court finds that the rights of that party were prejudiced by:

(1) Corruption, fraud, or misconduct in procuring the award;

(2) Partiality of an arbitrator appointed as a neutral;

(3) An overstepping by the arbitrators of their authority or such imperfect execution of it that a final and definite award upon the subject matter submitted was not made;

(4) A failure to follow the procedure of this part, unless the party applying to vacate the award continued with the arbitration with notice of this failure and without objection; or

(5) The arbitrator's manifest disregard of the law.

(c) The award shall be vacated on the application of a party who neither participated in the arbitration nor was served with a demand for arbitration or order to compel arbitration if the court finds that:

(1) The rights of the party were prejudiced by one of the grounds specified in subsection (b) of this Code section;

(2) A valid agreement to arbitrate was not made;

(3) The agreement to arbitrate has not been complied with; or

(4) The arbitrated claim was barred by limitation of time, as provided by this part.

(d) The fact that the relief was such that it could not or would not be granted by a court of law or equity is not ground for vacating or refusing to confirm the award.

(e) Upon vacating an award, the court may order a rehearing and determination of all or any of the issues either before the same arbitrators or before new arbitrators appointed as provided by this part. In any provision of an agreement limiting the time for a hearing or award, time shall be measured from the date of such order or rehearing, whichever is appropriate, or a time may be specified by the court. The court's ruling or order under this Code section shall constitute a final judgment and shall be subject to appeal in accordance with the appeal provisions of this part.

Amended by 2003 Ga. Laws 363, § 2, eff. 7/1/2003.

Section 9-9-14 - Modification of award by court; application; grounds; subsequent confirmation of award

(a) An application to modify the award shall be made to the court within three months after delivery of a copy of the award to the applicant.

(b) The court shall modify the award if:

(1) There was a miscalculation of figures or a mistake in the description of any person, thing, or property referred to in the award;

(2) The arbitrators awarded on a matter not submitted to them and the award may be corrected without affecting the merits of the decision upon the issues submitted; or

(3) The award is imperfect in a manner of form, not affecting the merits of the controversy.

(c) If the court modifies the award, it shall confirm the award as modified. If the court denies modification, it shall confirm the award made by the arbitrators.

Section 9-9-15 - Judgment on award

(a) Upon confirmation of the award by the court, judgment shall be entered in the same manner as provided by Chapter 11 of this title and be enforced as any other judgment or decree.

(b) The judgment roll shall consist of the following:

(1) The agreement and each written extension of time within which to make the award;

(2) The award;

(3) A copy of the order confirming, modifying, or correcting the award; and

(4) A copy of the judgment.

Section 9-9-16 - Appeals authorized

Any judgment or any order considered a final judgment under this part may be appealed pursuant to Chapter 6 of Title 5.

Section 9-9-17 - Arbitrators' fees and expenses

Unless otherwise provided in the agreement to arbitrate, the arbitrators' expenses and fees, together with other expenses, not including counsel fees, incurred in the conduct of the arbitration, shall be paid as provided in the award.

Section 9-9-18 - Commencement or continuation of proceedings upon death or incompetency of party

Where a party dies or becomes incompetent after making a written agreement to arbitrate, the proceedings may be begun or continued upon the application of, or upon notice to, his executor or administrator or trustee or guardian or, where it relates to real property, his distributee or devisee who has succeeded to his interest in the real property. Upon the death or incompetency of a party, the court may extend the time within which an application to confirm, vacate, or modify the award or to stay arbitration must be made. Where a party has died since an award was delivered, the proceedings thereupon are the same as where a party dies after a verdict.

Part 2 - GEORGIA INTERNATIONAL COMMERCIAL ARBITRATION CODE

Section 9-9-20 - Short title; statement of purpose

(a) This part shall be known and may be cited as the "Georgia International Commercial Arbitration Code."

(b) The purpose of this part is to encourage international commercial arbitration in this state, to enforce arbitration agreements and arbitration awards, to facilitate prompt and efficient arbitration proceedings consistent with this part, and to provide a conducive environment for international business and trade.

Added by 2012 Ga. Laws 713, § 1, eff. 7/1/2012.

Section 9-9-21 - Applicability

(a) This part shall apply to international commercial arbitration, subject to any agreement in force between the United States and any other country.

(b) The provisions of this part, except for Code Sections 9-9-29 and 9-9-30, subsections (f) through (h) of Code Section 9-9-38, and Code Sections 9-9-39, 9-9-57, and 9-9-58, shall apply only if the place of arbitration is in this state.

(c) An arbitration shall be considered international if:

(1) The parties to an arbitration agreement have their places of business in different countries at the time of the conclusion of such arbitration agreement;

(2) One of the following places is situated outside the country in which the parties have their places of business:

(A) The place of arbitration, if determined in or pursuant to the arbitration agreement; or

(B) Any place where a substantial part of the obligations of the commercial relationship is to be performed or the place with which the subject matter of the dispute is most closely connected; or

(3) The parties have expressly agreed that the subject matter of the arbitration agreement relates to more than one country.

(d) For the purposes of subsection (c) of this Code section:

(1) If a party has more than one place of business, the place of business is that which has the closest relationship to the arbitration agreement; and

(2) If a party does not have a place of business, reference is to be made to such party's habitual residence.

(e) This part shall not affect any other law of this state by virtue of which certain disputes shall not be submitted to arbitration or may be submitted to arbitration only according to provisions other than those of this part.

Added by 2012 Ga. Laws 713,§ 1, eff. 7/1/2012.

Section 9-9-22 - Definitions

(a) As used in this part, the term:

(1) "Arbitration" means any arbitration, whether or not administered by a permanent arbitral institution.

(2) "Arbitration agreement" means an agreement by the parties to submit to arbitration all or certain disputes that have arisen or may arise between them in respect of a defined legal relationship, whether contractual or not, and may be in the form of an arbitration clause in a contract or in the form of a separate agreement.

(3) "Arbitration award" means a decision of an arbitration tribunal on the substance of a dispute submitted to it and shall include an interim, interlocutory, or partial award.

(4) "Arbitration tribunal" means a sole arbitrator or a panel of arbitrators.

(b)

(1) Where a provision of this part, except Code Section 9-9-50, leaves the parties free to determine a certain issue, such freedom shall include the right of the parties to authorize a third party, including an institution, to make that determination.

(2) Where a provision of this part refers to the fact that the parties have agreed or that they may agree or in any other way refers to an agreement of the parties, such agreement shall include any arbitration rule referred to in such agreement.

(3) Where a provision of this part, other than in paragraph (1) of Code Section 9-9-47 and paragraph (1) of subsection (b) of Code Section 9-9-54, refers to a claim, it shall also apply to a counterclaim, and where it refers to a defense, it shall also apply to a defense to such counterclaim.

Added by 2012 Ga. Laws 713,§ 1, eff. 7/1/2012.

Section 9-9-23 - Interpretation

(a) In the interpretation of this part, regard shall be given to its international origin and to the need to promote uniformity in its application and the observance of good faith.

(b) Questions concerning matters governed by this part which are not expressly settled in it are to be settled in conformity with the general principles on which this part is based.

Added by 2012 Ga. Laws 713,§ 1, eff. 7/1/2012.

Section 9-9-24 - Receipt of written communications

(a) Unless otherwise agreed by the parties:

(1) Any written communication shall be deemed to have been received if it is delivered to the addressee personally or if it is delivered at his or her place of business, habitual residence, or mailing address; if none of these can be found after making a reasonable inquiry, a written communication shall be deemed to have been received if it is sent to the addressee's last known place of business, habitual residence, or mailing address by registered mail or any other means which provides a record of the attempt to deliver it; and

(2) Communications shall be deemed to have been received on the day it is delivered.

(b) The provisions of this Code section shall not apply to communications in court proceedings.

Added by 2012 Ga. Laws 713,§ 1, eff. 7/1/2012.

Section 9-9-25 - Waiver of right to object to violations of arbitration agreement

A party who knows that any provision of this part from which the parties may derogate or any requirement under the arbitration agreement has not been complied with and yet proceeds with the arbitration without objecting to such noncompliance without undue delay or, if a time limit is provided therefor, within such period of time, shall be deemed to have waived the right to object.

Added by 2012 Ga. Laws 713,§ 1, eff. 7/1/2012.

Section 9-9-26 - Judicial intervention and enforcement

In matters governed by this part, no court shall intervene except where provided in this part. If the controversy is within the scope of this part, the arbitration agreement shall be enforced by the courts of this state in accordance with this part without regard to the justiciable character of the controversy.

Added by 2012 Ga. Laws 713,§ 1, eff. 7/1/2012.

Section 9-9-27 - County where agreement to be enforced

The functions referred to in subsections (c) and (d) of Code Section 9-9-32, subsection (c) of Code Section 9-9-34, Code Section 9-9-35, paragraph (3) of Code Section 9-9-37, Code Section 9-9-49, and subsection (b) of Code Section 9-9-56 shall be performed by the superior court in the county agreed upon by the parties. Barring such agreement, these functions shall be performed by the superior court:

(1) In any county where any portion of the hearing has been conducted;

(2) If no portion of the hearing has been conducted in this state, in the county where any party resides or does business; or

(3) If there is no such county, in any county.

Added by 2012 Ga. Laws 713,§ 1, eff. 7/1/2012.

Section 9-9-28 - Arbitration agreements to be in writing; definitions

(a) All arbitration agreements shall be in writing.

(b) A written arbitration agreement means that its contents are recorded in any form, whether or not the arbitration agreement or contract has been concluded orally, by conduct, or by other means.

(c)

    (1) As used in this subsection, the term:

        (A) "Data message" means information generated, sent, received or stored by electronic, magnetic, optical, or similar means, including, but not limited to, electronic data interchange (EDI), e-mail, telegram, telex, or telecopy.

        (B) "Electronic communication" means any communication that the parties make by means of data messages.

    (2) The requirement that an arbitration agreement be in writing may be met by an electronic communication if the information contained therein is accessible so as to be useable for subsequent reference.

(d) An arbitration agreement shall be deemed to be in writing if it is contained in an exchange of statements of claim and defense in which the existence of an arbitration agreement is alleged by one party and not denied by the other.

(e) The reference in a contract to any document containing an arbitration clause shall constitute an arbitration agreement in writing, provided that the reference is such as to make that clause a part of the contract.

Added by 2012 Ga. Laws 713,§ 1, eff. 7/1/2012.

Section 9-9-29 - Arbitration referrals

(a) A court before which a civil action is brought in a matter which is the subject of an arbitration agreement shall, if a party so requests not later than when submitting the party's first statement on the substance of the dispute, refer the parties to arbitration unless it finds that the arbitration agreement is null and void, inoperative, or incapable of being performed.

(b) Where an action referred to in subsection (a) of this Code section has been brought, arbitral proceedings may nevertheless be commenced or continued, and an arbitration award may be made, while the action is pending before the court.

Added by 2012 Ga. Laws 713,§ 1, eff. 7/1/2012.

Section 9-9-30 - Interim measures of protection

Before or during arbitral proceedings, a party may request from a court an interim measure of protection, and a court may grant such measure, and such request shall not be deemed to be incompatible with an arbitration agreement.

Added by 2012 Ga. Laws 713,§ 1, eff. 7/1/2012.

Former 9-9-30 repealed by 2012 Ga. Laws 713,§ 1, eff. 7/1/2012.

Section 9-9-31 - Number of arbitrators

The parties shall be free to determine the number of arbitrators, and if no determination is stated, the number of arbitrators shall be one.

Added by 2012 Ga. Laws 713,§ 1, eff. 7/1/2012.

Former 9-9-31 repealed by 2012 Ga. Laws 713,§ 1, eff. 7/1/2012.

Section 9-9-32 - Appointment of arbitrators; immunity from liability

(a) No person shall be precluded by reason of nationality from acting as an arbitrator, unless otherwise agreed by the parties.

(b) The parties shall be free to agree on a procedure to appoint the arbitrator or arbitrators, subject to the provisions of subsections (d) and (e) of this Code section.

(c) If the parties do not agree on the procedure to appoint the arbitrator or arbitrators:

    (1) In an arbitration with three arbitrators, each party shall appoint one arbitrator, and the two arbitrators thus appointed shall appoint the third arbitrator; if a party fails to appoint the arbitrator within 30 days of receipt of a request to do so from the other party, or if the two arbitrators fail to agree on the third arbitrator within 30 days of their appointment, the appointment shall be made, upon request of a party, by the court specified in Code Section 9-9-27; or

    (2) In an arbitration with a sole arbitrator, if the parties are unable to agree on the arbitrator within 30 days, the arbitrator shall be appointed, upon request of a party, by the court specified in Code Section 9-9-27.

(d) Where, under an appointment procedure agreed upon by the parties:

    (1) A party fails to act as required under such procedure;

    (2) The parties, or two arbitrators, are unable to reach an agreement expected of them under such procedure; or

    (3) A third party, including an institution, fails to perform any function entrusted to it under such procedure, any party may request the court specified in Code Section 9-9-27 to take the necessary measure, unless the arbitration agreement on the appointment procedure provides other means for securing the appointment.

(e) A decision on a matter entrusted by subsection (c) or (d) of this Code section to the court specified in Code Section 9-9-27 shall not be subject to appeal. The court, in appointing an arbitrator, shall have due regard to any qualifications required of the arbitrator by the arbitration agreement and to such considerations as are likely to secure the appointment of an independent and impartial arbitrator and, in the case of a sole or third arbitrator, shall take into account as well the advisability of appointing an arbitrator of a nationality other than those of the parties.

(f) An arbitrator shall not be liable for:

(1) Anything done or omitted in the discharge or purported discharge of arbitral functions, unless the act or omission is shown to have been in bad faith; or

(2) Any mistake of law, fact, or procedure made in the course of arbitration proceedings or in the making of an arbitration award.

(g) Subsection (f) of this Code section shall apply to an employee or agent of an arbitrator and to an appointing authority, arbitral institution, or person designated or requested by the parties to appoint or nominate an arbitrator or provide other administrative services in support of the arbitration.

Amended by 2017 Ga. Laws 275,§ 9, eff. 5/9/2017.

Added by 2012 Ga. Laws 713,§ 1, eff. 7/1/2012.

Former 9-9-32 repealed by 2012 Ga. Laws 713,§ 1, eff. 7/1/2012.

Section 9-9-33 - Arbitrator disclosure requirements; challenge of arbitrator for doubts as to impartiality or independence

(a) When a person is approached in connection with the possible appointment of such person as an arbitrator, such person shall disclose any circumstances likely to give rise to justifiable doubts as to his or her impartiality or independence. An arbitrator, from the time of appointment and throughout the arbitral proceedings, shall without delay disclose any such circumstances to the parties unless they have already been informed of them by the arbitrator.

(b) An arbitrator may be challenged only if circumstances exist that give rise to justifiable doubts as to the arbitrator's impartiality or independence, or if the arbitrator does not possess qualifications agreed to by the parties. A party may challenge an arbitrator appointed by the party, or in whose appointment the party has participated, only for reasons of which the party becomes aware after the appointment has been made.

Added by 2012 Ga. Laws 713,§ 1, eff. 7/1/2012.

Former 9-9-33 repealed by 2012 Ga. Laws 713,§ 1, eff. 7/1/2012.

Section 9-9-34 - Procedure for challenging arbitrator

(a) The parties shall be free to agree on a procedure for challenging an arbitrator, subject to the provisions of subsection (c) of this Code section.

(b) If the parties fail to agree on a procedure for challenging an arbitrator, a party who intends to challenge an arbitrator shall, within 15 days after becoming aware of the constitution of the arbitration tribunal or after becoming aware of any circumstance referred to in subsection (b) of Code Section 9-9-33, send a written statement of the reasons for the challenge to the arbitration tribunal. Unless the challenged arbitrator withdraws from office or the other party agrees to the challenge, the arbitration tribunal shall decide on the challenge.

(c) If a challenge under the procedure set forth in subsection (b) of this Code section is not successful, within 30 days after having received notice of the decision rejecting the challenge, the challenging party may request that the court specified in Code Section 9-9-27 decide on the challenge, which decision shall not be subject to appeal; while such a request is pending, the arbitration tribunal, including the challenged arbitrator, may continue the arbitral proceedings and make an arbitration award.

Added by 2012 Ga. Laws 713,§ 1, eff. 7/1/2012.

Former 9-9-34 repealed by 2012 Ga. Laws 713,§ 1, eff. 7/1/2012.

Section 9-9-35 - Inability of arbitrator to carry out or perform functions; termination of mandate

(a) If an arbitrator becomes de jure or de facto unable to perform his or her functions or for other reasons fails to act without undue delay, the arbitrator's mandate terminates if he or she withdraws from office or if the parties agree on the termination. Otherwise, if a controversy remains concerning any of these grounds, any party may request that the court specified in Code Section 9-9-27 decide on the termination of the mandate, which decision shall not be subject to appeal.

(b) If, under this Code section or subsection (b) of Code Section 9-9-34, an arbitrator withdraws from office or a party agrees to the termination of the mandate of an arbitrator, this shall not imply acceptance of the validity of any ground referred to in this Code section or subsection (b) of Code Section 9-9-33.

Added by 2012 Ga. Laws 713,§ 1, eff. 7/1/2012.

Former 9-9-35 repealed by 2012 Ga. Laws 713,§ 1, eff. 7/1/2012.

Section 9-9-36 - Appointment of substitute arbitrator

Where the mandate of an arbitrator terminates under Code Section 9-9-34 or 9-9-35 or because of withdrawal from office for any other reason or because of the revocation of the arbitrator's mandate by agreement of the parties or in any other case of termination of the arbitrator's mandate, a substitute arbitrator shall be appointed according to the rules that were applicable to the appointment of the arbitrator being replaced.

Added by 2012 Ga. Laws 713,§ 1, eff. 7/1/2012.

Former 9-9-36 repealed by 2012 Ga. Laws 713,§ 1, eff. 7/1/2012.

Section 9-9-37 - Disputes as to jurisdiction

Unless otherwise agreed by the parties:

(1) The arbitration tribunal may rule on its own jurisdiction, including any objections with respect to the existence or validity of the arbitration agreement. For that purpose, an arbitration clause which forms part of a contract shall be treated as an agreement independent of the other terms of the contract. A decision by the arbitration tribunal that the contract is null and void shall not thereby invalidate the arbitration clause;

(2) A plea that the arbitration tribunal does not have jurisdiction shall be raised not later than the submission of the statement of defense. A party shall not be precluded from raising such a plea by the fact that the party has appointed, or participated in the appointment of, an arbitrator. A plea that the arbitration tribunal is exceeding the scope of its authority shall be raised as soon as the matter alleged to be beyond the scope of its authority is raised during the arbitral proceedings. The arbitration tribunal may, in either case, admit a later plea if it considers the delay justified; and

(3) The arbitration tribunal may rule on a plea referred to in paragraph (2) of this Code section either as a preliminary question or in an arbitration award on the merits. If the arbitration tribunal rules as a preliminary question that it has jurisdiction or only partial jurisdiction, within 30 days after having received notice of such ruling and subject to the permission of the arbitration tribunal, any party may request that the court specified in Code Section 9-9-27 decide the matter, which decision shall not be subject to appeal; while such a request is pending, the arbitration tribunal may continue the arbitral proceedings and make an arbitration award.

Added by 2012 Ga. Laws 713,§ 1, eff. 7/1/2012.

Former 9-9-37 repealed by 2012 Ga. Laws 713,§ 1, eff. 7/1/2012.

Section 9-9-38 - Interim measures

(a) Unless otherwise agreed by the parties, the arbitration tribunal may, at the request of a party, grant interim measures as it deems appropriate.

(b) The arbitration tribunal may modify, suspend, or terminate an interim measure it has granted, upon application of any party or, in exceptional circumstances and upon prior notice to the parties, on the arbitration tribunal's own initiative.

(c) The arbitration tribunal may require the party requesting an interim measure to provide appropriate security in connection with the measure.

(d) The arbitration tribunal may require any party promptly to disclose any material change in the circumstances on the basis of which the measure was requested or granted.

(e) If a measure ordered under subsection (a) of this Code section proves to have been unjustified from the outset, the party which obtained its enforcement may be obliged to compensate the other party for damage resulting from the enforcement of such measure or from its providing security in order to avoid enforcement. This claim may be put forward in the pending arbitral proceedings.

(f) An interim measure issued by an arbitration tribunal shall be recognized as binding and, unless otherwise provided by the arbitration tribunal, enforced upon application to the competent court, irrespective of the country in which it was issued, subject to the provisions of Code Section 9-9-39.

(g) The party who is seeking or has obtained recognition or enforcement of an interim measure shall promptly inform the court of any termination, suspension, or modification of that interim measure.

(h) Where recognition or enforcement of an interim measure is sought in a court of this state, such court may order the requesting party to provide appropriate security if the arbitration tribunal has not already made a determination with respect to security or where such a decision is necessary to protect the rights of third parties.

Added by 2012 Ga. Laws 713,§ 1, eff. 7/1/2012.

Former 9-9-38 repealed by 2012 Ga. Laws 713,§ 1, eff. 7/1/2012.

Section 9-9-39 - When recognition or enforcement of interim measure may be refused

(a) Recognition or enforcement of an interim measure may be refused only:

  (1) At the request of the party against whom it is invoked if the court is satisfied that:

    (A) Such refusal is warranted on the grounds set forth in subparagraphs (a)(1)(A) through (a)(1)(D) of Code Section 9-9-58;

    (B) The arbitration tribunal's decision with respect to the provision of security in connection with the interim measure issued by the arbitration tribunal has not been complied with; or

    (C) The interim measure has been terminated or suspended by the arbitration tribunal or, where so empowered, by the court of the state in which the arbitration takes place or under the law of which that interim measure was granted; or

  (2) If the court finds that:

    (A) The interim measure is incompatible with the powers conferred upon the court, unless the court decides to reformulate the interim measure to the extent necessary to adapt it to its own powers and procedures for the purposes of enforcing that interim measure and without modifying its substance; or

    (B) Any of the grounds set forth in subparagraph (a)(2)(A) or (a)(2)(B) of Code Section 9-9-58 shall apply to the recognition and enforcement of the interim measure.

(b) Any determination made by the court on any ground in subsection (a) of this Code section shall be effective only for the purposes of the application to recognize and enforce the interim measure. Where recognition or enforcement is sought, the court shall not undertake a review of the substance of the interim measure in determining any ground specified in subsection (a) of this Code section.

Added by 2012 Ga. Laws 713,§ 1, eff. 7/1/2012.

Former 9-9-39 repealed by 2012 Ga. Laws 713,§ 1, eff. 7/1/2012.

Section 9-9-40 - Treatment of parties

The parties shall be treated with equality, and each party shall be given a full opportunity of presenting its case.

Added by 2012 Ga. Laws 713,§ 1, eff. 7/1/2012.

Former 9-9-40 repealed by 2012 Ga. Laws 713,§ 1, eff. 7/1/2012.

Section 9-9-41 - Procedure to be followed by arbitration tribunal

(a) Subject to the provisions of this part, the parties shall be free to agree on the procedure to be followed by the arbitration tribunal in conducting the proceedings.

(b) If the parties fail to agree on the procedure to be followed by the arbitration tribunal in conducting proceedings, the arbitration tribunal may, subject to the provisions of this part, conduct the arbitration in such manner as it considers appropriate. The power conferred upon the arbitration tribunal includes the power to determine the admissibility, relevance, materiality, and weight of any evidence.

Added by 2012 Ga. Laws 713,§ 1, eff. 7/1/2012.

Former 9-9-41 repealed by 2012 Ga. Laws 713,§ 1, eff. 7/1/2012.

Section 9-9-42 - Place of arbitration

(a) The parties shall be free to agree on the place of arbitration; provided, however, that failing such agreement, the place of arbitration shall be determined by the arbitration tribunal having regard to the circumstances of the case, including the convenience of the parties.

(b) Notwithstanding the provisions of subsection (a) of this Code section, the arbitration tribunal may, unless otherwise agreed by the parties, meet at any place it considers appropriate for consultation among its members, for hearing witnesses, experts, or the parties, or for inspection of goods, other property, or documents.

Added by 2012 Ga. Laws 713,§ 1, eff. 7/1/2012.

Former 9-9-42 repealed by 2012 Ga. Laws 713,§ 1, eff. 7/1/2012.

Section 9-9-43 - Date of commencement of arbitral proceedings

Unless otherwise agreed by the parties, the arbitral proceedings in respect of a particular dispute shall commence on the date on which a request for that dispute to be referred to arbitration is received by the respondent.

Added by 2012 Ga. Laws 713,§ 1, eff. 7/1/2012.

Former 9-9-43 repealed by 2012 Ga. Laws 713,§ 1, eff. 7/1/2012.

Section 9-9-44 - Languages to be used in arbitral proceedings; translation of documentary evidence

(a) The parties shall be free to agree on the language or languages to be used in the arbitral proceedings; provided, however, that failing such agreement, the arbitration tribunal shall determine the language or languages to be used in the proceedings. Such agreement or determination, unless otherwise specified therein, shall apply to any written statement by a party, any hearing, and any arbitration award, decision, or other communication by the arbitration tribunal.

(b) The arbitration tribunal may order that any documentary evidence be accompanied by a translation into the language or languages agreed upon by the parties or determined by the arbitration tribunal.

Added by 2012 Ga. Laws 713,§ 1, eff. 7/1/2012.

Section 9-9-45 - Facts supporting claim; amendment or supplementing of claim

(a) Within the period of time agreed by the parties or determined by the arbitration tribunal, the claimant shall state the facts supporting his or her claim, the points at issue, and the relief or remedy sought, and the respondent shall state his or her defense in respect of these particulars, unless the parties have otherwise agreed as to the required elements of such statements. The parties may submit with their statements all documents they consider to be relevant or may add a reference to the documents or other evidence they will submit.

(b) Unless otherwise agreed by the parties, either party may amend or supplement his or her claim or defense during the course of the arbitral proceedings, unless the arbitration tribunal considers it inappropriate to allow such amendment having regard to the delay in making it.

Added by 2012 Ga. Laws 713,§ 1, eff. 7/1/2012.

Section 9-9-46 - How proceedings to be conducted; oral hearings; notice; consolidation of proceedings or hearings

(a) Subject to any contrary agreement by the parties, the arbitration tribunal shall decide whether to hold oral hearings for the presentation of evidence or for oral argument, or whether the proceedings shall be conducted on the basis of documents and other materials; provided, however, that unless the parties have agreed that no hearings shall be held, the arbitration tribunal shall hold hearings at an appropriate stage of the proceedings, if requested by a party.

(b) The parties shall be given sufficient advance notice of any hearing and of any meeting of the arbitration tribunal for the purposes of inspection of goods, other property, or documents.

(c) All statements, documents, or other information supplied to the arbitration tribunal by one party shall be communicated to the other party. Any expert report or evidentiary document on which the arbitration tribunal may rely in making its decision shall be communicated to the parties.

(d) Unless the parties agree to confer such power on the tribunal, the tribunal shall not have the power to order consolidation of proceedings or concurrent hearings; provided, however, that the parties shall be free to agree:

   (1) That the arbitral proceedings shall be consolidated with other arbitral proceedings; or

   (2) That concurrent hearings shall be held, on such terms as may be agreed.

Added by 2012 Ga. Laws 713,§ 1, eff. 7/1/2012.

Section 9-9-47 - Effects of failure to state facts supporting claim, failure to put forward statement of defense, or failure to appear at hearing or to produce documentary evidence

Unless otherwise agreed by the parties, if, without showing sufficient cause:

(1) The claimant fails to communicate his or her statement of claim in accordance with subsection (a) of Code Section 9-9-45, the arbitration tribunal shall terminate the proceedings;

(2) The respondent fails to communicate his or her statement of defense in accordance with subsection (a) of Code Section 9-9-45, the arbitration tribunal shall continue the proceedings without treating such failure in itself as an admission of the claimant's allegations; and

(3) Any party fails to appear at a hearing or to produce documentary evidence, the arbitration tribunal may continue the proceedings and make the arbitration award on the evidence before it.

Added by 2012 Ga. Laws 713,§ 1, eff. 7/1/2012.

Section 9-9-48 - Appointment of experts

(a) Unless otherwise agreed by the parties, the arbitration tribunal:

   (1) May appoint one or more experts to report to it on specific issues to be determined by the arbitration tribunal; and

   (2) May require a party to give the expert any relevant information or to produce, or to provide access to, any relevant documents, goods, or other property for the expert's inspection.

(b) Unless otherwise agreed by the parties, if a party requests or if the arbitration tribunal considers it necessary, the expert shall, after delivery of the expert's written or oral report, participate in a hearing where the parties have the opportunity to put questions to the expert and to present expert witnesses in order to testify on the points at issue.

Added by 2012 Ga. Laws 713,§ 1, eff. 7/1/2012.

Section 9-9-49 - Subpoenas for witnesses and other evidence; compensation of witnesses

(a) The arbitrators may issue subpoenas for the attendance of witnesses and for the production of books, records, documents, and other evidence. Subpoenas shall be served and, upon application to the court specified in Code Section 9-9-27 by a party or the arbitrators, enforced in the same manner provided by law for the service and enforcement of subpoenas in a civil action.

(b) Notices to produce books, writings, and other documents or tangible things, depositions, and other discovery may be used in the arbitration according to procedures established by the arbitrators.

(c) A party shall have the opportunity to obtain a list of witnesses and to examine and copy documents relevant to the arbitration.

(d) Witnesses shall be compensated in the same amount and manner set forth in Title 24.

Added by 2012 Ga. Laws 713,§ 1, eff. 7/1/2012.

Section 9-9-50 - Rules applicable to disputes

(a) The arbitration tribunal shall decide the dispute in accordance with such rules of law as are chosen by the parties as applicable to the substance of the dispute. Any designation of the law or legal system of a given state shall be construed, unless otherwise expressed, as directly referring to the substantive law of that state and not to its conflict of laws rules.

(b) Failing any designation by the parties, the arbitration tribunal shall apply the law determined by the conflict of laws rules which it considers applicable.

(c) The arbitration tribunal shall decide ex aequo et bono or as amiable compositeur only if the parties have expressly authorized it to do so.

(d) In all cases, the arbitration tribunal shall decide in accordance with the terms of the contract and shall take into account the usages of the trade applicable to the transaction.

Added by 2012 Ga. Laws 713,§ 1, eff. 7/1/2012.

Section 9-9-51 - Decision-making when more than one arbitrator

In arbitral proceedings with more than one arbitrator, any decision of the arbitration tribunal shall be made, unless otherwise agreed by the parties, by a majority of all its members; provided, however, that questions of procedure may be decided by a presiding arbitrator, if authorized by the parties or all members of the arbitration tribunal.

Added by 2012 Ga. Laws 713,§ 1, eff. 7/1/2012.

Section 9-9-52 - Settlement; arbitration award on agreed terms

(a) If, during arbitral proceedings, the parties settle the dispute, the arbitration tribunal shall terminate the proceedings and, if requested by the parties and not objected to by the arbitration tribunal, record the settlement in the form of an arbitration award on agreed terms.

(b) An arbitration award on agreed terms shall be made in accordance with the provisions of Code Section 9-9-53 and shall state that it is an arbitration award. Such an arbitration award shall have the same status and effect as any other arbitration award on the merits of the case.

Added by 2012 Ga. Laws 713,§ 1, eff. 7/1/2012.

Section 9-9-53 - Arbitration award

(a) An arbitration award shall be made in writing and shall be signed by the arbitrator or arbitrators. In arbitral proceedings with more than one arbitrator, the signatures of the majority of all members of the arbitration tribunal shall suffice, provided that the reason for any omitted signature is stated.

(b) The arbitration award shall state the reasons upon which it is based, unless the parties have agreed that no reasons are to be given or the arbitration award is an arbitration award on agreed terms pursuant to Code Section 9-9-52.

(c) The arbitration award shall state its date and the place of arbitration as determined in accordance with subsection (a) of Code Section 9-9-42. The arbitration award shall be deemed to have been made at that place.

(d) After the arbitration award is made, a copy signed by the arbitrators in accordance with subsection (a) of this Code section shall be delivered to each party.

(e) The arbitrators may award reasonable fees and expenses actually incurred, including, without limitation, fees and expenses of legal counsel, to any party to the arbitration and shall allocate the costs of the arbitration among the parties as it determines appropriate.

Added by 2012 Ga. Laws 713,§ 1, eff. 7/1/2012.

Section 9-9-54 - Termination of arbitral proceedings

(a) The arbitral proceedings shall be terminated by the final arbitration award or by an order of the arbitration tribunal in accordance with subsection (b) of this Code section.

(b) The arbitration tribunal shall issue an order for the termination of the arbitral proceedings when:

    (1) The claimant withdraws his or her claim, unless the respondent objects thereto and the arbitration tribunal recognizes a legitimate interest by the respondent in obtaining a final settlement of the dispute;

    (2) The parties agree on the termination of the proceedings; or

    (3) The arbitration tribunal finds that the continuation of the proceedings has for any other reason become unnecessary or impossible.

(c) The mandate of the arbitration tribunal shall terminate with the termination of the arbitral proceedings, subject to the provisions of Code Section 9-9-55 and subsection (d) of Code Section 9-9-56.

Added by 2012 Ga. Laws 713,§ 1, eff. 7/1/2012.

Section 9-9-55 - Correction or interpretation of arbitration award; additional arbitration awards; extension of time for correction, interpretation, or additional award

(a)

(1) Within 30 days of receipt of the arbitration award, unless another period of time has been agreed upon by the parties:

(A) A party, with notice to the other party, may request the arbitration tribunal to correct in the arbitration award any errors in computation, any clerical or typographical errors, or any errors of similar nature; and

(B) If agreed by the parties, a party, with notice to the other party, may request the arbitration tribunal to give an interpretation of a specific point or part of the arbitration award.

(2) If the arbitration tribunal considers any request under paragraph (1) of this subsection to be justified, it shall make the correction or give the interpretation within 30 days of receipt of the request. The interpretation shall form part of the arbitration award.

(b) The arbitration tribunal may correct any error of the type referred to in subparagraph (a)(1)(A) of this Code section on its own initiative within 30 days of the date of the arbitration award.

(c) Unless otherwise agreed by the parties, a party, with notice to the other party, may request, within 30 days of receipt of the arbitration award, the arbitration tribunal to make an additional award as to claims presented in the arbitration proceedings but omitted from the arbitration award. If the arbitration tribunal considers such request to be justified, it shall make the additional award within 60 days of receipt of the request.

(d) The arbitration tribunal may extend, if necessary, the period of time within which it shall make a correction, interpretation, or an additional award under subsection (a) or (c) of this Code section.

(e) The provisions of Code Section 9-9-53 shall apply to a correction or interpretation of the arbitration award or to an additional award.

Added by 2012 Ga. Laws 713,§ 1, eff. 7/1/2012.

Section 9-9-56 - Recourse against arbitration award; criteria for setting aside award; time for making application to set aside

(a) Recourse to a court against an arbitration award may be made only by an application for setting aside in accordance with subsections (b) and (c) of this Code section.

(b) An arbitration award may be set aside by the court specified in Code Section 9-9-27 only if:

(1) The party making the application furnishes proof that:

(A) A party to the arbitration agreement referred to in Code Section 9-9-28 was under some incapacity; or that said arbitration agreement is not valid under the law to which the parties have subjected it or, failing any indication thereon, under the law of this state;

(B) The party making the application was not given proper notice of the appointment of an arbitrator or of the arbitral proceedings or was otherwise unable to present his or her case;

(C) The arbitration award deals with a dispute not contemplated by or not falling within the terms of the submission to arbitration or contains decisions on matters beyond the scope of the submission to arbitration, provided that, if the decisions on matters submitted to arbitration can be separated from those not so submitted, only that part of the arbitration award which contains decisions on matters not submitted to arbitration may be set aside; or

(D) The composition of the arbitration tribunal or the arbitral procedure was not in accordance with the arbitration agreement of the parties, unless such arbitration agreement was in conflict with a provision of this part from which the parties cannot derogate, or, failing such agreement, was not in accordance with this part; or

(2) The court finds that:

(A) The subject matter of the dispute is not capable of settlement by arbitration under the law of the United States; or

(B) The arbitration award is in conflict with the public policy of the United States.

(c) An application for setting aside an arbitration award may not be made after three months have elapsed from the date on which the party making that application had received the arbitration award or, if a request had been made under Code Section 9-9-55, from the date on which that request had been disposed of by the arbitration tribunal.

(d) The court, when asked to set aside an arbitration award, may, where appropriate and requested by a party, suspend the setting aside proceedings for a period of time determined by it in order to give the arbitration tribunal an opportunity to resume the arbitral proceedings or to take such other action as in the arbitration tribunal's opinion will eliminate the grounds for setting aside.

(e) Where none of the parties is domiciled or has its place of business in this state, they may, by written agreement referencing this subsection, limit any of the grounds for recourse against the arbitration award under this Code section, with the exception of paragraph (2) of subsection (b) of this Code section.

Added by 2012 Ga. Laws 713,§ 1, eff. 7/1/2012.

Section 9-9-57 - Arbitration award recognized as binding; enforcement

(a) An arbitration award, irrespective of the country in which it was made, shall be recognized as binding and, upon application in writing to the competent court, shall be enforced subject to the provisions of this Code section and of Code Section 9-9-58.

(b) The party relying on an arbitration award or applying for its enforcement shall supply the original arbitration award or a copy thereof. The court may request the party to supply a translation of the arbitration award.

Added by 2012 Ga. Laws 713,§ 1, eff. 7/1/2012.

Section 9-9-58 - Grounds for refusing recognition or enforcement of arbitration award

(a) Recognition or enforcement of an arbitration award, irrespective of the country in which it was made, may be refused only:

(1) At the request of the party against whom it is invoked, if that party furnishes to the competent court where recognition or enforcement is sought proof that:

(A) A party to the arbitration agreement referred to in Code Section 9-9-28 was under some incapacity; or the arbitration agreement is not valid under the law to which the parties have subjected it or, failing any indication thereon, under the law of the country where the arbitration award was made;

(B) The party against whom the arbitration award is invoked was not given proper notice of the appointment of an arbitrator or of the arbitral proceedings or was otherwise unable to present his or her case;

(C) The arbitration award deals with a dispute not contemplated by or not falling within the terms of the submission to arbitration, or it contains decisions on matters beyond the scope of the submission to arbitration, provided that, if the decisions on matters submitted to arbitration can be separated from those not so submitted, that part of the arbitration award which contains decisions on matters submitted to arbitration may be recognized and enforced;

(D) The composition of the arbitration tribunal or the arbitral procedure was not in accordance with the arbitration agreement of the parties or, failing such agreement, was not in accordance with the law of the country where the arbitration took place; or

(E) The arbitration award has not yet become binding on the parties or has been set aside or suspended by a court of the country in which, or under the law of which, that arbitration award was made; or

(2) If the court finds that:

(A) The subject matter of the dispute is not capable of settlement by arbitration under the law of the United States; or

(B) The recognition or enforcement of the arbitration award would be contrary to the public policy of the United States.

(b) If an application for setting aside or suspension of an arbitration award has been made to a court referred to in subparagraph (a)(1)(E) of this Code section, the court where recognition or enforcement is sought may, if it considers it proper, adjourn its decision and may also, on the application of the party claiming recognition or enforcement of the arbitration award, order the other party to provide appropriate security.

Added by 2012 Ga. Laws 713,§ 1, eff. 7/1/2012.

Section 9-9-59 - Appeal of final judgment

Any judgment considered a final judgment under this part may be appealed pursuant to Chapter 6 of Title 5.

Added by 2012 Ga. Laws 713,§ 1, eff. 7/1/2012.

Article 2 - MEDICAL MALPRACTICE

Section 9-9-60 - "Medical malpractice claim" defined

For the purposes of this article, the term "medical malpractice claim" means any claim for damages resulting from the death of or injury to any person arising out of:

(1) Health, medical, dental, or surgical service, diagnosis, prescription, treatment, or care, rendered by a person authorized by law to perform such service or by any person acting under the supervision and control of a lawfully authorized person; or

(2) Care or service rendered by any public or private hospital, nursing home, clinic, hospital authority, facility, or institution, or by any officer, agent, or employee thereof acting within the scope of his employment.

Section 9-9-61 - Medical malpractice arbitration authorized

In addition to any other legal procedure for the resolution of medical malpractice claims, the parties to a medical malpractice claim may submit the claim for arbitration in accordance with this article.

Section 9-9-62 - Petition for arbitration; arbitration order and appointment of referee; conditions precedent to enforceability

If the parties to a medical malpractice claim agree in writing to arbitrate the claim pursuant to this article, they shall file a petition in the superior court of the county where any party resides for an order authorizing the arbitration of the claim in accordance with this article and for the appointment of a referee for the arbitration. If the judge determines that the claim is a medical malpractice claim subject to this article, within 30 days of the filing of the petition for such order he shall issue an order authorizing the arbitration and appointing a referee. However, no agreement to arbitrate shall be enforceable unless the agreement was made subsequent to the alleged malpractice and after a dispute or controversy has occurred and unless the claimant is represented by an attorney at law at the time the agreement is entered into.

Section 9-9-63 - Tolling of statute of limitations; when action permitted after filing of petition for arbitration

(a) The filing of the petition for an order authorizing arbitration as provided in Code Section 9-9-62 shall toll any applicable statute of limitations, and the statute of limitations shall remain tolled until the earliest of:

(1) Thirty days after the filing of the petition, when the judge has failed within the 30 days to issue an order authorizing arbitration as provided in Code Section 9-9-62;

(2) Sixty days after the issuance of the judge's order authorizing arbitration, when the parties or their representatives have failed by such time to sign the arbitration submission as provided in Code Section 9-9-65; or

(3) The date the arbitration submission is revoked as provided in Code Section 9-9-65.

(b) If any of the contingencies listed in subsection (a) of this Code section occur and if the statute of limitations has not yet run, the medical malpractice claim may be brought in any court of this state having jurisdiction.

Section 9-9-64 - Appointment of reporter; duties; compensation

The judge of the superior court of the county in which was issued the order authorizing arbitration shall appoint a reporter to attend the proceedings of the medical malpractice arbitration panel and to record exactly and truly the testimony and proceedings in the case being arbitrated, except the arguments of counsel. All provisions relating to court reporter fees, compensation, contingent expenses, and travel allowance, as well as those relating to the furnishing of transcripts and the style and form of transcripts, shall be the same for reporters appointed to attend the arbitration panel proceedings as those applicable to reporters of the superior court of the county in which the arbitration was authorized.

Section 9-9-65 - Arbitration submission; irrevocability absent consent

(a) The referee shall meet with the parties or their representatives, or both, prior to the arbitration. The referee shall assist the parties in preparing an arbitration submission which shall contain the following:

(1) A clear and accurate statement of the matters in controversy;

(2) An agreement as to the payment of the costs of the arbitration;

(3) The procedure to be followed in the arbitration;

(4) A list of the witnesses whose testimony the parties desire to present to the arbitrators;

(5) The names of the arbitrators chosen by each party;

(6) The time and place of meeting of the arbitrators; and

(7) Any other matters that may be pertinent to the arbitration.

(b) The submission shall be in writing and shall be signed by the parties or their representatives. When signed, the submission shall be irrevocable except by consent of all the parties.

Section 9-9-66 - Qualifications and status of referee

The referee shall be an attorney who is an active member of the State Bar of Georgia. The referee shall be a nonvoting member of the arbitration panel.

Section 9-9-67 - Arbitrators - How chosen

(a) Every arbitration pursuant to this article shall be conducted by three arbitrators, one of whom shall be chosen by each of the parties prior to the execution of the submission provided for in Code Section 9-9-65 and one of whom shall be chosen by the arbitrators named in the submission. The third arbitrator shall be chosen after the parties sign the submission provided in Code Section 9-9-65 and before arbitration begins.

(b) If the arbitrators chosen by the parties are unable to agree upon the third arbitrator as provided in subsection (a) of this Code section, the judge authorizing the arbitration and appointing the referee or the judge's successor shall appoint the third arbitrator.

(c) In cases involving a medical malpractice claim where there are multiple plaintiffs or defendants, there shall be only one arbitrator chosen by each side. The plaintiff parties shall have the right to choose one arbitrator and the defendant parties shall have the right to choose one arbitrator.

Section 9-9-68 - Arbitrators - How vacancy filled

If an arbitrator selected by one of the parties should cease to serve for any reason, the party who chose the arbitrator shall then choose another in his place. If the arbitrator chosen by the other arbitrators shall cease to serve for any reason, the arbitrators chosen by the parties shall choose another in his place. If the arbitrators chosen by the parties are unable to agree upon the third arbitrator, the third arbitrator shall be appointed as provided in subsection (b) of Code Section 9-9-67. An arbitrator chosen pursuant to this Code section shall have all the powers of the original arbitrator.

Section 9-9-69 - Arbitrators - Oath and affidavit

(a) Before the arbitrators begin the arbitration, they shall be sworn by the referee to determine impartially the matters submitted to them according to law and the justice and equity of the case without favor or affection to either party.

(b) Each arbitrator selected under this article shall sign the following affidavit before the selection is effective and before acting as an arbitrator: State of Georgia County I, , first being duly sworn, make this affidavit: I, , agree to serve as arbitrator in the case of v. and will decide any issue put before me without favor or affection to any party and without prejudice for or against any party. I will follow and apply the law as given to me by the referee and will accept and abide by all decisions of the referee. I also agree not to discuss this case or any issue with any person except when all other arbitrators and the referee are present. , L. S.

Section 9-9-70 - Postponement of arbitration

When, upon the meeting of the arbitrators, either party is not ready for trial, the referee may postpone the hearing of the case to a future day, which day shall be as early as may be consistent with the ends of justice, considering all the circumstances of the case. If one party is not ready for trial at the time appointed for the hearing of the case and the party has previously required two or more postponements of the trial, the referee shall determine whether the arbitration panel shall nonetheless hear the case or whether another postponement shall be granted, the determination to be consistent with the ends of justice, considering all the circumstances of the case.

Section 9-9-71 - Adjournments by arbitrators; no meeting outside group

After the arbitrators have commenced their investigations, they may adjourn from day to day or for a longer time, if the ends of justice require it, until their investigations are completed and they have made up their award. The arbitrators shall not meet or discuss the case or any issue except as a group and with the referee present.

Section 9-9-72 - Discovery

The parties to the arbitration may obtain discovery in the same manner as provided by law for discovery in civil cases in the superior courts.

Section 9-9-73 - Subpoena power of referee; compensation of witnesses

The referee shall have all the powers of the superior courts to compel the attendance of witnesses before the arbitrators, to compel witnesses to testify, and to issue subpoenas requiring the attendance of witnesses at the time and place of the meeting of the arbitrators. Subpoenas shall be served in the manner provided by law for the service of subpoenas in cases pending in the superior courts. Witnesses shall be entitled to the same compensation as witnesses in the superior courts, and the compensation may be collected in the same manner.

Section 9-9-74 - Powers of referee to compel production of documentary evidence

The referee shall have all the powers of the superior courts to compel parties to produce books and all other papers which may be deemed necessary and proper for the investigation of the matters submitted to arbitration, giving to the party, his agent, or his attorney, from whom the production is required, such notice as is required in the superior courts for the production of papers.

Section 9-9-75 - Competency of witnesses

All persons who are competent as witnesses in the superior courts shall be competent in all cases before the arbitrators.

Section 9-9-76 - Rules governing examination of witnesses and admission of evidence

The examination of witnesses and the admission of evidence shall be governed by the rules applicable to the superior courts.

Section 9-9-77 - Administration of oaths by referee

The referee shall have power to administer oaths to witnesses and to administer all other oaths that may be necessary for carrying this article into full effect.

Section 9-9-78 - Findings by arbitrators; concurrence of two sufficient

The arbitrators shall make a written finding on each of the matters in controversy contained in the submission. If the arbitrators shall fail to agree on any finding, then any two of them may make the finding, which shall have the same force and effect as if made by all.

Section 9-9-79 - Copy of findings furnished parties; entry of original on court's minutes; effect and enforcement; clerk's fees

After the arbitrators have made their findings, the referee shall furnish each of the parties with a copy thereof. The original shall be entered on the minutes of the court authorizing the arbitration; it shall have all the force and effect of a judgment or decree of the court and may be enforced in the same manner at any time after the adjournment of the court. For the entering of the findings upon the minutes of the court, the clerk shall be entitled to the same fees allowed by law for the entering of judgments in other cases, to be paid by the parties as provided in the submission.

Section 9-9-80 - Finality of findings absent appeal; appeals to superior courts; transmittal of record; when findings set aside; disposition of case; supersedeas

(a) All findings of the arbitrators with respect to which no application for a review thereof is filed in due time shall be final and conclusive between the parties as to all matters submitted to the arbitrators; but either party to the dispute may, within 30 days from the date the findings are entered upon the minutes of the court authorizing the arbitration, appeal from the findings to the superior court of the county in which the arbitration was authorized. When an appeal is made, all findings shall be final and conclusive between the parties as to all matters submitted to the arbitrators only upon the final disposition of the appeal as provided by this article.

(b) The party conceiving himself to be aggrieved may file an application in writing to the referee of the arbitration panel asking for an appeal from the findings, stating generally the grounds upon which the appeal is sought. In the event the appeal is filed as provided in this Code section, the referee shall, within 30 days from the filing of the same, cause a true copy of the submission, findings, and all other parts of the record, including a transcript of evidence and proceedings, to be transmitted to the clerk of the superior court to which the case is appealable. The case so appealed may thereupon be brought on for a hearing before the superior court upon such record by either party on ten days' written notice to the other; subject, however, to an assignment of the same for hearing by the court.

(c) The findings of fact made by the arbitrators shall, in the absence of fraud, be conclusive but, upon the hearing, the court shall set aside the findings if it is found that:

(1) The findings were procured by fraud;

(2) There is no evidence to support the findings of fact by the arbitrators; or

(3) The findings are contrary to law.

(d) No findings shall be set aside by the court upon any grounds other than one or more of the grounds above-stated. If not set aside upon one or more of the stated grounds, the court shall affirm the findings so appealed from. Upon the setting aside of any such findings, the court may recommit the controversy to the arbitration panel for further hearing or proceeding in conformity with the judgment and opinion of the court or the court may enter the proper judgment upon the findings, as the nature of the case may demand. The decree of the court shall have the same effect and all proceedings in relation thereto shall thereafter be the same as though rendered in an action heard and determined by the court.

(e) An appeal from the decision of the arbitration panel shall operate as a supersedeas and no defendant shall be required to make payment of the amount involved in the submission in the case so appealed until the question at issue therein has been fully determined in accordance with this article. The defendant may voluntarily make payment, however, prior to final disposition of the appeal.

Section 9-9-81 - Costs; how taxed

The arbitrators shall return in their award the costs of the case, which they shall tax against the parties in accordance with the submission.

Section 9-9-82 - Compensation of arbitrators and referee

The arbitrators and referee shall have such compensation for their services as may be agreed upon by the parties in the submission.

Section 9-9-83 - Civil and criminal immunity of arbitrators

An arbitrator shall not be civilly or criminally liable for libel, slander, or defamation of any of the parties to the arbitration for any statement or action taken within the official capacity of the arbitrator during the arbitration.

Section 9-9-84 - [Repealed] Governor's Commission on Obstetrics

Repealed by Ga. L. 1990, p. 573, § 1, effective December 1, 1990.

Chapter 10 - CIVIL PRACTICE AND PROCEDURE GENERALLY
Article 1 - GENERAL PROVISIONS

Section 9-10-1 - Preference given to cases in which state is plaintiff

Where civil cases are pending in the superior courts, the Court of Appeals, or the Supreme Court in which the state is a party plaintiff, preference shall be given to such cases over all other cases so pending; and the judges or Justices, as the case may be, shall use all the power vested in them by law to bring the cases to a speedy trial and, whenever required to do so by counsel for the state, shall take up the cases for trial and proceed to try the same, unless the defendant shows some good cause for continuance, when the case shall be continued to a future time in the same term, or to the next term, in the discretion of the court. Nothing in this Code section shall affect the right of the state to a continuance on a proper showing.

Section 9-10-2 - Actions against state void absent notice or waiver

Any verdict, decision, judgment, decree, order, ruling, or other judicial action by any court in this state in any matter in which this state or an official of this state in his official capacity is a party defendant, intervenor, respondent, appellee, or plaintiff in fi. fa. shall be void unless it affirmatively appears as a matter of record either:

(1) That the Attorney General was given five days' advance written notice by the adverse party or his attorney of the time set for the particular trial, hearing, or other proceeding as a result of which the verdict, decision, judgment, decree, order, ruling, or other judicial action was entered;

(2) That the Attorney General or an assistant attorney general was present in person at the trial, hearing, or other proceeding; or

(3) That the Attorney General or an assistant attorney general has, in writing, waived the notice.

Amended by 2007 Ga. Laws 18,§ 9, eff. 5/11/2007.

Section 9-10-3 - Closed trials authorized in certain cases

During the trial in any court of any case in which the evidence is vulgar and obscene or relates to improper sexual acts and tends to debauch the morals of the young, the presiding judge shall have the right, in his discretion and on his own motion, or on motion of the plaintiff or the defendant or their attorneys, to hear and try the case after clearing the courtroom of all or any portion of the audience.

Section 9-10-4 - Trial of collateral issues

All collateral issues in the superior, state, or city courts, unless otherwise directed by law, shall be tried by jury.

Section 9-10-5 - Charges to be written out on request; exception; filing of written charges; copies

(a) The judges of the superior, state, and city courts, when counsel for either party requests it before argument begins, shall write out their charges and read them to the jury; and it shall be error to give any other or additional charge than that so written and read; provided, however, that this Code section shall not apply when there is an official court reporter in attendance thereon who records the full charge of the trial judge in the case upon the direction of the court.

(b) In any civil action, upon motion by a party, upon request by the jury, or sua sponte, a judge of a superior, state, or city court is authorized, but shall not be required, to reduce all of the charge to the jury to writing and send all of the charge so reduced to writing out with the jury during its deliberation.

(c) Any charge reduced to writing under subsection (a) or (b) of this Code section shall be filed with the clerk of the court in which it was given and shall be accessible to all persons interested in it. The clerk shall give certified copies of the charge to any person applying therefor, upon payment of the usual fee.

Section 9-10-6 - Juror's private knowledge

A juror shall not act on his or her private knowledge respecting the facts, witnesses, or parties.

Amended by 2011 Ga. Laws 52,§; 9, eff. 1/1/2013.

Section 9-10-7 - Expression by judge of opinion in case reversible error

It is error for any judge, during the progress of any case, or in his charge to the jury, to express or intimate his opinion as to what has or has not been proved. Should any judge violate this Code section, the violation shall be held by the Supreme Court or Court of Appeals to be error, the decision in the case shall be reversed, and a new trial shall be granted in the court below with such directions as the Supreme Court or the Court of Appeals may lawfully give.

Section 9-10-8 - Approval or disapproval of verdict by judge forbidden; discharge or commendation of jury for verdict not permitted; judge expressing approval or disapproval disqualified from presiding at new trial

(a) No judge of any court shall either directly or indirectly express in open court his approval or disapproval of the verdict of any jury in any case tried before him, except as provided in this Code section; nor may the judge discharge any jury upon the ground that the verdict rendered in any case does not meet with his approval.

(b) No judge of any court may commend or compliment a jury during the term of any court for discharging its duty if the commendation or compliment has the effect of approving a verdict.

(c) If any judge of any court either directly or indirectly expresses in open court his approval or disapproval of the verdict of the jury in any case tried before him, he shall be disqualified from presiding in the case in the event a new trial is granted.

(d) Nothing in this Code section shall have the effect of prohibiting a judge of any court from approving or disapproving the verdict of a jury in any case tried before him in hearing a motion for a new trial that comes on before him; however, the approval or disapproval on the hearing of a motion for new trial shall be expressed in the formal order of the judge in granting or overruling the motion and not otherwise.

Section 9-10-9 - [Repealed] Jurors' affidavits permitted to uphold but not impeach verdict

Repealed by 2011 Ga. Laws 52,§ 10, eff. 1/1/2013.

Reserved. Repealed by Ga. L. 2011, p. 99, § 10/HB 24, effective January 1, 2013.

Section 9-10-10 - Cash bonds permitted; docketing

(a) Any party, litigant, or other person required or permitted by law to give or post bond or bail as surety or security for the happening of any event or act in all civil matters may discharge the requirement by depositing cash in the amount of the bond so required with the appropriate person, official, or other depository.

(b) Any official or other person receiving any such bond shall give a receipt therefor and shall cause the fact of the receipt to be entered and recorded on the docket of the case in which it was given. If bond is given in a matter not appearing as a separate court case on a docket, a docket shall be prepared, maintained, and kept of all such transactions. The name and address of the person giving or making the bond, the date of the receipt of the bond, the name of the person receiving the bond, the amount of the bond, and a description of the cause for giving the bond, together with any and all other desirable information concerning the bond, shall be a part of the record in that separate docket.

Section 9-10-11 - When appearance bond not forfeited by failure to attend; setting aside forfeiture of appearance bond

(a) No judgment decreeing the forfeiture of any appearance bond shall be rendered:

(1) If it is shown to the satisfaction of the court by the sworn statement of a reputable physician that the principal in the bond was prevented from attending by some physical disability; or

(2) If it is shown to the satisfaction of the court that the principal in the bond was prevented from attending because he was detained in a penal institution in another jurisdiction. A sworn affidavit of the warden or other responsible officer of the penal institution in which the principal is being detained shall be considered adequate proof of the principal's detention.

(b) If adequate proof is furnished within 60 days of the forfeiture of an appearance bond that the principal failed to appear on the date of forfeiture for one of the reasons set forth in subsection (a) of this Code section, the forfeiture shall be set aside.

Section 9-10-12 - Certified mail equivalent to registered mail; sufficient compliance for notice by statutory overnight delivery

(a) Whenever any law, statute, Code section, ordinance, rule, or regulation of this state or any officer, department, agency, municipality, or governmental subdivision thereof provides that a notice shall be given by "registered mail," the notice may be given by "certified mail."

(b) Whenever any law, statute, Code section, ordinance, rule, or regulation of this state or any officer, department, agency, municipality, or governmental subdivision thereof provides that a notice may be given by "statutory overnight delivery," it shall be sufficient compliance if:

(1) Such notice is delivered through the United States Postal Service or through a commercial firm which is regularly engaged in the business of document delivery or document and package delivery;

(2) The terms of the sender's engagement of the services of the United States Postal Service or commercial firm call for the document to be delivered not later than the next business day following the day on which it is received for delivery by the United States Postal Service or the commercial firm; and

(3) The sender receives from the United States Postal Service or the commercial firm a receipt acknowledging receipt of the document which receipt is signed by the addressee or an agent of the addressee.

Section 9-10-13 - Effect of judgment on party vouched into court

Where a defendant may have a remedy over against another person and vouches him into court by giving notice of the pendency of the action, the judgment rendered therein shall be conclusive upon the person vouched, as to the amount and right of the plaintiff to recover.

Section 9-10-14 - Promulgation of form for use by inmates in actions against government

(a) The Administrative Office of the Courts shall, with the approval of the Supreme Court, promulgate and from time to time amend as necessary a form or forms for use by inmates of state and local penal and correctional institutions in actions against the state and local governments and government agencies and officers. In addition to any other appropriate provisions, such form or forms shall clearly identify the nature of the action, the subject matter and disposition of all previous actions filed against any unit or officer of government by the inmate during his incarceration, the law and facts on which the action is based, the parties to be served, the parties against whom relief is requested, and the specific relief requested against each party. If an affidavit of indigency accompanies the pleading, it shall include a sworn financial statement which shall include but not be limited to any custodial account of the inmate with the institution wherein he is incarcerated.

(b) No clerk of any court shall accept for filing any action by an inmate of a state or local penal or correctional institution against the state or a local government or against any agency or officer of state or local government unless the complaint or other initial pleading is on a form or forms promulgated by the Administrative Office of the Courts and such form or forms are appropriately and legibly completed. Any inmate filing such an action may submit with the complaint or other initial pleading any additional matter in any form if the pleading includes the form or forms required by this Code section. If the pleading is accompanied by an affidavit of indigency, the clerk shall not accept the pleading for filing unless the pleading is also accompanied by a certification from the institution wherein the inmate is incarcerated that the financial statement correctly states the amount of funds in any and all custodial accounts of the inmate with the institution.

(c) Upon request of an inmate or the order of a court wherein an inmate has filed an action subject to this Code section, the officials in charge of a state or local institution may remit to the court amounts from an inmate's custodial account for payment of court costs, deposits, or filing fees. Such officials shall upon request of an inmate provide the certification required by subsection (b) of this Code section.

(d) The Administrative Office of the Courts shall cause to be printed such number of the forms provided for in this Code section as is necessary to furnish such forms to attorneys and to the Department of Corrections and local penal and correctional institutions for use by their inmates. Such forms shall be distributed to such institutions by the Administrative Office of the Courts without cost, and such forms shall be provided in reasonable numbers to inmates without cost. The cost of printing and distributing such forms shall be paid from funds appropriated to the judicial branch of government.

Article 2 - VENUE

Part 1 - GENERAL PROVISIONS

Section 9-10-30 - Proceedings in equity generally; injunctions to stay pending litigation; divorce cases

All actions seeking equitable relief shall be filed in the county of the residence of one of the defendants against whom substantial relief is prayed, except in cases of injunctions to stay pending proceedings, when the action may be filed in the county where the proceedings are pending, provided no relief is prayed as to matters not included in such litigation, and except in divorce cases, venue in which is governed by Article VI, Section II, Paragraph I of the Constitution of this state.

Section 9-10-31 - Actions against certain codefendants residing in different counties; pleading requirements; application

(a) The General Assembly finds that Paragraph IV of Section II of Article VI of the Georgia Constitution permits a trial and entry of judgment against a resident of Georgia in a county other than the county of the defendant's residence only if the Georgia resident defendant is a joint obligor, joint tort-feasor, joint promisor, copartner, or joint trespasser.

(b) Subject to the provisions of Code Section 9-10-31.1, joint tort-feasors, obligors, or promisors, or joint contractors or copartners, residing in different counties, may be subject to an action as such in the same action in any county in which one or more of the defendants reside.

(c) In any action involving a medical malpractice claim as defined in Code Section 9-9-60, a nonresident defendant may require that the case be transferred to the county of that defendant's residence if the tortious act upon which the medical malpractice claim is based occurred in the county of that defendant's residence.

(d) If all defendants who reside in the county in which an action is pending are discharged from liability before or upon the return of a verdict by the jury or the court hearing the case without a jury, a nonresident defendant may require that the case be transferred to a county and court in which venue would otherwise be proper. If venue would be proper in more than one county, the plaintiff may elect from among the counties in which venue is proper the county and the court in which the action shall proceed.

(e) Nothing in this Code section shall be deemed to alter or amend the pleading requirements of Chapter 11 of this title relating to the filing of complaints or answers.

Added by 2005 Ga. Laws 1,§ 2, eff. 2/16/2005.

Added by 2005 Ga. Laws 1,§ 2, eff. 2/16/2005.

Amended by 2001 Ga. Laws 2, § 9, eff. 2/12/2001.

Section 9-10-31.1 - Forums outside this state; waiver of statute of limitations defense

(a) If a court of this state, on written motion of a party, finds that in the interest of justice and for the convenience of the parties and witnesses a claim or action would be more properly heard in a forum outside this state or in a different county of proper venue within this state, the court shall decline to adjudicate the matter under the doctrine of forum non conveniens. As to a claim or action that would be more properly heard in a forum outside this state, the court shall dismiss the claim or action. As to a claim or action that would be more properly heard in a different county of proper venue within this state, the venue shall be transferred to the appropriate county. In determining whether to grant a motion to dismiss an action or to transfer venue under the doctrine of forum non conveniens, the court shall give consideration to the following factors:

   (1) Relative ease of access to sources of proof;

   (2) Availability and cost of compulsory process for attendance of unwilling witnesses;

   (3) Possibility of viewing of the premises, if viewing would be appropriate to the action;

   (4) Unnecessary expense or trouble to the defendant not necessary to the plaintiff's own right to pursue his or her remedy;

   (5) Administrative difficulties for the forum courts;

   (6) Existence of local interests in deciding the case locally; and

   (7) The traditional deference given to a plaintiff's choice of forum.

(b) A court may not dismiss a claim under this Code section until the defendant files with the court or with the clerk of the court a written stipulation that, with respect to a new action on the claim commenced by the plaintiff, all the defendants waive the right to assert a statute of limitations defense in all other states of the United States in which the claim was not barred by limitations at the time the claim was filed in this state as necessary to effect a tolling of the limitations periods in those states beginning on the date the claim was filed in this state and ending on the date the claim is dismissed.

Added by 2005 Ga. Laws 1,§ 2, eff. 2/16/2005.

Section 9-10-32 - Action against maker and endorser residing in different counties

Where the maker and endorser of a promissory note who reside in different counties are subjected to an action in the county where the maker resides, as provided by Article VI, Section II, Paragraph V of the Constitution of this state, service of a copy of the original pleading and process on the endorser, as provided in the case of joint obligors and promisors, shall be deemed sufficient.

Section 9-10-33 - Action against nonresident found in state

A person who is not a citizen of this state, passing through or sojourning temporarily in the state, may be subject to an action in any county thereof in which he may be found at the time when the action is brought.

Section 9-10-34 - Action against third-party defendant

(a) As used in this Code section, the term:

   (1) "Defending party" means a party to a civil action who is:

      (A) A defendant who contends that a person or entity not a party to the action is or may be liable to the defendant for all or part of a plaintiff's claim against the defendant;

      (B) A plaintiff who contends that a person or entity not a party to the action is or may be liable to the plaintiff for all or part of another party's claim against the plaintiff; or

      (C) A third-party defendant who contends that a person or entity not a party to the action is or may be liable to the third-party defendant for all or part of a claim made in the action against the third-party defendant.

   (2) "Third-party defendant" means any person or entity whom a defending party contends may be liable to the defending party for all or part of the claim made against the defending party in the action.

(b) The claim of a defending party against a third-party defendant may be tried in the county where the action in which the claim for which the third-party defendant may be wholly or partially liable to the defending party is pending; and such claim may be tried in such county even though the third-party defendant is not a resident of such county.

(c) The venue established under this Code section against a third-party defendant is dependent upon the venue over the defending party who brought the third-party defendant into the action, and if venue is lost over said defending party, whether through dismissal or otherwise, venue shall likewise be lost as to the third-party defendant.

Part 2 - CHANGE OF VENUE

Section 9-10-50 - When venue may be changed; how county for transfer to be selected; subsequent change of venue

(a) Whenever, by an examination voir dire of the persons whose names are on the jury list and who are compellable to serve on the jury, the presiding judge is satisfied that an impartial jury cannot be obtained in the county where any civil case is pending, the civil case may be transferred to any county that may be agreed upon by the parties or their counsel.

(b) In the event the parties or their counsel fail or refuse to agree upon any county in which to try the case pending, the judge may select the county in which the same shall be tried and have the case transferred accordingly.

(c) When any civil case has been once transferred, the judge may again change the venue from the county to which the transfer was first made to any other county, in the same manner as the venue was first changed from the county in which the civil case was originally commenced.

Section 9-10-51 - Change of venue in action by county against county

In all actions brought by one county against another county in the defending county, the judge shall change the venue to a county adjoining the one in which the action is brought, on the motion of the plaintiff, supported by the oath of the chairman or presiding official of the county governing authority of the county bringing the action, that in his opinion a fair and impartial trial cannot be had in the county in which the action is brought.

Section 9-10-52 - Transmittal of transcript of order and record to court of transfer

The clerk of the court from which a case has been transferred shall send a true transcript of the order for the change of venue, together with the original record in the case, including depositions and orders and all pleadings, to the court of the county to which the case has been transferred.

Section 9-10-53 - Conduct of proceedings following transfer

After a case has been transferred, all further proceedings shall be conducted as if the case had been originally commenced in the court to which the same was transferred.

Section 9-10-54 - Payment of costs accrued at time of transfer

All costs which have accrued at the time of the transfer of a case shall, at the termination of the case, be paid by the party or parties against whom the same are assessed to the proper officers of the county from which the case was transferred.

Article 3 - SERVICE

Section 9-10-70 - Service on resident minor over 14 temporarily outside state; return or refusal of receipt; time for filing defensive pleadings; appointment of guardian ad litem; effect of service on guardian or trustee

(a) Anything to the contrary notwithstanding, in all instances where a minor, 14 years of age or older, is a legal resident of the county wherein the legal proceeding concerning such service is sought to be made but is temporarily residing or sojourning outside this state or outside the United States, service may be perfected upon the minor by registered or certified United States mail with return receipt attached or by statutory overnight delivery.

(b) When service is to be perfected by registered or certified mail or statutory overnight delivery, as provided for in subsection (a) of this Code section, the clerk or the judge of the court in which the matter is proceeding shall enclose a copy of the petition, order, or other document sought to be served on the minor in an envelope addressed to the minor at his or her last known address and shall mail the same forthwith with postage prepaid, noting on the records of the court the date and hour of mailing, or shall send the same by statutory overnight delivery as provided in Code Section 9-10-12. When a receipt therefor is returned or if the sealed envelope in which the notice was mailed to the minor is returned to the sender by the appropriate postal authorities or commercial delivery company marked "Refused," giving the date of refusal, and the notation of refusal is signed or initialed by a postal employee or mail carrier or commercial delivery company employee to whom the refusal was made, then the clerk or judge shall attach the same to the original papers in the case or shall otherwise file it as a part of the records in the case and it shall be prima-facie evidence of service on the minor.

(c) When service upon a minor is perfected as set forth in subsections (a) and (b) of this Code section, the minor shall have 60 days from the date of receipt of the registered letter or statutory overnight delivery or the refusal thereof as shown on the receipt of refusal in which to file such defensive pleadings as may be necessary. No judgment or decree shall be rendered in the proceeding which shall adversely affect the interest of the minor until the 60 day period has elapsed unless the judgment or decree is expressly agreed or consented to by the duly appointed guardian ad litem of the minor as being in the best interest of the minor and unless the 60 day period provided for in this subsection has been expressly waived by the guardian ad litem. Each process issued in such cases shall be conformed to the 60 day provision set forth in this subsection.

(d) When the return of service provided for in this Code section is made to the proper court and an order is taken to appoint for the minor a guardian ad litem, and the guardian ad litem agrees to serve in writing, all of which shall be shown in the proceedings of the court, the minor shall be considered a party to the proceedings.

(e) In cases concerning minors 14 years of age or older who are temporarily sojourning or living outside this state or the United States, where the minor has a statutory or testamentary guardian or trustee representing the interest of the minor to be affected by a legal proceeding, service as usual on the guardian or trustee shall be sufficient to bind the minor's interest in his control to be affected by the proceedings.

Section 9-10-71 - Service by publication on nonresidents or unknown persons with interest in property in state

(a) Where any nonresident or person unknown claims or owns title to or an interest, present or contingent, in any real or personal property in this state, service on the nonresident or unknown owner or claimant may be made by publication in cases affecting such property in proceedings brought:

(1) To remove a cloud therefrom or quiet title thereto;

(2) To cancel or set aside deeds, mortgages, liens, or encumbrances thereon;

(3) To establish, enforce, or foreclose liens thereon;

(4) To enforce, by decree for specific performance, any contract in reference thereto;

(5) To order the partition thereof by division or sale;

(6) To make any decree or order in which the subject of the action is real or personal property in this state in which a nonresident or unknown person has or may have or claims an interest, actual or contingent, and in which the relief demanded consists wholly or in part in excluding him from an interest therein;

(7) Where a nonresident or person unknown has or may have or may claim a present, future, or contingent interest in any property in this state; or

(8) Where a nonresident or person unknown may have or claim any interest in any trust estate in this state and it becomes necessary or proper or advantageous to order a sale of the whole or any part of the property.

(b) This Code section shall be supplemental to the other provisions in this Code providing for service by publication.

Section 9-10-72 - Issuance of second original where defendants reside out of county

If the defendant or any of the defendants reside outside the county where the action is filed, the clerk shall issue a second original and copy for such other county or counties and forward the same to the sheriff, who shall serve the copy and return the second original, with his entry thereon, to the clerk of the court from which the same issued.

Section 9-10-73 - Acknowledgment of service or waiver of process

The defendant may acknowledge service or waive process by a writing signed by the defendant or someone authorized by him.

Article 4 - PERSONAL JURISDICTION OVER NONRESIDENTS

Section 9-10-90 - "Nonresident" defined

As used in this article, the term "nonresident" includes an individual, or a partnership, association, or other legal or commercial entity (other than a corporation) not residing, domiciled, organized, or existing in this state at the time a claim or cause of action under Code Section 9-10-91 arises, or a corporation which is not organized or existing under the laws of this state and is not authorized to do or transact business in this state at the time a claim or cause of action under Code Section 9-10-91 arises. The term "nonresident" shall also include an individual, or a partnership, association, or other legal or commercial entity (other than a corporation) who, at the time a claim or cause of action arises under Code Section 9-10-91, was residing, domiciled, organized, or existing in this state and subsequently becomes a resident, domiciled, organized, or existing outside of this state as of the date of perfection of service of process as provided by Code Section 9-10-94.

Section 9-10-91 - Grounds for exercise of personal jurisdiction over nonresident

A court of this state may exercise personal jurisdiction over any nonresident or his or her executor or administrator, as to a cause of action arising from any of the acts, omissions, ownership, use, or possession enumerated in this Code section, in the same manner as if he or she were a resident of this state, if in person or through an agent, he or she:

(1) Transacts any business within this state;

(2) Commits a tortious act or omission within this state, except as to a cause of action for defamation of character arising from the act;

(3) Commits a tortious injury in this state caused by an act or omission outside this state if the tort-feasor regularly does or solicits business, or engages in any other persistent course of conduct, or derives substantial revenue from goods used or consumed or services rendered in this state;

(4) Owns, uses, or possesses any real property situated within this state;

(5) With respect to proceedings for divorce, separate maintenance, annulment, or other domestic relations action or with respect to an independent action for support of dependents, maintains a matrimonial domicile in this state at the time of the commencement of this action or if the defendant resided in this state preceding the commencement of the action, whether cohabiting during that time or not. This paragraph shall not change the residency requirement for filing an action for divorce; or

(6) Has been subject to the exercise of jurisdiction of a court of this state which has resulted in an order of alimony, child custody, child support, equitable apportionment of debt, or equitable division of property if the action involves modification of such order and the moving party resides in this state or if the action involves enforcement of such order notwithstanding the domicile of the moving party.

Amended by 2011 Ga. Laws 186,§ 3, eff. 7/1/2011.

Amended by 2010 Ga. Laws 611,§ 1, eff. 7/1/2010.

Section 9-10-92 - Effect of appearance

Where personal jurisdiction is based solely upon this article, an appearance does not confer such jurisdiction with respect to causes of action not arising from the conduct enumerated in Code Section 9-10-91.

Section 9-10-93 - Venue

Venue in cases under this article shall lie in any county wherein a substantial part of the business was transacted, the tortious act, omission, or injury occurred, or the real property is located. Where an action is brought against a resident of this state, any nonresident of this state who is involved in the same transaction or occurrence and who is suable under the provisions of this article may be joined as a defendant in the county where a resident defendant is suable. Under such circumstances, jurisdiction and venue of the court of and over such nonresident defendant shall not be affected or lost if at trial a verdict or judgment is returned in favor of such resident defendant. If such resident defendant is dismissed from the action prior to commencement of the trial, the action against the nonresident defendant shall not abate but shall be transferred to a court in a county where venue is proper.

Section 9-10-94 - Service

A person subject to the jurisdiction of the courts of the state under Code Section 9-10-91, or his executor or administrator, may be served with a summons outside the state in the same manner as service is made within the state by any person authorized to make service by the laws of the state, territory, possession, or country in which service is made or by any duly qualified attorney, solicitor, barrister, or the equivalent in such jurisdiction.

Article 5 - VERIFICATION

Section 9-10-110 - Petitions for extraordinary equitable relief to be verified or supported by proof

Petitions for a restraining order, injunction, receiver, or other extraordinary equitable relief shall be verified positively by the petitioner or supported by other satisfactory proofs.

Section 9-10-111 - When verified answer required; by whom made for corporate defendant

In all cases where the plaintiff files a pleading with an affidavit attached to the effect that the facts stated in the pleading are true to the best of his knowledge and belief, the defendant shall in like manner verify any answer. If the defendant is a corporation, the affidavit may be made by the president, vice-president, superintendent, or any officer or agent who knows, or whose official duty it is to know, about the matters set out in the answer.

Section 9-10-112 - Verification of answer in action on open account

Whenever an action is brought on an open account and the same is verified by the plaintiff as provided by law, the answer either shall deny that the defendant is indebted in any sum or shall specify the amount in which the defendant admits he may be indebted and it shall be verified as required by law.

Section 9-10-113 - When verification sufficient

All affidavits, petitions, answers, defenses, or other proceedings required to be verified or sworn to under oath shall be held to be sufficient when the same are sworn to before any notary public, magistrate, judge of any court, or any other officer of the state or county where the oath is made who is authorized by the laws thereof to administer oaths. The oath if made outside this state shall have the same force and effect as if it had been made before an officer of this state authorized to administer the same. The official attestation of the officer before whom the oath or affidavit is made shall be prima-facie evidence of the official character of the officer and that he was authorized by law to administer oaths. However, this Code section shall not apply to such affidavits as may be expressly required by statute to be made before some particular officer within the state.

Section 9-10-114 - Use of verified answer as evidence; amendment of sworn answer

The defendant shall always have the privilege of filing an answer under oath for the purpose of using the same as evidence on any motion to dissolve an injunction or to set aside any extraordinary process or remedy granted. A sworn answer may be amended at any time, by leave of the court, as other pleadings; but an admission made in the answer shall always be evidence when offered by the other party.

Article 6 - AMENDMENTS

Section 9-10-130 - When affidavits amendable

All affidavits for the foreclosure of liens, including mortgages, all affidavits that are the foundation of legal proceedings, and all counter affidavits shall be amendable to the same extent as ordinary pleadings and with only the restrictions, limitations, and consequences of ordinary pleadings.

Section 9-10-131 - Bonds in judicial proceedings amendable

All bonds taken under requirement of law in the course of a judicial proceeding may be amended and new security given if necessary.

Section 9-10-132 - Amendment of misnomers on motion

All misnomers, whether in the Christian name or surname, made in writs, pleadings, or other civil judicial proceedings, shall, on motion, be amended and corrected instanter without working unnecessary delay to the party making the same.

Section 9-10-133 - Mistake by clerk or ministerial officer

The mistake or misprision of a clerk or other ministerial officer shall in no case work to the injury of a party where by amendment justice may be promoted.

Section 9-10-134 - Amendment by negligent party; payment of costs; terms

If a party must apply for leave to amend his pleadings and has been negligent or dilatory in respect to the subject of the amendment, the court may order the party to pay to his adversary the cost of any proceedings which he proposes by amendment and, in the court's discretion, may order reasonable and equitable terms for amendment not affecting the merits of the case.

Section 9-10-135 - Amendment of pleadings on court ruling not waiver of objection thereto

Either party who amends or attempts to amend his complaint or other pleadings in response to an order or other ruling of the court shall not be held to have waived his objection to the order or ruling but may thereafter take exception thereto as in other cases.

Article 7 - CONTINUANCES

Section 9-10-150 - Grounds for continuance and stay - Attendance of party or attorney in General Assembly; writing requirement; considerations

(a) A member of the General Assembly who is a party to or the attorney for a party to a case; any member of the Office of Legislative Counsel, including the legislative counsel and persons provided for under subsection (d) of Code Section 28-4-3, appearing on behalf of the General Assembly in a case; or any member of the staff of the Lieutenant Governor, the Speaker of the House of Representatives, the President Pro Tempore of the Senate, the Speaker Pro Tempore of the House of Representatives, or the chairperson of the Judiciary Committee or Special Judiciary Committee of the Senate or of the Judiciary Committee or Judiciary, Non-civil Committee of the House of Representatives who is the lead counsel for a party to a case pending in any trial or appellate court or before any administrative agency of this state, shall be granted a continuance and stay of the case. The continuance and stay shall apply to all aspects of the case, including, but not limited to, the filing and serving of an answer to a complaint, the making of any discovery or motion, or of any response to any subpoena, discovery, or motion, and appearance at any hearing, trial, or argument. Unless a shorter length of time is requested by the member, the continuance and stay shall last for the seven days prior to the regular or extraordinary session of the General Assembly; the length of any regular or extraordinary session of the General Assembly; during the first three weeks following any recess or adjournment, including an adjournment sine die of any regular or extraordinary session; and the entirety of any day during the calendar year on which a legislative committee for which the member serves or is staff holds a scheduled meeting, the member attends a national legislative conference or board meeting, the member attends a caucus meeting, or the member attends a meeting of a study committee of the General Assembly. Notwithstanding any other provision of law, rule of court, or administrative rule or regulation, the time for doing any act in the case which is delayed by the continuance provided by this Code section shall be automatically extended by the same length of time as the continuance or stay covered.

(b)

(1) For such other times not provided for in subsection (a) of this Code section, a member of the General Assembly who is a party to a case or the lead counsel for a party to a case may request a continuance or stay as the member of the General Assembly certifies to the court that his or her presence elsewhere is required by his or her duties with the General Assembly. The certification by the member of the General Assembly shall be in writing and shall state with particularity the nature of the General Assembly duties that require the continuance or stay. Opposing counsel, a party to the case, or the court on its own motion shall have ten days from receipt of the request for a continuance or stay to object to the request by stating with particularity the grounds upon which it is determined that such stay or continuance will cause significant harm to the rights of a party or would otherwise be detrimental to the interest of justice. The court upon receipt of the objection, or on its own motion, shall consider the following in determining whether to grant or deny the continuance or stay:

(A) The length of time that the case has been pending;

(B) The length of delay that such stay or continuance will cause in the resolution of the case;

(C) The nature of the General Assembly duties that require the continuance or stay; and

(D) Such other factors that the court determines to be relevant in determining the harm to the rights of the parties or the interest of justice in the granting or denial of the request for a continuance or stay.

(2) Absent a ruling by the court denying the continuance or stay certified by the member under paragraph (1) of this subsection, such continuance or stay shall be considered granted as a matter of law.

Amended by 2019 Ga. Laws 253,§ 1, eff. 5/7/2019.

Amended by 2009 Ga. Laws 74,§ 18, eff. 4/30/2009.

Amended by 2006 Ga. Laws 608,§ 1, eff. 7/1/2006.

Amended by 2002 Ga. Laws 459, § 1, eff. 4/15/2002.

Section 9-10-151 - Grounds for continuance - Attendance at board of regents or education meeting

Should any member of the Board of Regents of the University System of Georgia or any member of the State Board of Education be otherwise occupied, at the time of any meeting of the board, as counsel or party in any case pending in the courts of this state and should the case be called for trial during the regular session of the board, the absence of the member to attend the session shall be good ground for a postponement or continuance of the case until the session of the board has come to an end.

Amended by 2019 Ga. Laws 253,§ 2, eff. 5/7/2019.

Section 9-10-152 - Grounds for continuance - Attendance at meeting of Board of Human Services or Board of Behavioral Health and Developmental Disabilities

Should any member of the Board of Human Services or the Board of Behavioral Health and Developmental Disabilities be engaged, at the time of any meeting of the board, as counsel or party in any case pending in the courts of this state and should the case be called for trial during the regular session of the board, the absence of the member to attend the session shall be good ground for a postponement or a continuance of the case until the session of the board has come to an end.

Amended by 2010 Ga. Laws 418,§ 9, eff. 7/1/2010.

Amended by 2009 Ga. Laws 102,§ 2-3, eff. 7/1/2009.

Section 9-10-153 - Grounds for continuance - Service in National Guard; oath of party or statement of counsel

It shall be the duty of any judge of a court of this state, on or without motion, to continue any case in the court when the case is reached and any party thereto or his leading counsel is absent from the court by reason of his service in the armed forces when such service directly prevents his attendance in court or by reason of his attendance as a member of the National Guard upon any duty prescribed by the Governor or the adjutant general, unless the party, in the absence of his leading counsel, or the leading counsel, in the absence of the party, on the call of the case, announces ready for trial. If counsel is absent it shall be necessary for his client to make oath that he cannot safely go to trial without the absent counsel; and, if the party plaintiff or defendant is absent, his counsel shall state in his place that he cannot safely go to trial without the client.

Section 9-10-154 - Grounds for continuance - Party providentially prevented from attendance; statement of counsel

If either party is providentially prevented from attending the trial of a case, and the counsel of the absent party will state in his place that he cannot go safely to trial without the presence of the absent party, the case shall be continued, provided the continuances of the party have not been exhausted.

Section 9-10-155 - Grounds for continuance - Illness or absence of counsel; oath of party

The illness or absence, from providential cause, of counsel where there is but one, or of the leading counsel where there are more than one, shall be a sufficient ground for continuance, provided that the party making the application for a continuance will swear that he cannot go safely to trial without the services of the absent counsel, that he expects his services at the next term, and that the application is not made for delay only.

Section 9-10-156 - Grounds for continuance - Occupation of counsel as Attorney General in aid of General Assembly

When any case pending in the courts of this state in which the Attorney General is of counsel is scheduled to be called for any purpose during sessions of the General Assembly or during a period of 15 days preceding or following sessions of the General Assembly, on motion of the Attorney General or an assistant attorney general, it shall be a good ground for continuance that the Attorney General and his staff are occupied in aid of the business of the General Assembly.

Section 9-10-157 - When amending party granted continuance

The party amending pleadings or other proceedings in any of the courts of this state shall not be entitled to delay or continuance on account of the amendment, except by leave of the court to enable him to make the amendment.

Section 9-10-158 - Continuance to enable opposite party to meet amendment; when charged to amending party

When a pleading is amended, if the opposite party makes oath or his counsel states in his place that he is surprised and not fully prepared for trial because of the amendment, upon a showing of the manner of unpreparedness and that surprise is not claimed for the purpose of delay, the case may be continued and the continuance charged to the amending party.

Section 9-10-159 - Legislator attending General Assembly excused as witness; deposition in civil case

Any person summoned as a witness in any case shall be excused by the judge from attending the court by reason of his attendance as a legislator in the General Assembly. In all civil cases it shall be the right of either party thereto to take the deposition, as provided by law, of any person desired to be used as a witness in the case who is a member of the General Assembly when the session of the General Assembly conflicts with the session of the court in which such case is to be tried.

Section 9-10-160 - Continuance for absence of witness; what application to show

All applications for continuances upon the ground of the absence of a witness shall show to the court:

(1) That the witness is absent;

(2) That he has been subpoenaed;

(3) That he does not reside outside of the state;

(4) That his testimony is material;

(5) That the witness is not absent by the permission, directly or indirectly, of the applicant;

(6) That the applicant expects he will be able to procure the testimony of the witness at the next term of the court;

(7) That the application is not made for the purpose of delay but to enable the party to procure the testimony of the absent witness; and

(8) The facts expected to be proved by the absent witness.

Section 9-10-161 - Denial of continuance for absence of witness or testimony where opposite party makes admission

No continuance shall be allowed in any court on account of the absence of a witness or for the purpose of procuring testimony when the opposite party is willing to admit and does not contest the truth of the facts expected to be proved by the testimony of the witness. The court shall order the admission to be reduced to writing.

Section 9-10-162 - Continuance after case sent back by appellate court

When any case is sent back for trial by the Supreme Court or the Court of Appeals, the same shall be in order for trial; and, if the continuances of a party are exhausted, the trial court may grant one continuance to the party as the ends of justice may require.

Section 9-10-163 - Continuance of appeals case

No appeal case shall be continued more than twice by the same party, except for providential cause, for which it may be continued as often as justice may require.

Section 9-10-164 - Continuances for one term only

A continuance requested by a party in a pending case in any court shall not be granted for longer than one term.

Section 9-10-165 - Case not reached continued

A case not reached at the trial term stands over as continued.

Section 9-10-166 - Diligence to be shown by applicant for continuance

In all cases, the party making an application for a continuance must show that he has used due diligence.

Section 9-10-167 - Continuance in discretion of court; countershowing to motion for continuance

(a) All applications for continuances are addressed to the sound legal discretion of the court and, if not expressly provided for, shall be granted or refused as the ends of justice may require.

(b) In all cases the presiding judge may, in his discretion, admit a countershowing to a motion for a continuance and, after a hearing, may decide whether the motion shall prevail.

Section 9-10-168 - When postponement substituted for continuance

No continuance shall be granted in any of the courts in this state which have a continuous session for 30 days or more, over the objection of the adverse party, where the cause for the same can be obviated by a postponement to a later day during the term. It shall be the duty of the presiding judge, whenever a motion and a proper showing for a continuance are made by either party at any time, to set the case down for a later day during the same term if it is practicable thereby to avoid the continuance of the case.

Section 9-10-169 - Announcement and docketing of continuance

Continuances of cases in the superior, state, county, and city courts and the dates thereof shall be entered on the docket. Upon the call of the calendar which includes such case, the judge shall announce the continuance.

Article 8 - ARGUMENT AND CONDUCT OF COUNSEL

Section 9-10-180 - Time limit for arguments

Counsel shall be limited in their arguments to two hours on a side.

Section 9-10-181 - Extension of time limit for argument after application therefor

If counsel on either side, before argument begins, applies to the court for extension of the time prescribed for argument and states in his place or on oath, in the discretion of the court, that he or they cannot do the case justice within the time prescribed and that it will require for that purpose additional time, stating how much additional time will be necessary, the court shall grant such extension of time as may seem reasonable and proper.

Section 9-10-182 - Number of counsel who may argue case

Not more than two counsel for each side shall be permitted to argue any case, except by express leave of the court; and in no case shall more than one counsel be heard in conclusion.

Section 9-10-183 - Use of blackboard, models, etc., in argument

In the trial of any civil action, counsel for either party shall be permitted to use a blackboard and models or similar devices in connection with his argument to the jury for the purpose of illustrating his contentions with respect to the issues which are to be decided by the jury, provided that counsel shall not in writing present any argument that could not properly be made orally.

Section 9-10-184 - Value of pain and suffering may be argued

In the trial of a civil action for personal injuries, counsel shall be allowed to argue the worth or monetary value of pain and suffering to the jury; provided, however, that any such argument shall conform to the evidence or reasonable deductions from the evidence in the case.

Section 9-10-185 - Prejudicial statements by counsel; prevention by court; rebuke of counsel and instruction to jury; mistrial

Where counsel in the hearing of the jury make statements of prejudicial matters which are not in evidence, it is the duty of the court to interpose and prevent the same. On objection made, the court shall also rebuke counsel and by all needful and proper instructions to the jury endeavor to remove the improper impression from their minds. In its discretion, the court may order a mistrial if the plaintiff's attorney is the offender.

Section 9-10-186 - Opening and closing arguments

In civil actions, where the burden of proof rests with the plaintiff, the plaintiff is entitled to the opening and concluding arguments except that if the defendant introduces no evidence or admits a prima-facie case, the defendant shall be entitled to open and conclude. In civil actions for personal injuries, the defendant shall be deemed not to have admitted a prima-facie case if such defendant introduces any evidence as to the extent of damages, other than cross-examination of the plaintiff and witnesses called by the plaintiff.

Article 9 - GENERAL CIVIL FORMS

Section 9-10-200 - Action for recovery of realty and mesne profits

The form of an action for the recovery of real estate and mesne profits may be as follows:

IN THE COURT OF COUNTY STATE OF GEORGIA A.B.,) Plaintiff)) v.) Civil action) File no. C.D.,) (Clerk will insert Defendant) number.) COMPLAINT The defendant herein named is a resident of (street), (city), County, Georgia, and is subject to the jurisdiction of this court.

1. Defendant C.D. of said county is in possession of a certain tract of land in said county (here describe the land) to which plaintiff claims title.

2. Defendant has received the profits of said land since the day of , , of the yearly value of $ and refuses to deliver said land to plaintiff or to pay him the profits thereof. Wherefore, plaintiff demands judgment against defendant (here list the relief prayed for). Attorney for plaintiff Address

Section 9-10-201 - Action for recovery of personalty

The form of an action for the recovery of personal property may be as follows:

IN THE COURT OF COUNTY STATE OF GEORGIA A.B.,) Plaintiff)) v.) Civil action) File no. C.D.,) (Clerk will insert Defendant) number.) COMPLAINT The defendant herein named is a resident of (street), (city), County, Georgia, and is subject to the jurisdiction of this court.

1. Defendant C.D. is in possession of a certain (here describe the property) of the value of $, to which plaintiff claims title.

2. Defendant refuses to deliver the said to plaintiff or to pay plaintiff the profits thereof. Wherefore, plaintiff demands judgment against defendant (here list the relief prayed for). Attorney for plaintiff Address

Section 9-10-202 - Action to recover money on a judgment

The form of an action to recover money on a judgment may be as follows:

IN THE COURT OF COUNTY STATE OF GEORGIA A.B.,) Plaintiff)) v.) Civil action) File no. C.D.,) (Clerk will insert Defendant) number.) COMPLAINT The defendant herein named is a resident of (street), (city), County, Georgia, and is subject to the jurisdiction of this court.

1. Defendant C.D. is indebted to plaintiff in the sum of $, plus interest, on a judgment obtained by plaintiff against defendant.

2. Said judgment was obtained in the (name of court) held on the day of , , in (county, city, or town and state), as fully appears in the properly authenticated certified copies of the proceeding attached to this complaint as Exhibit A.

3. Said judgment has not been satisfied and defendant C.D. has not paid the same. Wherefore, plaintiff demands judgment against defendant (here list the relief prayed for). Attorney for plaintiff Address

Section 9-10-203 - Action for breach of warranty in deed

The form of an action for a breach of warranty in a deed may be as follows:

IN THE COURT OF COUNTY STATE OF GEORGIA A.B.,) Plaintiff)) v.) Civil action) File no. C.D.,) (Clerk will insert Defendant) number.) COMPLAINT The defendant herein named is a resident of (street), (city), County, Georgia, and is subject to the jurisdiction of this court.

1. On the day of , , defendant C.D. executed to plaintiff a warranty deed to a certain tract of land (here describe the land), for the sum of $, paid by plaintiff to defendant C.D.

2. Plaintiff has been evicted from said lot of land and defendant refuses to indemnify plaintiff from his damages in that behalf.

3. Because of said eviction, plaintiff has suffered damages in the amount of $, for which defendant is indebted to plaintiff. Wherefore, plaintiff demands judgment against defendant (here list the relief prayed for). Attorney for plaintiff Address

Section 9-10-204 - Action for words

The form of an action for words may be as follows:

IN THE COURT OF COUNTY STATE OF GEORGIA A.B.,) Plaintiff)) v.) Civil action) File no. C.D.,) (Clerk will insert Defendant) number.) COMPLAINT The defendant herein named is a resident of (street), (city), County, Georgia, and is subject to the jurisdiction of this court. Defendant C.D. has injured and damaged plaintiff in the sum of $, by falsely and maliciously saying of and concerning plaintiff, on the day of , , the following false and malicious words to (name of person): (here give the words). Wherefore, plaintiff demands judgment against defendant (here list the relief prayed for). Attorney for plaintiff Address

Chapter 11 - CIVIL PRACTICE ACT

Article 1 - SCOPE OF RULES AND FORM OF ACTION

Section 9-11-1 - Scope of chapter; construction

This chapter governs the procedure in all courts of record of this state in all actions of a civil nature whether cognizable as cases at law or in equity, with the exceptions stated in Code Section 9-11-81. This chapter shall be construed to secure the just, speedy, and inexpensive determination of every action. This chapter shall also apply to courts which are not courts of record to the extent that no other rule governing a particular practice or procedure of such courts is prescribed by general or local law applicable to such courts.

Section 9-11-2 - One form of action

There shall be one form of action, to be known as "civil action."

Article 2 - COMMENCEMENT OF ACTION AND SERVICE

Section 9-11-3 - Commencement of action; filing of civil case filing form

(a) A civil action is commenced by filing a complaint with the court.

(b) At the time of filing the complaint for a civil action in superior court or state court, the plaintiff shall file the appropriate civil case filing form with the clerk of the court. The form shall contain complete information and shall be substantially in the form prescribed by the Judicial Council of Georgia. The filing of the complaint shall not be delayed for the filing of the case filing form. If, after a civil action has been filed, the court presiding over the civil action decides that the civil case filing form has not been filed or has been filed incorrectly, the court shall require the plaintiff to file the civil case filing form or an amended form. In no case shall the failure to accurately complete the civil case filing form required by this Code section provide a basis to dismiss a civil action.

Amended by 2017 Ga. Laws 240,§ 2-1, eff. 1/1/2018.

Amended by 2006 Ga. Laws 660,§ 1, eff. 7/1/2006.

Amended by 2001 Ga. Laws 2, § 9, eff. 2/12/2001.

Section 9-11-4 - Process

(a)Summons -- Issuance. Upon the filing of the complaint, the clerk shall forthwith issue a summons and deliver it for service. Upon request of the plaintiff, separate or additional summons shall issue against any defendants.

(b)Summons -- Form. The summons shall be signed by the clerk; contain the name of the court and county and the names of the parties; be directed to the defendant; state the name and address of the plaintiff's attorney, if any, otherwise the plaintiff's address; and state the time within which this chapter requires the defendant to appear and file appropriate defensive pleadings with the clerk of the court, and shall notify the defendant that in case of the defendant's failure to do so judgment by default will be rendered against him or her for the relief demanded in the complaint.

(c)Summons -- By whom served. Process shall be served by:

(1) The sheriff of the county where the action is brought or where the defendant is found or by such sheriff's deputy;

(2) The marshal or sheriff of the court or by such official's deputy;

(3) Any citizen of the United States specially appointed by the court for that purpose;

(4) A person who is not a party, not younger than 18 years of age, and has been appointed by the court to serve process or as a permanent process server; or

(5) A certified process server as provided in Code Section 9-11-4.1.Where the service of process is made outside of the United States, after an order of publication, it may be served either by any citizen of the United States or by any resident of the country, territory, colony, or province who is specially appointed by the court for that purpose. When service is to be made within this state, the person making such service shall make the service within five days from the time of receiving the summons and complaint; but failure to make service within the five-day period will not invalidate a later service.

(d)Waiver of service.

(1) A defendant who waives service of a summons does not thereby waive any objection to the venue or to the jurisdiction of the court over the person of the defendant.

(2) Upon receipt of notice of an action in the manner provided in this subsection, the following defendants have a duty to avoid unnecessary costs of serving the summons:

(A) A corporation or association that:

(i) Is subject to service under paragraph (1) or (2) of subsection (e) of this Code section; and

(ii) Receives notice of such action by an agent other than the Secretary of State; and

(B) A natural person who:

(i) Is not a minor; and

(ii) Has not been judicially declared to be of unsound mind or incapable of conducting his or her own affairs.

(3) To avoid costs, the plaintiff may notify such a defendant of the commencement of the action and request that the defendant waive service of a summons. The notice and request shall:

(A) Be in writing and shall be addressed directly to the defendant, if an individual, or else to an officer or managing or general agent or other agent authorized by appointment to receive service of process for a defendant subject to service under paragraph (1) or (2) of subsection (e) of this Code section;

(B) Be dispatched through first-class mail or other reliable means;

(C) Be accompanied by a copy of the complaint and shall identify the court in which it has been filed;

(D) Make reference to this Code section and shall inform the defendant, by means of the text prescribed in subsection (l) of this Code section, of the consequences of compliance and of failure to comply with the request;

(E) Set forth the date on which the request is sent;

(F) Allow the defendant a reasonable time to return the waiver, which shall be at least 30 days from the date on which the request is sent, or 60 days from that date if the defendant is addressed outside any judicial district of the United States; and

(G) Provide the defendant with an extra copy of the notice and request, as well as a prepaid means of compliance in writing.

(4) If a defendant located within the United States that is subject to service inside or outside the state under this Code section fails to comply with a request for a waiver made by a plaintiff located within the United States, the court shall impose the costs subsequently incurred in effecting service on the defendant unless good cause for the failure is shown.

(5) A defendant that, before being served with process, returns a waiver so requested in a timely manner is not required to serve an answer to the complaint until 60 days after the date on which the request for waiver of service was sent, or 90 days after that date if the defendant was addressed outside any judicial district of the United States.

(6) When the plaintiff files a waiver of service with the court, the action shall proceed, except as provided in paragraph (5) of this subsection, as if a summons and complaint had been served at the time of filing the waiver, and no proof of service shall be required.

(7) The costs to be imposed on a defendant under paragraph (4) of this subsection for failure to comply with a request to waive service of summons shall include the costs subsequently incurred in effecting service, together with the costs, including a reasonable attorney's fee, of any motion required to collect the costs of service.

(e)Summons -- Personal service. Except for cases in which the defendant has waived service, the summons and complaint shall be served together. The plaintiff shall furnish the clerk of the court with such copies as are necessary. Service shall be made by delivering a copy of the summons attached to a copy of the complaint as follows:

(1)

(A) If the action is against a corporation incorporated or domesticated under the laws of this state or a foreign corporation authorized to transact business in this state, to the president or other officer of such corporation or foreign corporation, a managing agent thereof, or a registered agent thereof, provided that when for any reason service cannot be had in such manner, the Secretary of State shall be an agent of such corporation or foreign corporation upon whom any process, notice, or demand may be served. Service on the Secretary of State of any such process, notice, or demand shall be made by delivering to and leaving with him or her or with any other person or persons designated by the Secretary of State to receive such service a copy of such process, notice, or demand, along with a copy of the affidavit to be submitted to the court pursuant to this Code section. The plaintiff or the plaintiff's attorney shall certify in writing to the Secretary of State that he or she has forwarded by registered mail or statutory overnight delivery such process, service, or demand to the last registered office or registered agent listed on the records of the Secretary of State, that service cannot be effected at such office, and that it therefore appears that such corporation or foreign corporation has failed either to maintain a registered office or to appoint a registered agent in this state. Further, if it appears from such certification that there is a last known address of a known officer of such corporation or foreign corporation outside this state, the plaintiff shall, in addition to and after such service upon the Secretary of State, mail or cause to be mailed to the known officer at the address by registered or certified mail or statutory overnight delivery a copy of the summons and a copy of the complaint. Any such service by certification to the Secretary of State shall be answerable not more than 30 days from the date the Secretary of State receives such certification.

(B) As used in this paragraph, the term "managing agent" means a person employed by a corporation or a foreign corporation who is at an office or facility in this state and who has managerial or supervisory authority for such corporation or foreign corporation;

(2)

(A) If the action is against a foreign corporation doing business in this state without authorization to transact business in this state that has a managing agent or against a nonresident individual, partnership, joint-stock company, or association doing business in this state that has a managing agent, to such agent, or to a registered agent designated for service of process.

(B) As used in this paragraph, the term "managing agent" means a person employed by a foreign corporation doing business in this state without authorization to transact business in this state or a nonresident individual, partnership, joint-stock company, or association doing business in this state who is at an office or facility in this state and who has managerial or supervisory authority for such foreign corporation, nonresident individual, partnership, joint-stock company, or association;

(3) If against a minor, to the minor, personally, and also to such minor's father, mother, guardian, or duly appointed guardian ad litem unless the minor is married, in which case service shall not be made on the minor's father, mother, or guardian;

(4) If against a person residing within this state who has been judicially declared to be of unsound mind or incapable of conducting his or her own affairs and for whom a guardian has been appointed, to the person and also to such person's guardian and, if there is no guardian appointed, then to his or her duly appointed guardian ad litem;

(5) If against a county, municipality, city, or town, to the chairman of the board of commissioners, president of the council of trustees, mayor or city manager of the city, or to an agent authorized by appointment to receive service of process. If against any other public body or organization subject to an action, to the chief executive officer or clerk thereof;

(6) If the principal sum involved is less than $200.00 and if reasonable efforts have been made to obtain personal service by attempting to find some person residing at the most notorious place of abode of the defendant, then by securely attaching the service copy of the complaint in a conspicuously marked and waterproof packet to the upper part of the door of the abode and on the same day mailing by certified or registered mail or statutory overnight delivery an additional copy to the defendant at his or her last known address, if any, and making an entry of this action on the return of service; or

(7) In all other cases to the defendant personally, or by leaving copies thereof at the defendant's dwelling house or usual place of abode with some person of suitable age and discretion then residing therein, or by delivering a copy of the summons and complaint to an agent authorized by appointment or by law to receive service of process.

(f)Summons -- Other service.

(1)Service by publication.

(A)General. When the person on whom service is to be made resides outside the state, or has departed from the state, or cannot, after due diligence, be found within the state, or conceals himself or herself to avoid the service of the summons, and the fact shall appear, by affidavit, to the satisfaction of the judge or clerk of the court, and it shall appear, either by affidavit or by a verified complaint on file, that a claim exists against the defendant in respect to whom the service is to be made, and that he or she is a necessary or proper party to the action, the judge or clerk may grant an order that the service be made by the publication of summons, provided that when the affidavit is based on the fact that the party on whom service is to be made resides outside the state, and the present address of the party is unknown, it shall be a sufficient showing of such fact if the affiant shall state generally in the affidavit that at a previous time such person resided outside this state in a certain place (naming the place and stating the latest date known to affiant when the party so resided there); that such place is the last place in which the party resided to the knowledge of affiant; that the party no longer resides at the place; that affiant does not know the present place of residence of the party or where the party can be found; and that affiant does not know and has never been informed and has no reason to believe that the party now resides in this state; and, in such case, it shall be presumed that the party still resides and remains outside the state, and the affidavit shall be deemed to be a sufficient showing of due diligence to find the defendant. This Code section shall apply to all manner of civil actions, including those for divorce.

(B)Property. In any action which relates to, or the subject of which is, real or personal property in this state in which any defendant, corporate or otherwise, has or claims a lien or interest, actual or contingent, or in which the relief demanded consists wholly or in part of excluding such defendant from any interest therein, where the defendant resides outside the state or has departed from the state, or cannot, after due diligence, be found within the state, or conceals himself or herself to avoid the service of summons, the judge or clerk may make an order that the service be made by publication of summons. The service by publication shall be made in the same manner as provided in all cases of service by publication.

(C)Publication. When the court orders service by publication, the clerk shall cause the publication to be made in the paper in which sheriff's advertisements are printed, four times within the ensuing 60 days, publications to be at least seven days apart. The party obtaining the order shall, at the time of filing, deposit the cost of publication. The published notice shall contain the name of the parties plaintiff and defendant, with a caption setting forth the court, the character of the action, the date the action was filed, the date of the order for service by publication, and a notice directed and addressed to the party to be thus served, commanding him or her to file with the clerk and serve upon the plaintiff's attorney an answer within 60 days of the date of the order for service by publication and shall bear teste in the name of the judge and shall be signed by the clerk of the court. Where the residence or abiding place of the absent or nonresident party is known, the party obtaining the order shall advise the clerk thereof; and it shall be the duty of the clerk, within 15 days after filing of the order for service by publication, to enclose, direct, stamp, and mail a copy of the notice, together with a copy of the order for service by publication and complaint, if any, to the party named in the order at his or her last known address, if any, and make an entry of this action on the complaint or other pleadings filed in the case. The copy of the notice to be mailed to the nonresident shall be a duplicate of the one published in the newspaper but need not necessarily be a copy of the newspaper itself. When service by publication is ordered, personal service of a copy of the summons, complaint, and order of publication outside the state in lieu of publication shall be equivalent to serving notice by publication and to mailing when proved to the satisfaction of the judge or otherwise. The defendant shall have 30 days from the date of such personal service outside the state in which to file defensive pleadings.

(2)Personal service outside the state. Personal service outside the state upon a natural person may be made:

(A) in any action where the person served is a resident of this state, and

(B) in any action affecting specific real property or status, or in any other proceeding in rem without regard to the residence of the person served. When such facts shall appear, by affidavit, to the satisfaction of the court and it shall appear, either by affidavit or by a verified complaint on file, that a claim is asserted against the person in respect to whom the service is to be made, and that he or she is a necessary or proper party to the action, the court may grant an order that the service be made by personal service outside the state. Such service shall be made by delivering a copy of the process together with a copy of the complaint in person to the persons served.

(3)Service upon persons in a foreign country. Unless otherwise provided by law, service upon a person from whom a waiver has not been obtained and filed, other than an infant or an incompetent person, may be effected in a place not within the United States:

(A) By any internationally agreed means reasonably calculated to give notice, such as those means authorized by the Hague Convention on the Service Abroad of Judicial and Extrajudicial Documents;

(B) If there is no internationally agreed means of service or the applicable international agreement allows other means of service, provided that service is reasonably calculated to give notice:

(i) In the manner prescribed by the law of the foreign country for service in that country in an action in any of its courts of general jurisdiction;

(ii) As directed by the foreign authority in response to a letter rogatory or letter of request; or

(iii) Unless prohibited by the law of the foreign country, by:

(I) Delivery to the person of a copy of the summons and the complaint; or

(II) Any form of mail requiring a signed receipt, to be addressed and dispatched by the clerk of the court to the party to be served; or

(C) By other means not prohibited by international agreement as may be directed by the court.

(4)Service upon persons residing in gated and secured communities.

(A) As used in this paragraph, the term "gated and secured communities" means multiple residential or commercial properties, such as houses, condominiums, offices, or apartments, where access to the multiple residential or commercial properties is restricted by a gate, security device, or security attendant that restricts public entrance onto the property; provided, however, that a single residence, farm, or commercial property with its own fence or gate shall not be included in this definition.

(B) Any person authorized to serve process shall be granted access to gated and secured communities for a reasonable period of time during reasonable hours for the purpose of performing lawful service of process upon:

(i) Identifying to the guard or managing agent the person, persons, entity, or entities to be served;

(ii) Displaying a current driver's license or other government issued identification which contains a photograph; and

(iii) Displaying evidence of current appointment as a process server pursuant to this Code section.

(C) Any person authorized to serve process shall promptly leave gated and secured communities upon perfecting service of process or upon a determination that process cannot be effected at that time.

(g)Territorial limits of effective service. All process may be served anywhere within the territorial limits of the state and, when a statute so provides, beyond the territorial limits of the state.

(h)Return. The person serving the process shall make proof of such service with the court in the county in which the action is pending within five business days of the service date. If the proof of service is not filed within five business days, the time for the party served to answer the process shall not begin to run until such proof of service is filed. Proof of service shall be as follows:

(1) If served by a sheriff or marshal, or such official's deputy, the affidavit or certificate of the sheriff, marshal, or deputy;

(2) If by any other proper person, such person's affidavit;

(3) In case of publication, the certificate of the clerk of court certifying to the publication and mailing; or

(4) The written admission or acknowledgment of service by the defendant.In the case of service otherwise than by publication, the certificate or affidavit shall state the date, place, and manner of service. Failure to make proof of service shall not affect the validity of the service.

(i)Amendment. At any time in its discretion and upon such terms as it deems just, the court may allow any process or proof of service thereof to be amended, unless it clearly appears that material prejudice would result to the substantial rights of the party against whom the process issued.

(j)Alternative service. The methods of service provided in this Code section are cumulative and may be utilized with, after, or independently of other methods of service. Whenever a statute provides for another method of service, service may be made under the circumstances and in the manner prescribed by the statute or under any other methods prescribed in this Code section. The provisions for service by publication provided in this Code section shall apply in any action or proceeding in which service by publication may be authorized by law; and, where by law special provision is made for service by publication, the procedure for such service by publication provided in this Code section may be utilized in lieu thereof. In all cases or special proceedings where the requirements or procedure for service, or both, are not prescribed by law and in any situation where the provisions therefor are not clear or certain, the court may prescribe service according to the exigencies of each case, consistent with the Constitution.

(k)Service in probate courts and special statutory proceedings. The methods of service provided in this Code section may be used as alternative methods of service in proceedings in the probate courts and in any other special statutory proceedings and may be used with, after, or independently of the method of service specifically provided for in any such proceeding; and, in any such proceeding, service shall be sufficient when made in accordance with the statutes relating particularly to the proceeding or in accordance with this Code section.

(l) $ B Forms. $

R

NOTICE OF LAWSUIT AND REQUEST FOR WAIVER OF SERVICE OF SUMMONS TO: (Name of individual defendant or name of officer or agent of corporate defendant) as (title, or other relationship of individual to corporate defendant) of (name of corporate defendant to be served, if any) A lawsuit has been commenced against you (or the entity on whose behalf you are addressed). A copy of the complaint is attached to this notice. The complaint has been filed in the (court named on the complaint) for the State of Georgia in and for the County of (county) and has been assigned (case number of action). This is not a formal summons or notification from the court, but rather my request pursuant to Code Section 9-11-4 of the Official Code of Georgia Annotated that you sign and return the enclosed Waiver of Service in order to save the cost of serving you with a judicial summons and an additional copy of the complaint. The cost of service will be avoided if I receive a signed copy of the waiver within 30 days (or 60 days if located outside any judicial district of the United States) after the date designated below as the date on which this Notice of Lawsuit and Request for Waiver of Service of Summons is sent. I enclose a stamped and addressed envelope (or other means of cost-free return) for your use. An extra copy of the Waiver of Service is also attached for your records. YOU ARE ENTITLED TO CONSULT WITH YOUR ATTORNEY REGARDING THIS MATTER. If you comply with this request and return the signed Waiver of Service, the waiver will be filed with the court and no summons will be served on you. The action will then proceed as if you had been served on the date the waiver is filed except that you will not be obligated to answer or otherwise respond to the complaint within 60 days from the date designated below as the date on which this notice is sent (or within 90 days from that date if your address is not in any judicial district of the United States). If you do not return the signed waiver within the time indicated, I will take appropriate steps to effect formal service in a manner authorized by the Georgia Rules of Civil Procedure and then, to the extent authorized by those rules, I will ask the court to require you (or the party on whose behalf you are addressed) to pay the full cost of such service. In that connection, please read the statement concerning the duty of parties to avoid unnecessary costs of service of summons, which is set forth on the Notice of Duty to Avoid Unnecessary Costs of Service of Summons enclosed herein. I affirm that this Notice of Lawsuit and Request for Waiver of Service of Summons is being sent to you on behalf of the Plaintiff on this day of .
Signature of plaintiff's attorney or Unrepresented plaintiff WAIVER OF SERVICE OF SUMMONS To: (Name of plaintiff's attorney or unrepresented plaintiff) I acknowledge receipt of your request that I waive service of a summons in the action of (caption of action), which is case number (docket number) in the (name of court) of the State of Georgia in and for the County of (county). I have also received a copy of the complaint in the action, two copies of this instrument, and a means by which I can return the signed waiver to you without cost to me. I understand that I am entitled to consult with my own attorney regarding the consequences of my signing this waiver. I agree to save the cost of service of a summons and an additional copy of the complaint in this lawsuit by not requiring that I (or the entity on whose behalf I am acting) be served with judicial process in the manner provided by the Georgia Rules of Civil Procedure. I (or the entity on whose behalf I am acting) will retain all defenses or objections to the lawsuit or to the

jurisdiction or venue of the court except for objections based on a defect in the summons or in the service of the summons. I understand that a judgment may be entered against me (or the entity on whose behalf I am acting) if an answer is not served upon you within 60 days after the date this waiver was sent, or within 90 days after that date if the request for the waiver was sent outside the United States. This day of , . (Signed) (Printed or typed name of defendant) as (title) of (name of corporate defendant, if any) NOTICE OF DUTY TO AVOID UNNECESSARY COSTS OF SERVICE OF SUMMONS Subsection (d) of Code Section 9-11-4 of the Official Code of Georgia Annotated requires certain parties to cooperate in saving unnecessary costs of service of the summons and the pleading. A defendant located in the United States who, after being notified of an action and asked by a plaintiff located in the United States to waive service of a summons, fails to do so will be required to bear the cost of such service unless good cause be shown for such defendant's failure to sign and return the waiver. It is not good cause for a failure to waive service that a party believes that the complaint is unfounded, or that the action has been brought in an improper place or in a court that lacks jurisdiction over the subject matter of the action or over its person or property. A party who waives service of the summons retains all defenses and objections (except any relating to the summons or to the service of the summons), and may later object to the jurisdiction of the court or to the place where the action has been brought. A defendant who waives service must, within the time specified on the waiver form, serve on the plaintiff's attorney (or unrepresented plaintiff) a response to the complaint and also must file a signed copy of the response with the court. If the answer is not served within this time, a default judgment may be taken against that defendant. By waiving service, a defendant is allowed more time to answer than if the summons had been actually served when the request for waiver of service was received.

Amended by 2013 Ga. Laws 182,§ 1, eff. 7/1/2013.

Amended by 2012 Ga. Laws 695,§ 1, eff. 7/1/2012.

Amended by 2010 Ga. Laws 611,§ 4, eff. 7/1/2010.

Amended by 2010 Ga. Laws 611,§ 3, eff. 7/1/2010.

Amended by 2010 Ga. Laws 611,§ 2, eff. 7/1/2010.

Amended by 2002 Ga. Laws 949, § 1, eff. 7/1/2002.

Section 9-11-4.1 - Certified process servers

(a)Certified process servers. A person at least 18 years of age who files with a sheriff of any county of this state an application stating that the movant complies with this Code section and any procedures and requirements set forth in any rules or regulations promulgated by the Judicial Council of Georgia regarding this Code section shall, absent good cause shown, be certified as a process server. Such certification shall be effective for a period of three years or until such approval is withdrawn by a superior court judge upon good cause shown, whichever shall first occur. Such certified process server shall be entitled to serve in such capacity for any court of the state, anywhere within the state, provided that the sheriff of the county for which process is to be served allows such servers to serve process in such county.

(b)Certification procedures.

(1) Any person seeking certification under this Code section shall upon applying for certification present evidence that he or she:

(A) Has undergone a criminal record check based on fingerprints and has never been convicted of a felony or of impersonating a peace officer or other public officer or employee under Code Section 16-10-23;

(B) Completed a 12 hour course of instruction relating to service of process which course has been approved by the Administrative Office of the Courts in consultation with the Georgia Sheriffs' Association;

(C) Passed a test approved by the Administrative Office of the Courts which will measure the applicant's knowledge of state law regarding serving of process and other papers on various entities and persons;

(D) Obtained a commercial surety bond or policy of commercial insurance conditioned to protect members of the public and persons employing the certified process server against any damage arising from any actionable misconduct, error, or omission on the part of the applicant while serving as a certified process server; and

(E) Is a citizen of the United States.

(2) A sheriff of any county of this state shall review the application, test score, criminal record check, and such other information or documentation as required by that sheriff and determine whether the applicant shall be approved for certification and authorized to act as a process server in this state.

(3) Upon approval the applicant shall complete a written oath as follows: "I do solemnly swear (or affirm) that I will conduct myself as a process server truly and honestly, justly and uprightly, and according to law; and that I will support the Constitution of the State of Georgia and the Constitution of the United States. I further swear (or affirm) that I will not serve any papers or process in any action where I have a financial or personal interest in the outcome of the matter or where any person to whom I am related by blood or marriage has such an interest."

(c)Renewal and revocation of certification. A certified process server shall be required to renew his or her certification every three years. Any certified process server failing to renew his or her certification shall no longer be approved to serve as a certified process server. At the time of renewal, the certified process server shall provide evidence that he or she has completed three annual five-hour courses of continuing education which courses have been approved by the Administrative Office of the Courts and has undergone an updated criminal record check. The certification of a process server may be revoked or suspended by a superior court judge for cause at any time. If a complaint has been filed by a sheriff alleging serious misconduct by the process server, such judge may suspend the certification for up to five business days while the matter is considered by the judge.

(d)Fees. The sheriff shall collect a fee of $80.00 for processing the application required by this Code section.

(e)Registry. The sheriff shall forward $30.00 of each fee received to the Georgia Sheriffs' Association. The Georgia Sheriffs' Association shall maintain a registry of certified process servers.

(f)Service by off-duty deputy sheriff. An off-duty deputy sheriff may serve process with the approval of the sheriff by whom he or she is employed and shall be exempt from certification under this Code section.

(g)Impersonation of public officer or employee. It shall be unlawful for a certified process server to falsely hold himself or herself out as a peace officer or public officer or employee and any violation shall be punished as provided in Code Section 16-10-23.

(h)Notice to sheriff.

(1) Prior to the first time that a certified process server serves process in any county, he or she shall file with the sheriff of the county a written notice, in such form as shall be prescribed by the Georgia Sheriffs' Association, of his or her intent to serve process in that county. Such notice shall only be accepted by a sheriff who allows certified process servers to serve process in his or her county. Such notice shall be effective for a period of one year; and a new notice shall be filed before the certified process server again serves process in that county after expiration of the one-year period.

(2) The provisions of this subsection shall not apply to a certified process server who was appointed by the court to serve process or who was appointed as a permanent process server by a court.

(i)Credentials. A sheriff of any county of this state shall at the time of certification provide credentials in the form of an identification card to each certified process server. The identification card shall be designed to clearly distinguish it from any form of credentials issued to certified peace officers and will not be in the shape or form of a law enforcement badge. A certified process server shall display his or her credentials at all times while engaged in the service of process.

(j)False representation. It shall be unlawful for any person who is not a certified process server to hold himself or herself out as being a certified process server. Any person who violates this subsection shall upon conviction be guilty of a misdemeanor.

Amended by 2017 Ga. Laws 275,§ 9, eff. 5/9/2017.

Amended by 2015 Ga. Laws 181,§ 1-1, eff. 5/6/2015.

Added by 2010 Ga. Laws 611,§ 5, eff. 7/1/2010.

Section 9-11-5 - Service and filing of pleadings subsequent to the original complaint and other papers

(a)Service -- When required. Except as otherwise provided in this chapter, every order required by its terms to be served, every pleading subsequent to the original complaint unless the court otherwise orders because of numerous defendants, every written motion other than one which may be heard ex parte, and every written notice, appearance, demand, offer of judgment, and similar paper shall be served upon each of the parties. However, the failure of a party to file pleadings in an action shall be deemed to be a waiver by him or her of all notices, including notices of time and place of trial and entry of judgment, and all service in the action, except service of pleadings asserting new or additional claims for relief, which shall be served as provided by subsection (b) of this Code section.

(b)Same -- How made. Whenever under this chapter service is required or permitted to be made upon a party represented by an attorney, the service shall be made upon the attorney unless service upon the party is ordered by the court. Service upon the attorney or upon a party shall be made by delivering a copy to the person to be served or by mailing it to the person to be served at the person's last known address or, if no address is known, by leaving it with the clerk of the court. As used in this Code section, the term "delivery of a copy" means handing it to the person to be served or leaving it at the person to be served's office with a person in charge thereof or, if such office is closed or the person to be served has no office, leaving it at the person to be served's dwelling house or usual place of abode with some person of suitable age and discretion residing therein. "Delivery of a copy" also means transmitting a copy via email in portable document format (PDF) to the person to be served using all email addresses provided pursuant to subsection (f) of this Code section and showing in the subject line of the email message the words "STATUTORY ELECTRONIC SERVICE" in capital letters. Service by mail is complete upon mailing. Proof of service may be made by certificate of an attorney or of his or her employee, by written admission, by affidavit, or by other proof satisfactory to the court. Failure to make proof of service shall not affect the validity of service.

(c)Same -- Numerous defendants. In any action in which there are unusually large numbers of defendants, the court, upon motion or of its own initiative, may order that service of the pleadings of the defendants and replies thereto need not be made as between the defendants, and that any cross-claim, counterclaim, or matter constituting an avoidance or affirmative defense contained therein shall be deemed to be denied or avoided by all other parties, and that the filing of any such pleading and service thereof upon the plaintiff constitutes due notice of it to the parties. A copy of every such order shall be served upon the parties in such manner and form as the court directs.

(d)Filing. All papers after the complaint required to be served upon a party shall be filed with the court within the time allowed for service.

(e)"Filing with the court" defined. The filing of pleadings and other papers with the court as required by this chapter shall be made by filing them with the clerk of the court, except that the judge may permit the papers to be filed with him, in which event he shall note thereon the filing date and forthwith transmit them to the office of the clerk.

(f)Electronic service of pleadings.

(1) A person to be served may consent to being served with pleadings electronically by:

(A) Filing a notice of consent to electronic service and including the person to be served's email address or addresses in such pleading; or

(B) Including the person to be served's email address or addresses in or below the signature block of the complaint or answer, as applicable to the person to be served.

(2) A person who is not an attorney may rescind his or her election to be served with pleadings electronically by filing and serving a notice of such rescission.

(3) If a person to be served agrees to electronic service of pleadings, such person to be served bears the responsibility of providing notice of any change in his or her email address or addresses.

(4) When an attorney files a pleading in a case via an electronic filing service provider, such attorney shall be deemed to have consented to be served electronically with future pleadings for such case at the primary email address on record with the electronic filing service provider. An attorney may not rescind his or her election to be served with pleadings electronically in cases that were initiated using an electronic filing service provider.

(5) If electronic service of a pleading is made upon a person to be served, and such person certifies to the court under oath that he or she did not receive such pleading, it shall be presumed that such pleading was not received unless the serving party disputes the assertion of nonservice, in which case the court shall decide the issue of service of such pleading.

Amended by 2022 Ga. Laws 782,§ 9, eff. 5/2/2022.
Amended by 2020 Ga. Laws 521,§ 9, eff. 7/29/2020.
Amended by 2019 Ga. Laws 271,§ 4-1, eff. 5/7/2019.
Amended by 2018 Ga. Laws 416,§ 1A-1, eff. 7/1/2018.
Amended by 2009 Ga. Laws 25,§ 2, eff. 7/1/2009.
Amended by 2009 Ga. Laws 25,§ 1, eff. 7/1/2009.
Amended by 2001 Ga. Laws 264, § 1, eff. 7/1/2001.

Section 9-11-6 - Time

(a)Computation. In computing any period of time prescribed or allowed by this chapter, by the rules of any court, by order of court, or by an applicable statute, the computation rules prescribed in paragraph (3) of subsection (d) of Code Section 1-3-1 shall be used.

(b)Extension of time. When by this chapter or by a notice given thereunder or by order of court an act is required or allowed to be done at or within a specified time, the parties, by written stipulation of counsel filed in the action, may extend the period, or the court for cause shown may at any time in its discretion (1) with or without motion or notice, order the period extended if request therefor is made before the expiration of the period originally prescribed or as extended by a previous order, or (2) upon motion made after the expiration of the specified period, permit the act to be done where the failure to act was the result of excusable neglect; provided, however, that no extension of time shall be granted for the filing of motions for new trial or for judgment notwithstanding the verdict.

(c)Unaffected by expiration of term. The period of time provided for the doing of any act or the taking of any proceeding is not affected or limited by the continued existence or expiration of a term of court, except as otherwise specifically provided by law. The continued existence or expiration of a term of court in no way affects the power of a court to do any act or take any proceeding in any civil action which has been pending before it, except as otherwise specifically provided by law.

(d)For motions; for affidavits. A written motion, other than one which may be heard ex parte, and notice of the hearing thereof shall be served not later than five days before the time specified for the hearing, unless a different period is fixed by this chapter or by order of the court. Such an order may for cause shown be made on ex parte application. When a motion is supported by affidavit, the affidavit shall be served with the motion. Opposing affidavits may be served not later than one day before the hearing, unless the court permits them to be served at some other time.

(e)Additional time after service by mail or e-mail. Whenever a party has the right or is required to do some act or take some proceedings within a prescribed period after the service of a notice or other paper, other than process, upon him or her, and the notice or paper is served upon the party by mail or e-mail, three days shall be added to the prescribed period.
Amended by 2009 Ga. Laws 25,§ 3, eff. 7/1/2009.

Article 3 - PLEADINGS AND MOTIONS

Section 9-11-7 - Pleadings allowed; form of motions

(a)Pleadings. There shall be a complaint and an answer; a third-party complaint, if a person who is not an original party is summoned under Code Section 9-11-14; and a third-party answer, if a third-party complaint is served. There may be a reply to a counterclaim denominated as such and an answer to a cross-claim, if the answer contains a cross-claim. No other pleading shall be allowed, except that the court may order a reply to an answer or a third-party answer.

(b)Motions and other papers.

(1) An application to the court for an order shall be by motion which, unless made during a hearing or trial, shall be made in writing, shall state with particularity the grounds therefor, and shall set forth the relief or order sought. The requirement of writing is fulfilled if the motion is stated in a written notice of the hearing of the motion.

(2) The rules applicable to captions, signing, and other matters of form of pleadings apply to all motions and other papers provided for by this chapter.

(c)Demurrers, pleas, etc., abolished. Demurrers, pleas, and exceptions for insufficiency of a pleading shall not be used.

Section 9-11-7.1 - Redacted information; exceptions and filings under seal; correction; protective orders; waivers

(a)Redacted filings. Except as provided in subsections (b) and (c) of this Code section or unless the court orders otherwise, a filing with the court that contains a social security number, taxpayer identification number, financial account number, or birth date shall include only:

(1) The last four digits of a social security number;

(2) The last four digits of a taxpayer identification number;

(3) The last four digits of a financial account number; and

(4) The year of an individual's birth.

(b)Garnishment. A summons of garnishment that is filed with a court shall only include the last four digits of the defendant's social security number, taxpayer identification number, or financial account number; provided, however, that the plaintiff shall provide the defendant's full social security number, taxpayer identification number, or financial account number, if reasonably available to the plaintiff, on the copies of the summons of garnishment served on the garnishee and defendant.

(c)Exemptions from redaction requirement. Subsection (a) of this Code section shall not apply to the following:

(1) A financial account number that identifies property allegedly subject to forfeiture in a civil forfeiture proceeding;

(2) The official record of an administrative or agency proceeding;

(3) The official record of a court or tribunal in another case or proceeding;

(4) A filing made in a probate court; and

(5) A filing made under seal as provided in subsection (d) of this Code section.

(d)Filings made under seal. The court may order that a filing be made under seal without redaction. The court may later unseal the filing or order the filer to file a redacted version for the public record. A filer may petition the court to file an unredacted filing under seal. The court shall retain all filings made under seal as part of the record.

(e)Correction of unredacted information. An inadvertent failure to redact information which is required to be redacted shall be a curable defect and shall not preclude a document from being filed with the court. The court may order an unredacted filing be sealed and may also order that a redacted version of the same filing be filed for the public record.

(f)Protective orders. For good cause, the court may:

(1) Order a filing which contains additional personal or confidential information, other than the information required to be redacted pursuant to this Code section, be sealed and may also order that a redacted version of the same filing be filed for the public record; and

(2) Limit or prohibit a nonparty's remote electronic access to a document filed with the court.

(g)Option for reference list. A filing that contains redacted information may be filed together with a reference list that identifies each item of redacted information and specifies an appropriate identifier that uniquely corresponds to each item listed. Such reference list shall be filed under seal and may be amended as of right. Any reference in a civil action to a listed identifier shall be construed to refer to the corresponding item of information.

(h)Waiver of protected identifiers. A filer waives the protections provided by subsection (a) of this Code section to the extent that he or she makes his or her own filing without redaction and not under seal.

Added by 2014 Ga. Laws 586,§ 2, eff. 7/1/2014.

Section 9-11-8 - General rules of pleading

(a)Claims for relief.

(1)"Action for medical malpractice" defined. As used in this Code section, the term "action for medical malpractice" means any claim for damages resulting from the death of or injury to any person arising out of:

(A) Health, medical, dental, or surgical service, diagnosis, prescription, treatment, or care rendered by a person authorized by law to perform such services or by any person acting under the supervision and control of a lawfully authorized person; or

(B) Care or service rendered by any public or private hospital, nursing home, clinic, hospital authority, facility, or institution, or by any officer, agent, or employee thereof acting within the scope of his employment.

(2)Form of complaint, generally; action for malpractice. An original complaint shall contain facts upon which the court's venue depends; and any pleading which sets forth a claim for relief, whether an original claim, counterclaim, a cross-claim, or a third-party claim, shall contain:

(A) A short and plain statement of the claims showing that the pleader is entitled to relief; and

(B) A demand for judgment for the relief to which the pleader deems himself entitled; provided, however, that in actions for medical malpractice, as defined in this Code section, in which a claim for unliquidated damages is made for $10,000.00 or less, the pleadings shall contain a demand for judgment in a sum certain; and, in actions for medical malpractice in which a claim for unliquidated damages is made for a sum exceeding $10,000.00, the demand for judgment shall state that the pleader "demands judgment in excess of $10,000.00," and no further monetary amount shall be stated.Relief in the alternative or of several different types may be demanded.

(3)Sanctions. If the provisions of subparagraph (B) of paragraph (2) of this subsection are violated, the court in which the action is pending shall, upon a proper motion, strike the improper portion of the demand for judgment and may impose such other sanctions, including disciplinary action against the attorney, found in Code Section 9-11-37 as are appropriate.

(b)Defenses; form of denials. A party shall state in short and plain terms his defenses to each claim asserted and shall admit or deny the averments upon which the adverse party relies. If he is without knowledge or information sufficient to form a belief as to the truth of an averment, he shall so state, and this has the effect of a denial. Denials shall fairly meet the substance of the averments denied. When a pleader intends in good faith to deny only a part or a qualification of an averment, he shall specify so much of it as is true and material and shall deny only the remainder. Unless the pleader intends in good faith to controvert all the averments of the preceding pleading, he may make his denials as specific denials of designated averments or paragraphs, or he may generally deny all the averments except such designated averments or paragraphs as he expressly admits; but, when he does so intend to controvert all its averments, he may do so by general denial subject to the obligations set forth in Code Section 9-11-11.

(c)Affirmative defenses. In pleading to a preceding pleading, a party shall set forth affirmatively accord and satisfaction, arbitration and award, discharge in bankruptcy, duress, estoppel, failure of consideration, fraud, illegality, injury by fellow servant, laches, license, payment, release, res judicata, statute of frauds, statute of limitations, and waiver. When a party has mistakenly designated a defense as a counterclaim or a counterclaim as a defense, the court on terms, if justice so requires, shall treat the pleadings as if there had been a proper designation.

(d)Effect of failure to deny. Averments in a pleading to which a responsive pleading is required, other than those as to the amount of damage, are admitted when not denied in the responsive pleading. Averments in a pleading to which no responsive pleading is required or permitted shall be taken as denied or avoided.

(e)Pleading to be concise and direct; alternative statements.

(1) Each averment of a pleading shall be simple, concise, and direct. No technical forms of pleading or motions are required.

(2) A party may set forth two or more statements of a claim or defense alternatively or hypothetically, either in one count or defense or in separate counts or defenses. When two or more statements are made in the alternative and one of them, if made independently, would be sufficient, the pleading is not made insufficient by the insufficiency of one or more of the alternative statements. A party may also state as many separate claims or defenses as he has, regardless of consistency and whether based on legal or on equitable grounds or on both. All statements shall be made subject to the obligations set forth in Code Section 9-11-11.

(f)Construction of pleadings. All pleadings shall be so construed as to do substantial justice.

Section 9-11-9 - Pleading special matters

(a)Capacity. It is not necessary to aver the capacity of a party to bring or defend an action, the authority of a party to bring or defend an action in a representative capacity, or the legal existence of an organized association of persons that is made a party. When a party desires to raise an issue as to the legal existence of any party, the capacity of any party to bring or defend an action, or the authority of a party to bring or defend an action in a representative capacity, he shall do so by specific negative averment, which shall include such supporting particulars as are peculiarly within the pleader's knowledge.

(b)Fraud, mistake, condition of the mind. In all averments of fraud or mistake, the circumstance constituting fraud or mistake shall be stated with particularity. Malice, intent, knowledge, and other condition of mind of a person may be averred generally.

(c)Conditions precedent. In pleading the performance or occurrence of conditions precedent, it is sufficient to aver generally that all conditions precedent have been performed or have occurred. A denial of performance or occurrence shall be made specifically and with particularity.

(d)Official document or act. In pleading an official document or official act, it is sufficient to aver that the document was issued or the act done in compliance with law.

(e)Judgment. In pleading a judgment or decision of a domestic or foreign court, of a judicial or quasi-judicial tribunal, or of a board or officer, it is sufficient to aver the judgment or decision without setting forth matter showing jurisdiction to render it.

(f)Time and place. For the purpose of testing the sufficiency of a pleading, averments of time and place are material and shall be considered like all other averments of material matter.

(g)Special damage. When items of special damage are claimed, they shall be specifically stated.

Amended by 2016 Ga. Laws 625,§ 9, eff. 5/3/2016.

Section 9-11-9.1 - Affidavit to accompany charge of professional malpractice

(a) In any action for damages alleging professional malpractice against:

(1) A professional licensed by the State of Georgia and listed in subsection (g) of this Code section;

(2) A domestic or foreign partnership, corporation, professional corporation, business trust, general partnership, limited partnership, limited liability company, limited liability partnership, association, or any other legal entity alleged to be liable based upon the action or inaction of a professional licensed by the State of Georgia and listed in subsection (g) of this Code section; or

(3) Any licensed health care facility alleged to be liable based upon the action or inaction of a health care professional licensed by the State of Georgia and listed in subsection (g) of this Code section, the plaintiff shall be required to file with the complaint an affidavit of an expert competent to testify, which affidavit shall set forth specifically at least one negligent act or omission claimed to exist and the factual basis for each such claim.

(b) The contemporaneous affidavit filing requirement pursuant to subsection (a) of this Code section shall not apply to any case in which the period of limitation will expire or there is a good faith basis to believe it will expire on any claim stated in the complaint within ten days of the date of filing the complaint and, because of time constraints, the plaintiff has alleged that an affidavit of an expert could not be prepared. In such cases, if the attorney for the plaintiff files with the complaint an affidavit in which the attorney swears or affirms that his or her law firm was not retained by the plaintiff more than 90 days prior to the expiration of the period of limitation on the plaintiff's claim or claims, the plaintiff shall have 45 days after the filing of the complaint to supplement the pleadings with the affidavit. The trial court shall not extend such time for any reason without consent of all parties. If either affidavit is not filed within the periods specified in this Code section, or it is determined that the law firm of the attorney who filed the affidavit permitted in lieu of the contemporaneous filing of an expert affidavit or any attorney who appears on the pleadings was retained by the plaintiff more than 90 days prior to the expiration of the period of limitation, the complaint shall be dismissed for failure to state a claim.

(c) This Code section shall not be construed to extend any applicable period of limitation, except that if the affidavits are filed within the periods specified in this Code section, the filing of the affidavit of an expert after the expiration of the period of limitations shall be considered timely and shall provide no basis for a statute of limitations defense.

(d) If a complaint alleging professional malpractice is filed without the contemporaneous filing of an affidavit as permitted by subsection (b) of this Code section, the defendant shall not be required to file an answer to the complaint until 30 days after the filing of the affidavit of an expert, and no discovery shall take place until after the filing of the answer.

(e) If a plaintiff files an affidavit which is allegedly defective, and the defendant to whom it pertains alleges, with specificity, by motion to dismiss filed on or before the close of discovery, that said affidavit is defective, the plaintiff's complaint shall be subject to dismissal for failure to state a claim, except that the plaintiff may cure the alleged defect by amendment pursuant to Code Section 9-11-15 within 30 days of service of the motion alleging that the affidavit is defective. The trial court may, in the exercise of its discretion, extend the time for filing said amendment or response to the motion, or both, as it shall determine justice requires.

(f) If a plaintiff fails to file an affidavit as required by this Code section and the defendant raises the failure to file such an affidavit by motion to dismiss filed contemporaneously with its initial responsive pleading, such complaint shall not be subject to the renewal provisions of Code Section 9-2-61 after the expiration of the applicable period of limitation, unless a court determines that the plaintiff had the requisite affidavit within the time required by this Code section and the failure to file the affidavit was the result of a mistake.

(g) The professions to which this Code section shall apply are:

(1) Architects;

(2) Attorneys at law;

(3) Audiologists;

(4) Certified public accountants;

(5) Chiropractors;

(6) Clinical social workers;

(7) Dentists;

(8) Dietitians;

(9) Land surveyors;

(10) Marriage and family therapists;

(11) Medical doctors;

(12) Nurses;

(13) Occupational therapists;

(14) Optometrists;

(15) Osteopathic physicians;

(16) Pharmacists;

(17) Physical therapists;

(18) Physicians' assistants;

(19) Podiatrists;

(20) Professional counselors;

(21) Professional engineers;

(22) Psychologists;

(23) Radiological technicians;

(24) Respiratory therapists;

(25) Speech-language pathologists; or

(26) Veterinarians.

Amended by 2007 Ga. Laws 125,§ 1, eff. 7/1/2007.

Amended by 2006 Ga. Laws 453,§ 9, eff. 4/14/2006.

Added by 2005 Ga. Laws 1,§ 3, eff. 2/16/2005.

Section 9-11-9.2 - Medical authorization forms; review of protected health information

(a) In any action for damages alleging medical malpractice against a professional licensed by the State of Georgia and listed in subsection (g) of Code Section 9-11-9.1, against a professional corporation or other legal entity that provides health care services through a professional licensed by the State of Georgia and listed in subsection (g) of Code Section 9-11-9.1, or against any licensed health care facility alleged to be liable based upon the action or inaction of a health care professional licensed by the State of Georgia and listed in subsection (g) of Code Section 9-11-9.1, contemporaneously with the filing of the complaint, the plaintiff shall be required to file a medical authorization form. Failure to provide this authorization shall subject the complaint to dismissal.

(b) The authorization shall provide that the attorney representing the defendant is authorized to obtain and disclose protected health information contained in medical records to facilitate the investigation, evaluation, and defense of the claims and allegations set forth in the complaint which pertain to the plaintiff or, where applicable, the plaintiff's decedent whose treatment is at issue in the complaint. This authorization includes the defendant's attorney's right to discuss the care and treatment of the plaintiff or, where applicable, the plaintiff's decedent with all of the plaintiff's or decedent's treating physicians.

(c) The authorization shall provide for the release of all protected health information except information that is considered privileged and shall authorize the release of such information by any physician or health care facility by which health care records of the plaintiff or the plaintiff's decedent would be maintained.

Amended by 2007 Ga. Laws 125,§ 2, eff. 7/1/2007.

Added by 2005 Ga. Laws 1,§ 4, eff. 2/16/2005.

Added by 2005 Ga. Laws 1,§ 4, eff. 2/16/2005.

Added by 2005 Ga. Laws 1,§ 4, eff. 2/16/2005.

Section 9-11-10 - Form of pleadings

(a)Caption; names of parties. Every pleading shall contain a caption setting forth the name of the court and county, the title of the action, the file number, and a designation as in subsection (a) of Code Section 9-11-7. In the complaint the title of the action shall include the names of all the parties, but in other pleadings it is sufficient to state the name of the first party on each side with an appropriate indication of other parties. A party whose name is not known may be designated by any name; and, when his true name is discovered, the pleading may be amended accordingly.

(b)Paragraphs; separate statements. All averments of claim or defense shall be made in numbered paragraphs, the contents of each of which shall be limited as far as practicable to a statement of a single set of circumstances; and a paragraph may be referred to by number in all succeeding pleadings. Each claim founded upon a separate transaction or occurrence and each defense other than denials shall be stated in a separate count or defense whenever a separation facilitates the clear presentation of the matters set forth.

(c)Adoption by reference; exhibits. Statements in a pleading may be adopted by reference in a different part of the same pleading or in another pleading or in any motion. A copy of any written instrument which is an exhibit to a pleading is a part thereof for all purposes.

Section 9-11-11 - Signing of pleadings; when verification required; rule abolished

(a) Every pleading of a party represented by an attorney shall be signed by at least one attorney of record in his individual name, whose address shall be stated. A party who is not represented by an attorney shall sign his pleading and state his address. The signature of an attorney constitutes a certificate by him that he has read the pleading and that it is not interposed for delay.

(b) Except when otherwise specifically provided by rule or statute, pleadings need not be verified or accompanied by affidavit.

(c) The rule in equity that the averments of an answer under oath must be overcome by the testimony of two witnesses or of one witness sustained by corroborating circumstances is abolished.

Section 9-11-11.1 - Exercise of rights of freedom of speech and to petition government for redress of grievances; legislative findings; verification of claims; definitions; procedure on motions; exception; fees and expenses

(a) The General Assembly of Georgia finds and declares that it is in the public interest to encourage participation by the citizens of Georgia in matters of public significance and public interest through the exercise of their constitutional rights of petition and freedom of speech. The General Assembly of Georgia further finds and declares that the valid exercise of the constitutional rights of petition and freedom of speech should not be chilled through abuse of the judicial process. To accomplish the declarations provided for under this subsection, this Code section shall be construed broadly.

(b)

(1) A claim for relief against a person or entity arising from any act of such person or entity which could reasonably be construed as an act in furtherance of the person's or entity's right of petition or free speech under the Constitution of the United States or the Constitution of the State of Georgia in connection with an issue of public interest or concern shall be subject to a motion to strike unless the court determines that the nonmoving party has established that there is a probability that the nonmoving party will prevail on the claim.

(2) In making the determination as provided for in paragraph (1) of this subsection, the court shall consider the pleadings and supporting and opposing affidavits stating the facts upon which the liability or defense is based; provided, however, that if there exists a claim that the nonmoving party is a public figure plaintiff, then the nonmoving party shall be entitled to discovery on the sole issue of actual malice whenever actual malice is relevant to the court's determination under paragraph (1) of this subsection.

(3) If the court determines that the nonmoving party under paragraph (1) of this subsection has established a probability that he or she would prevail on the claim, neither that determination nor the fact of such determination shall be admissible in evidence at any later stage of the case or in any subsequent action and no burden of proof or degree of proof otherwise applicable shall be affected by such determination in any later stage of the case or in any subsequent proceeding.

(b.1) In any action subject to subsection (b) of this Code section, a prevailing moving party on a motion to strike shall be granted the recovery of attorney's fees and expenses of litigation related to the action in an amount to be determined by the court based on the facts and circumstances of the case. If the court finds that a motion to strike is frivolous or is solely intended to cause unnecessary delay, the court shall award attorney's fees and expenses of litigation to the nonmoving party prevailing on the motion for the attorney's fees and expenses of litigation associated with the motion in an amount to be determined by the court based on the facts and circumstances of the case.

(c) As used in this Code section, the term "act in furtherance of the person's or entity's right of petition or free speech under the Constitution of the United States or the Constitution of the State of Georgia in connection with an issue of public interest or concern" shall include:

(1) Any written or oral statement or writing or petition made before a legislative, executive, or judicial proceeding, or any other official proceeding authorized by law;

(2) Any written or oral statement or writing or petition made in connection with an issue under consideration or review by a legislative, executive, or judicial body, or any other official proceeding authorized by law;

(3) Any written or oral statement or writing or petition made in a place open to the public or a public forum in connection with an issue of public interest or concern; or

(4) Any other conduct in furtherance of the exercise of the constitutional right of petition or free speech in connection with a public issue or an issue of public concern.

(d) All discovery and any pending hearings or motions in the action shall be stayed upon the filing of a motion to dismiss or a motion to strike made pursuant to subsection (b) of this Code section until a final decision on the motion. The motion shall be heard not more than 30 days after service unless the emergency matters before the court require a later hearing. The court, on noticed motion and for good cause shown, may order that specified discovery or other hearings or motions be conducted notwithstanding this subsection.

(e) An order granting or denying a motion to dismiss or a motion to strike shall be subject to direct appeal in accordance with subsection (a) of Code Section 5-6-34.

(f) Nothing in this Code section shall affect or preclude the right of any party to any recovery otherwise authorized by common law, statute, law, or rule.

(g) This Code section shall not apply to any action brought by the Attorney General or a prosecuting attorney, or a city attorney acting as a prosecutor, to enforce laws aimed at public protection.

(h) Attorney's fees and expenses of litigation under this Code section shall be requested by motion at any time during the course of the action but not later than 45 days after the final disposition, including but not limited to dismissal by the plaintiff, of the action. Amended by 2016 Ga. Laws 420,§ 2, eff. 7/1/2016.

Section 9-11-12 - Answer, defenses, and objections; when and how presented and heard; when defenses waived; stay of discovery

(a)When answer presented. A defendant shall serve his answer within 30 days after the service of the summons and complaint upon him, unless otherwise provided by statute. A cross-claim or counterclaim shall not require an answer, unless one is required by order of the court, and shall automatically stand denied.

(b)How defenses and objections presented. Every defense, in law or fact, to a claim for relief in any pleading, whether a claim, counterclaim, cross-claim, or third-party claim, shall be asserted in the responsive pleading thereto if one is required, except that the following defenses may, at the option of the pleader, be made by motion in writing:

(1) Lack of jurisdiction over the subject matter;

(2) Lack of jurisdiction over the person;

(3) Improper venue;

(4) Insufficiency of process;

(5) Insufficiency of service of process;

(6) Failure to state a claim upon which relief can be granted;

(7) Failure to join a party under Code Section 9-11-19.A motion making any of these defenses shall be made before or at the time of pleading if a further pleading is permitted. No defense or objection is waived by being joined with one or more other defenses or objections in a responsive pleading or motion. If a pleading sets forth a claim for relief to which the adverse party is not required to serve a responsive pleading, he may assert at the trial any defense in law or fact to that claim for relief. If, on a motion to dismiss for

failure of the pleading to state a claim upon which relief can be granted, matters outside the pleading are presented to and not excluded by the court, the motion shall be treated as one for summary judgment and disposed of as provided in Code Section 9-11-56, and all parties shall be given reasonable opportunity to present all material made pertinent to such a motion by Code Section 9-11-56.

(c)Motion for judgment on the pleadings. After the pleadings are closed but within such time as not to delay the trial, any party may move for judgment on the pleadings. If, on a motion for judgment on the pleadings, matters outside the pleadings are presented to and not excluded by the court, the motion shall be treated as one for summary judgment and disposed of as provided in Code Section 9-11-56, and all parties shall be given reasonable opportunity to present all material made pertinent to such a motion by Code Section 9-11-56.

(d)Preliminary hearings. The defenses specifically enumerated in paragraphs (1) through (7) of subsection (b) of this Code section, whether made in a pleading or by motion, and the motion for judgment mentioned in subsection (c) of this Code section shall be heard and determined before trial on application of any party unless the court orders that the hearing and determination thereof be deferred until the trial.

(e)Motion for more definite statement. If a pleading to which a responsive pleading is permitted is so vague or ambiguous that a party cannot reasonably be required to frame a proper responsive pleading, he shall nevertheless answer or respond to the best of his ability, and he may move for a more definite statement. The motion shall point out the defects complained of and the details desired. If the motion is granted and the order of the court is not obeyed within 15 days after notice of the order, or within such other time as the court may fix, the court may strike the pleading to which the motion was directed or make such order as it deems just.

(f)Motion to strike. Upon motion made by a party within 30 days after the service of the pleading upon him, or upon the court's own initiative at any time, the court may order stricken from any pleading any insufficient defense or any redundant, immaterial, impertinent, or scandalous matter.

(g)Consolidation of defenses in motion. A party who makes a motion under this Code section may join with it any other motions provided for in this Code section and then available to him. If a party makes a motion under this Code section but omits therefrom any defense or objection then available to him which this Code section permits to be raised by motion, he shall not thereafter make a motion based on the defense or objection so omitted, except a motion as provided in paragraph (2) of subsection (h) of this Code section on any of the grounds there stated.

(h)Waiver or preservation of certain defenses.

(1) A defense of lack of jurisdiction over the person, improper venue, insufficiency of process, or insufficiency of service of process is waived:

(A) If omitted from a motion in the circumstances described in subsection (g) of this Code section; or

(B) If it is neither made by motion under this Code section nor included in a responsive pleading, as originally filed.

(2) A defense of failure to state a claim upon which relief can be granted, a defense of failure to join a party indispensable under Code Section 9-11-19, and an objection of failure to state a legal defense to a claim may be made in any pleading permitted or ordered under subsection (a) of Code Section 9-11-7, or by motion for judgment on the pleadings, or at the trial on the merits.

(3) Whenever it appears, by suggestion of the parties or otherwise, that the court lacks jurisdiction of the subject matter, the court shall dismiss the action.

(i)Officer's defense of service. The officer making service of process and the principal officer in charge of service made by a deputy need not be made a party to any action or motion where the defense or defenses under paragraph (2), (4), or (5) of subsection (b) of this Code section are asserted by motion or by answer. Any party to the action may give notice of the objection to the service, made pursuant to such paragraphs, to the officer making the service and to the principal officer in case of service made by a deputy, and the court shall afford the officer or officers opportunity to defend the service, in which case the decision on the question of service shall be conclusive on the officer and on his principal in case of service by a deputy.

(j)Stay of discovery.

(1) If a party files a motion to dismiss before or at the time of filing an answer and pursuant to the provisions of this Code section, discovery shall be stayed for 90 days after the filing of such motion or until the ruling of the court on such motion, whichever is sooner. The court shall decide the motion to dismiss within the 90 days provided in this paragraph.

(2) The discovery period and all discovery deadlines shall be extended for a period equal to the duration of the stay imposed by this subsection.

(3) The court may upon its own motion or upon motion of a party terminate or modify the stay imposed by this subsection but shall not extend such stay.

(4) If a motion to dismiss raises defenses set forth in paragraph (2), (3), (5), or (7) of subsection (b) of this Code section or if any party needs discovery in order to identify persons who may be joined as parties, limited discovery needed to respond to such defenses or identify such persons shall be permitted until the court rules on such motion.

(5) The provisions of this subsection shall not modify or affect the provisions of paragraph (2) of subsection (f) of Code Section 9-11-23 or any other power of the court to stay discovery.

Amended by 2009 Ga. Laws 25,§ 4, eff. 7/1/2009.

Section 9-11-13 - Counterclaim and cross-claim

(a)Compulsory counterclaims. A pleading shall state as a counterclaim any claim which at the time of serving the pleading the pleader has against any opposing party, if it arises out of the transaction or occurrence that is the subject matter of the opposing party's claim and does not require for its adjudication the presence of third parties of whom the court cannot acquire jurisdiction. But the pleader need not state the claim if (1) at the time the action was commenced the claim was the subject of another pending action, or (2) the opposing party brought an action upon his claim by attachment or other process by which the court did not acquire jurisdiction to render a personal judgment on that claim, and the pleader is not stating any counterclaim under this Code section, or (3) the claim is not within the jurisdiction of the court.

(b)Permissive counterclaims. A pleading may state as a counterclaim any claim against an opposing party not arising out of the transaction or occurrence that is the subject matter of the opposing party's claim. But any such permissive counterclaim shall be separated for the purposes of trial, unless the parties otherwise agree.

(c)Counterclaim exceeding opposing claim. A counterclaim may or may not diminish or defeat the recovery sought by the opposing party. It may claim relief exceeding in amount or different in kind from that sought in the pleading of the opposing party.

(d)Counterclaim against the state. This Code section shall not be construed to enlarge beyond the limits fixed by law the right to assert counterclaims or to claim credits against the state or an officer or agency thereof.

(e)Counterclaim maturing or acquired after pleading. A claim which either matured or was acquired by the pleader after serving his pleading may, with the permission of the court, be presented as a counterclaim by supplemental pleading.

(f)Omitted counterclaim. When a pleader fails to set up a counterclaim through oversight, inadvertence, or excusable neglect, or when justice requires, he may by leave of court set up the counterclaim by amendment.

(g)Cross-claim against coparty. A pleading may state as a cross-claim any claim by one party against a coparty arising out of the transaction or occurrence that is the subject matter either of the original action or of a counterclaim therein or relating to any property that is the subject matter of the original action. The cross-claim may include a claim that the party against whom it is asserted is or may be liable to the cross-claimant for all or part of a claim asserted in the action against the cross-claimant.

(h)Additional parties may be brought in. When the presence of parties other than those to the original action is required for the granting of complete relief in the determination of a counterclaim or cross-claim, the court shall order them to be brought in as defendants as provided in this chapter, if jurisdiction of them can be obtained.

(i)Separate trials; separate judgments. If the court orders separate trials as provided in subsection (b) of Code Section 9-11-42, judgment on a counterclaim or cross-claim may be rendered in accordance with the terms of subsection (b) of Code Section 9-11-54 when the court has jurisdiction to do so, even if the claims of the opposing party have been dismissed or otherwise disposed of.

Section 9-11-14 - Third-party practice

(a)When defendant may bring in third party. At any time after commencement of the action a defendant, as a third-party plaintiff, may cause a summons and complaint to be served upon a person not a party to the action who is or may be liable to him for all or part of the plaintiff's claim against him. The third-party plaintiff need not obtain leave to make the service if he files the third-party complaint not later than ten days after he serves his original answer. Otherwise he must obtain leave on motion upon notice to all parties to the action. The person served with the summons and third-party complaint, hereinafter called the third-party defendant, shall make his defenses to the third-party plaintiff's claim as provided in Code Section 9-11-12 and his counterclaims against the third-party plaintiff and cross-claims against other third-party defendants as provided in Code Section 9-11-13. The third-party defendant may assert against the plaintiff any defenses which the third-party plaintiff has to the plaintiff's claim. The third-party defendant may also assert any claim against the plaintiff arising out of the transaction or occurrence that is the subject matter of the plaintiff's claim against the third-party plaintiff. The plaintiff may assert any claim against the third-party defendant arising out of the transaction or occurrence that is the subject matter of the plaintiff's claim against the third-party plaintiff, and the third-party defendant thereupon shall assert his defenses as provided in Code Section 9-11-12 and his counterclaims and cross-claims as provided in Code Section 9-11-13. Any party may move to strike the third-party claim, or for its severance or separate trial. A third-party defendant may proceed under this Code section against any person not a party to the action who is or may be liable to him for all or part of the claim made in the action against the third-party defendant.

(b)When plaintiff may bring in third party. When a counterclaim is asserted against a plaintiff, he may cause a third party to be brought in under circumstances which under this Code section would entitle a defendant to do so.

(c)Exhibits attached to third-party complaint. Any third-party complaint filed shall have attached thereto, as exhibits, a true and correct copy of the original complaint in the action and all other pleadings which have been filed in the action prior to the filing of the third-party complaint.

Section 9-11-15 - Amended and supplemental pleadings

(a)Amendments. A party may amend his pleading as a matter of course and without leave of court at any time before the entry of a pretrial order. Thereafter the party may amend his pleading only by leave of court or by written consent of the adverse party. Leave shall be freely given when justice so requires. A party may plead or move in response to an amended pleading and, when required by an order of the court, shall plead within 15 days after service of the amended pleading, unless the court otherwise orders.

(b)Amendments to conform to the evidence. When issues not raised by the pleadings are tried by express or implied consent of the parties, they shall be treated in all respects as if they had been raised in the pleadings. Such amendment of the pleadings as may be necessary to cause them to conform to the evidence and to raise these issues may be made upon motion of any party at any time, even after judgment; but failure so to amend does not affect the result of the trial of these issues. If evidence is objected to at the trial on the ground that it is not within the issues made by the pleadings, the court may allow the pleadings to be amended and shall do so freely when the presentation of the merits of the action will be subserved thereby and the objecting party fails to satisfy the court that the admission of the evidence would prejudice him in maintaining his action or defense upon the merits. The court may grant a continuance to enable the objecting party to meet the evidence.

(c)Relation back of amendments. Whenever the claim or defense asserted in the amended pleading arises out of the conduct, transaction, or occurrence set forth or attempted to be set forth in the original pleading, the amendment relates back to the date of the original pleading. An amendment changing the party against whom a claim is asserted relates back to the date of the original pleadings if the foregoing provisions are satisfied, and if within the period provided by law for commencing the action against him the party to be brought in by amendment (1) has received such notice of the institution of the action that he will not be prejudiced in maintaining his defense on the merits, and (2) knew or should have known that, but for a mistake concerning the identity of the proper party, the action would have been brought against him.

(d)Supplemental pleadings. Upon motion of a party the court may, upon reasonable notice and upon such terms as are just, permit him to serve a supplemental pleading setting forth transactions or occurrences or events which have happened since the date of the pleading sought to be supplemented. Permission may be granted even though the original pleading is defective in its statement of a claim for relief or defense. If the court deems it advisable that the adverse party plead to the supplemental pleading, it shall so order, specifying the time therefor.

Section 9-11-16 - Pretrial procedure; formulating issues; order; calendar

(a) Upon the motion of any party, or upon its own motion, the court shall direct the attorneys for the parties to appear before it for a conference to consider:

    (1) The simplification of the issues;

    (2) The necessity or desirability of amendments to the pleadings;

    (3) The possibility of obtaining admissions of fact and of documents which will avoid unnecessary proof;

    (4) The limitation of the number of expert witnesses; and

    (5) Such other matters as may aid in the disposition of the action.

(b) The court shall make an order which recites the action taken at the conference and the agreements made by the parties as to any of the matters considered and which limits the issues for trial to those not disposed of by admissions or agreements of counsel. The order, when entered, controls the subsequent course of the action unless modified at the trial to prevent manifest injustice. After entry of the pretrial order, it shall be within the discretion of the court to permit or disallow the presentation of testimony from any expert witness whose name is not contained in the pretrial order; provided, however, that if the additional expert witness is permitted to testify, any opposing party shall be permitted reasonable time to take the deposition of the additional expert witness. The court, in its discretion, may establish by rule a pretrial calendar on which actions may be placed for consideration as provided in subsection (a) of this Code section and may either confine the calendar to jury actions or to nonjury actions or extend it to all actions.

Amended by 2002 Ga. Laws 949, § 1.1, eff. 7/1/2002.

Article 4 - PARTIES

Section 9-11-17 - Real party in interest; capacity

(a)Real party in interest. Every action shall be prosecuted in the name of the real party in interest. A personal representative, a temporary administrator, a guardian, a conservator, a bailee, a trustee of an express trust, a party with whom or in whose name a contract has been made for the benefit of another, or a party authorized by statute may bring an action in his or her own name without joining with him or her the party for whose benefit the action is brought; and, when a statute so provides, an action for the use or benefit of another shall be brought in the name of the state. No action shall be dismissed on the ground that it is not prosecuted in the name of the real party in interest until a reasonable time has been allowed after objection for ratification of commencement of the action by, or joinder or substitution of, the real party in interest; and such ratification, joinder, or substitution shall have the same effect as if the action had been commenced in the name of the real party in interest.

(b)Capacity to bring or defend an action. The capacity of an individual, including one acting in a representative capacity, to bring or defend an action shall be determined by the law of this state. The capacity of a corporation to bring or defend an action shall be determined by the law under which it was organized, unless a statute of this state provides to the contrary.

(c)Infants or incompetent persons. Whenever an infant or incompetent person has a representative, such as a general guardian, committee, conservator, or other like fiduciary, the representative may bring or defend an action on behalf of the infant or incompetent person. If an infant or incompetent person does not have a duly appointed representative, he or she may bring an action by his or her next friend or by a guardian ad litem. The court shall appoint a guardian ad litem for an infant or incompetent person not otherwise represented in an action or shall make such other order as it deems proper for the protection of the infant or incompetent person. No next friend shall be permitted to receive the proceeds of any personal action, in the name and on behalf of an infant or incompetent person, until such next friend shall have entered into a sufficient bond to the Governor, for the use of the infant and the infant's representatives, conditioned well and fully to account for and concerning such trust, which bond may be sued on by order of the court in the name of the Governor and for the use of the infant. Such bond shall be approved by the court in which the action is commenced and such approval shall be filed in such clerk's office.

Amended by 2020 Ga. Laws 508,§ 2-7, eff. 1/1/2021.

Section 9-11-18 - Joinder of claims and remedies

(a)Joinder of claims. A party asserting a claim to relief as an original claim, counterclaim, cross-claim, or third-party claim may join, either as independent or as alternate claims, as many claims, legal or equitable, as he has against an opposing party.

(b)Joinder of remedies; fraudulent conveyances. Whenever a claim is one heretofore cognizable only after another claim has been prosecuted to a conclusion, the two claims may be joined in a single action; but the court shall grant relief in that action only in accordance with the relative substantive rights of the parties. In particular, a plaintiff may state a claim for money and a claim to have set aside a conveyance fraudulent as to him without first having obtained a judgment establishing the claim for money.

Section 9-11-19 - Joinder of persons needed for just adjudication

(a)Persons to be joined if feasible. A person who is subject to service of process shall be joined as a party in the action if:

    (1) In his absence complete relief cannot be afforded among those who are already parties; or

    (2) He claims an interest relating to the subject of the action and is so situated that the disposition of the action in his absence may:

        (A) As a practical matter impair or impede his ability to protect that interest; or

        (B) Leave any of the persons who are already parties subject to a substantial risk of incurring double, multiple, or otherwise inconsistent obligations by reason of his claimed interest.If he has not been so joined, the court shall order that he be made a party. If he should join as a plaintiff but refuses to do so, he may be made a defendant or, in a proper case, an involuntary plaintiff. If the joined party objects to venue and his joinder would render the venue of the action improper, he shall be dismissed from the action.

(b)Determination by court whenever joinder not feasible. If a person, as described in paragraphs (1) and (2) of subsection (a) of this Code section, cannot be made a party, the court shall determine whether in equity and good conscience the action should proceed among the parties before it or should be dismissed, the absent person being thus regarded as indispensable. The factors to be considered by the court include:

(1) To what extent a judgment rendered in the person's absence might be prejudicial to him or to those already parties;

(2) The extent to which, by protective provisions in the judgment, by the shaping of relief, or by other measures, the prejudice can be lessened or avoided;

(3) Whether a judgment rendered in the person's absence will be adequate;

(4) Whether the plaintiff will have an adequate remedy if the action is dismissed for nonjoinder; and

(5) Whether and by whom prejudice might have been avoided or may, in the future, be avoided.

(c)Pleading reasons for nonjoinder. A pleading asserting a claim for relief shall state the names, if known to the pleader, of any persons, as described in paragraphs (1) and (2) of subsection (a) of this Code section, who are not joined and the reasons why they are not joined.

(d)Exception of class actions. This Code section shall be subject to Code Section 9-11-23.

Section 9-11-20 - Permissive joinder of parties

(a)Permissive joinder. All persons may join in one action as plaintiffs if they assert any right to relief jointly, severally, or in the alternative in respect of or arising out of the same transaction, occurrence, or series of transactions or occurrences and if any question of law or fact common to all of them will arise in the action. All persons may be joined in one action as defendants if there is asserted against them jointly, severally, or in the alternative any right to relief in respect of or arising out of the same transaction, occurrence, or series of transactions or occurrences and if any question of law or fact common to all of them will arise in the action. A plaintiff or defendant need not be interested in obtaining or defending against all the relief demanded. Judgment may be given for one or more of the plaintiffs according to their respective rights to relief and against one or more of the defendants according to their respective liabilities.

(b)Separate trials. The court may make such orders as will prevent a party from being embarrassed, delayed, or put to expense by the inclusion of a party against whom he asserts no claim and who asserts no claim against him and may order separate trials or make other orders to prevent delay or prejudice.

Section 9-11-21 - Misjoinder and nonjoinder of parties

Misjoinder of parties is not ground for dismissal of an action. Parties may be dropped or added by order of the court on motion of any party or of its own initiative at any stage of the action and on such terms as are just. Any claim against a party may be severed and proceeded with separately.

Section 9-11-22 - Interpleader

(a) Persons having claims against the plaintiff may be joined as defendants and required to interplead when their claims are such that the plaintiff is or may be exposed to double or multiple liability. It is not ground for objection to the joinder that the claims of the several claimants or the titles on which their claims depend do not have a common origin or are not identical but are adverse to and independent of one another or that the plaintiff avers that he is not liable in whole or in part to any or all of the claimants. A defendant exposed to similar liability may obtain such interpleader by way of cross-claim or counterclaim. This Code section supplements and does not in any way limit the joinder of parties permitted in Code Section 9-11-20.

(b) The remedy provided in this Code section is in addition to and in no way supersedes or limits the remedy of equitable interpleader provided for in Code Sections 23-3-90 through 23-3-92.

Section 9-11-23 - Class actions

(a) One or more members of a class may sue or be sued as representative parties on behalf of all only if:

(1) The class is so numerous that joinder of all members is impracticable;

(2) There are questions of law or fact common to the class;

(3) The claims or defenses of the representative parties are typical of the claims or defenses of the class; and

(4) The representative parties will fairly and adequately protect the interests of the class.

(b) An action may be maintained as a class action if the prerequisites of subsection (a) of this Code section are satisfied, and, in addition:

(1) The prosecution of separate actions by or against individual members of the class would create a risk of:

(A) Inconsistent or varying adjudications with respect to individual members of the class which would establish incompatible standards of conduct for the party opposing the class; or

(B) Adjudications with respect to individual members of the class which would as a practical matter be dispositive of the interests of the other members not parties to the adjudications or substantially impair or impede their ability to protect their interests;

(2) The party opposing the class has acted or refused to act on grounds generally applicable to the class, thereby making appropriate final injunctive relief or corresponding declaratory relief with respect to the class as a whole; or

(3) The court finds that the questions of law or fact common to the members of the class predominate over any questions affecting only individual members, and that a class action is superior to other available methods for the fair and efficient adjudication of the controversy. The matters pertinent to the findings include:

(A) The interest of members of the class in individually controlling the prosecution or defense of separate actions;

(B) The extent and nature of any litigation concerning the controversy already commenced by or against members of the class;

(C) The desirability or undesirability of concentrating the litigation of the claims in the particular forum; and

(D) The difficulties likely to be encountered in the management of a class action.

(c)

(1) As soon as practicable after the commencement of an action brought as a class action, the court shall determine by order whether it is to be so maintained. An order under this subsection may be conditional, and may be altered or amended before the decision on the merits.

(2) In any class action maintained under paragraph (3) of subsection (b) of this Code section, the court shall direct to the members of the class the best notice practicable under the circumstances, including individual notice to all members who can be identified through reasonable effort. The notice shall advise each member that:

(A) The court will exclude the member from the class if the member so requests by a specified date;

(B) The judgment, whether favorable or not, will include all members who do not request exclusion; and

(C) Any member who does not request exclusion may, if the member desires, enter an appearance through counsel.

(3) The judgment in an action maintained as a class action under paragraph (1) or (2) of subsection (b) of this Code section, whether or not favorable to the class, shall include and describe those whom the court finds to be members of the class. The judgment in an action maintained as a class action under paragraph (3) of subsection (b) of this Code section, whether or not favorable to the class, shall include and specify or describe those to whom the notice provided in paragraph (2) of subsection (b) of this Code section was directed, and who have not requested exclusion, and whom the court finds to be members of the class.

(4) When appropriate:

(A) An action may be brought or maintained as a class action with respect to particular issues; or

(B) A class may be divided into subclasses and each subclass treated as a class, and the provisions of this rule shall then be construed and applied accordingly.

(d) In the conduct of actions to which this rule applies, the court may make appropriate orders:

(1) Determining the course of proceedings or prescribing measures to prevent undue repetition or complication in the presentation of evidence or argument;

(2) Requiring, for the protection of the members of the class or otherwise for the fair conduct of the action, that notice be given in such manner as the court may direct to some or all of the members of any step in the action, or of the proposed extent of the judgment, or of the opportunity of members to signify whether they consider the representation fair and adequate, to intervene and present claims or defenses, or otherwise to come into the action;

(3) Imposing conditions on the representative parties or on intervenors; and

(4) Requiring that the pleadings be amended to eliminate therefrom allegations as to representation of absent persons, and that the action proceed accordingly. The orders may be combined with other orders, and may be altered or amended by the court as may be desirable from time to time.

(e) A class action shall not be dismissed or compromised without the approval of the court, and notice of the proposed dismissal or compromise shall be given to all members of the class in such manner as the court directs.

(f)

(1) After the commencement of an action in which claims or defenses are purported to be asserted on behalf of or against a class, the court shall hold a conference among all named parties to the action for the purpose of establishing a schedule for any discovery germane to the issue of whether the requested class should or should not be certified. At this conference, the court shall set a date for a hearing on the issue of class certification. Except for good cause shown, such hearing may not be set sooner than 90 days nor later than 180 days after the date on which the court issues its scheduling order pursuant to the conference. If evidence is presented by affidavit, the parties shall have an opportunity to cross-examine affiants as to such testimony offered by affidavit.

(2) Except for good cause shown, the court shall stay all discovery directed solely to the merits of the claims or defenses in the action until the court has issued its written decision regarding certification of the class.

(3) When deciding whether a requested class is to be certified, the court shall enter a written order addressing whether the factors required by this Code section for certification of a class have been met and specifying the findings of fact and conclusions of law on which the court has based its decision with regard to whether each such factor has been established. In so doing, the court may treat a factor as having been established if all parties to the action have so stipulated on the record.

(4) Nothing in this Code section shall affect, or be construed to affect, any provision of Code Section 9-11-12 or Code Section 9-11-56.

(g) A court's order certifying a class or refusing to certify a class shall be appealable in the same manner as a final order to the appellate court which would otherwise have jurisdiction over the appeal from a final order in the action. The appellate courts shall expedite resolution of any appeals taken under this Code section. Such appeal may only be filed within 30 days of the order certifying or refusing to certify the class. During the pendency of any such appeal, the action in the trial court shall be stayed in all respects.

Amended by 2005 Ga. Laws 56,§ 1, eff. 4/22/2005.

Amended by 2003 Ga. Laws 363, § 3, eff. 7/1/2003.

Section 9-11-24 - Intervention

(a)Intervention of right. Upon timely application anyone shall be permitted to intervene in an action:

(1) When a statute confers an unconditional right to intervene; or

(2) When the applicant claims an interest relating to the property or transaction which is the subject matter of the action and he is so situated that the disposition of the action may as a practical matter impair or impede his ability to protect that interest, unless the applicant's interest is adequately represented by existing parties.

(b)Permissive intervention. Upon timely application anyone may be permitted to intervene in an action:

(1) When a statute confers a conditional right to intervene; or

(2) When an applicant's claim or defense and the main action have a question of law or fact in common.In exercising its discretion the court shall consider whether the intervention will unduly delay or prejudice the adjudication of the rights of the original parties.

(c)Procedure. A person desiring to intervene shall serve a motion to intervene upon the parties as provided in Code Section 9-11-5. The motion shall state the grounds therefor and shall be accompanied by a pleading setting forth the claim or defense for which intervention is sought. The same procedure shall be followed when a statute gives a right to intervene.

Section 9-11-25 - Substitution of parties

(a)Death.

(1) If a party dies and the claim is not thereby extinguished, the court may order substitution of the proper parties. The motion for substitution may be made by any party or by the successors or representative of the deceased party and, together with the notice of the hearing, shall be served on the parties as provided in Code Section 9-11-5 and upon persons not parties in the manner provided in Code Section 9-11-4 for the service of a summons. Unless the motion for substitution is made not later than 180 days after the death is suggested upon the record by service of a statement of the fact of the death, the action shall be dismissed as to the deceased party.

(2) In the event of the death of one or more of the plaintiffs or of one or more of the defendants in an action in which the right sought to be enforced survives only to the surviving plaintiffs or only against the surviving defendants, the action does not abate. The death shall be suggested upon the record and the action shall proceed in favor of or against the surviving parties.

(b)Incompetency. If a party becomes incompetent, the court, upon motion served as provided in subsection (a) of this Code section, may allow the action to be continued by or against his representative.

(c)Transfer of interest. In case of any transfer of interest, the action may be continued by or against the original party unless the court, upon motion, directs the person to whom the interest is transferred to be substituted in the action or joined with the original party. Service of the motion shall be made as provided in subsection (a) of this Code section.

(d)Public officers; death or separation from office.

(1) When a public officer is a party to an action in his official capacity and during its pendency dies, resigns, or otherwise ceases to hold office, the action does not abate, and his successor is automatically substituted as a party. Proceedings following the substitution shall be in the name of the substituted party, but any misnomer not affecting the substantial rights of the parties shall be disregarded. An order of substitution may be entered at any time, but the omission to enter such an order shall not affect the substitution.

(2) When a public officer brings or defends an action in his official capacity, he may be described as a party by his official title rather than by name; but the court may require his name to be added.

Article 5 - DEPOSITIONS AND DISCOVERY

Section 9-11-26 - General provisions governing discovery

(a)Discovery methods. Parties may obtain discovery by one or more of the following methods: depositions upon oral examination or written questions; written interrogatories; production of documents or things or permission to enter upon land or other property for inspection and other purposes; physical and mental examinations; and requests for admission. Unless the court orders otherwise under subsection (c) of this Code section, the frequency of use of these methods is not limited.

(b)Scope of discovery. Unless otherwise limited by order of the court in accordance with this chapter, the scope of discovery is as follows:

(1)In general. Parties may obtain discovery regarding any matter, not privileged, which is relevant to the subject matter involved in the pending action, whether it relates to the claim or defense of the party seeking discovery or to the claim or defense of any other party, including the existence, description, nature, custody, condition, and location of any books, documents, or other tangible things and the identity and location of persons having knowledge of any discoverable matter. It is not ground for objection that the information sought will be inadmissible at the trial if the information sought appears reasonably calculated to lead to the discovery of admissible evidence;

(2)Insurance agreements. A party may obtain discovery of the existence and contents of any insurance agreement under which any person carrying on an insurance business may be liable to satisfy part or all of a judgment which may be entered in the action or to indemnify or reimburse for payments made to satisfy the judgment. Information concerning the insurance agreement is not by reason of disclosure admissible in evidence at trial. For purposes of this paragraph, an application for insurance shall not be treated as part of an insurance agreement;

(3)Trial preparation; materials. Subject to paragraph (4) of this subsection, a party may obtain discovery of documents and tangible things otherwise discoverable under paragraph (1) of this subsection and prepared in anticipation of litigation or for trial by or for another party or by or for that other party's representative (including his attorney, consultant, surety, indemnitor, insurer, or agent) only upon a showing that the party seeking discovery has substantial need of the materials in the preparation of his case and that he is unable without undue hardship to obtain the substantial equivalent of the materials by other means. In ordering discovery of such materials when the required showing has been made, the court shall protect against disclosure of the mental impressions, conclusions, opinions, or legal theories of an attorney or other representative of a party concerning the litigation. A party may obtain, without the required showing, a statement concerning the action or its subject matter previously made by that party. Upon request, a person not a party may obtain, without the required showing, a statement concerning the action or its subject matter previously made by that person. If the request is refused, the person may move for a court order. Paragraph (4) of subsection (a) of Code Section 9-11-37 applies to the award of expenses incurred in relation to the motion. For purposes of this paragraph, a "statement previously made" is (A) a written statement signed or otherwise adopted or approved by the person making it, or (B) a stenographic, mechanical, electrical, or other recording, or a transcription thereof, which is a substantially verbatim recital of an oral statement by the person making it and contemporaneously recorded; and

(4)Trial preparation; experts. Discovery of facts known and opinions held by experts, otherwise discoverable under paragraph (1) of this subsection and acquired or developed in anticipation of litigation or for trial, may be obtained only as follows:

(A)

(i) A party may, through interrogatories, require any other party to identify each person whom the other party expects to call as an expert witness at trial, to state the subject matter on which the expert is expected to testify, and to state the substance of the facts and opinions to which the expert is expected to testify and a summary of the grounds for each opinion.

(ii) A party may obtain discovery under Code Section 9-11-30, 9-11-31, or 9-11-34 from any expert described in this paragraph, the same as any other witness, but the party obtaining discovery of an expert hereunder must pay a reasonable fee for the time spent in responding to discovery by that expert, subject to the right of the expert or any party to obtain a determination by the court as to the reasonableness of the fee so incurred;

(B) A party may discover facts known or opinions held by an expert who has been retained or specially employed by another party in anticipation of litigation or preparation for trial and who is not expected to be called as a witness at trial, only as provided in subsection (b) of Code Section 9-11-35 or upon a showing of exceptional circumstances under which it is impracticable for the party seeking discovery to obtain facts or opinions on the same subject by other means; and

(C) Unless manifest injustice would result:

(i) The court shall require the party seeking discovery to pay the expert a reasonable fee for time spent in responding to discovery under subparagraph (B) of this paragraph; and

(ii) With respect to discovery obtained under division (ii) of subparagraph (A) of this paragraph, the court may require, and with respect to discovery obtained under subparagraph (B) of this paragraph the court shall require, the party seeking discovery to pay the other party a fair portion of the fees and expenses reasonably incurred by the latter party in obtaining facts and opinions from the expert.

(c)Protective orders. Upon motion by a party or by the person from whom discovery is sought and for good cause shown, the court in which the action is pending or, alternatively, on matters relating to a deposition, the court in the county where the deposition is to be taken may make any order which justice requires to protect a party or person from annoyance, embarrassment, oppression, or undue burden or expense, including one or more of the following:

(1) That the discovery not be had;

(2) That the discovery may be had only on specified terms and conditions, including a designation of the time or place;

(3) That the discovery may be had only by a method of discovery other than that selected by the party seeking discovery;

(4) That certain matters not be inquired into or that the scope of the discovery be limited to certain matters;

(5) That discovery be conducted with no one present except persons designated by the court;

(6) That a deposition, after being sealed, be opened only by order of the court;

(7) That a trade secret or other confidential research, development, or commercial information not be disclosed or be disclosed only in a designated way; or

(8) That the parties simultaneously file specified documents or information enclosed in sealed envelopes to be opened as directed by the court.If the motion for a protective order is denied in whole or in part, the court may, on such terms and conditions as are just, order that any party or person provide or permit discovery. Paragraph (4) of subsection (a) of Code Section 9-11-37 applies to the award of expenses incurred in relation to the motion.

(d)Sequence and timing of discovery. Unless the court, upon motion, for the convenience of parties and witnesses and in the interests of justice, orders otherwise, methods of discovery may be used in any sequence; and the fact that a party is conducting discovery, whether by deposition or otherwise, shall not operate to delay any other party's discovery.

(e)Supplementation of responses. A party who has responded to a request for discovery with a response that was complete when made is under no duty to supplement his response to include information thereafter acquired, except as follows:

(1) A party is under a duty seasonably to supplement his response with respect to any question directly addressed to:

(A) The identity and location of persons having knowledge of discoverable matters; and

(B) The identity of each person expected to be called as an expert witness at trial, the subject matter on which he is expected to testify, and the substance of his testimony.

(2) A party is under a duty seasonably to amend a prior response if he obtains information upon the basis of which:

(A) He knows that the response was incorrect when made; or

(B) He knows that the response, though correct when made, is no longer true and the circumstances are such that a failure to amend the response is, in substance, a knowing concealment.

(3) A duty to supplement responses may be imposed by order of the court, agreement of the parties, or at any time prior to trial through new requests for supplementation of prior responses.

Section 9-11-27 - Depositions before action or pending appeal

(a)Before action.

(1)Petition. A person who desires to perpetuate such person's own testimony or that of another person regarding any matter that may be cognizable in any court may file a verified petition in the superior court of the county where the witness resides. The petition shall be entitled in the name of the petitioner and shall show that the petitioner expects to be a party to litigation but is presently unable to bring it or cause it to be brought, the subject matter of the expected action and the petitioner's interest therein, the facts which the petitioner desires to establish by the proposed testimony and the petitioner's reasons for desiring to perpetuate it, the names or a description of the persons the petitioner expects will be adverse parties and their addresses so far as known, and the names and addresses of the persons to be examined and the substance of the testimony which the petitioner expects to elicit from each, and shall ask for an order authorizing the petitioner to take the depositions of the persons to be examined named in the petition, for the purpose of perpetuating their testimony.

(2)Notice and service. The petitioner shall thereafter serve a notice upon each person named in the petition as an expected adverse party, together with a copy of the petition, stating that the petitioner will apply to the court at a time and place named therein for the order described in the petition. At least 20 days before the date of hearing the notice shall be served either within or outside the county in the manner provided for service of summons; but, if such service cannot with due diligence be made upon any expected adverse party named in the petition, the court may make such order as is just for service by publication or otherwise and shall appoint, for persons not served, an attorney who shall represent them and, in case they are not otherwise represented, shall cross-examine the deponent. The court may make such order as is just requiring the petitioner to pay a reasonable fee to an attorney so appointed. If any expected adverse party is a minor or an incompetent person and does not have a general guardian, the court shall appoint a guardian ad litem.

(3)Order and examination. If the court is satisfied that the perpetuation of the testimony may prevent a failure or delay of justice, it shall make an order designating or describing the persons whose depositions may be taken and specifying the subject matter of the examination and whether the depositions shall be taken upon oral examination or written interrogatories. The depositions may then be taken by a certified court reporter, or as otherwise provided by the rules of the Board of Court Reporting, in accordance with this chapter; and the court may make orders of the character provided for by Code Sections 9-11-34 and 9-11-35. For the purpose of applying this chapter to depositions for perpetuating testimony, each reference therein to the court in which the action is pending shall be deemed to refer to the court in which the petition for such deposition was filed.

(4)Use of deposition. If a deposition to perpetuate testimony is taken under this Code section or if, although not so taken, it would be otherwise admissible under the laws of this state, it may be used in any action involving the same parties and the same subject matter subsequently brought.

(b)Pending appeal. If an appeal has been taken from a judgment of a trial court or before the taking of an appeal if the time therefor has not expired, the court in which the judgment was rendered may allow the taking of the depositions of witnesses to perpetuate their testimony for use in the event of further proceedings in the trial court. In such case the party who desires to perpetuate the testimony may make a motion in the trial court for leave to take the depositions, upon the same notice and service thereof as if the action were pending in the court. The motion shall show the names and addresses of persons to be examined, the substance of the testimony which the movant expects to elicit from each, and the reasons for perpetuating their testimony. If the court finds that the perpetuation of the testimony is proper to avoid a failure or delay of justice, it may make an order allowing the depositions to be taken and may make orders of the character provided for by Code Sections 9-11-34 and 9-11-35; and thereupon the depositions may be taken before a certified court reporter, or as otherwise provided by the rules of the Board of Court Reporting, and used in the same manner and under the same conditions as are prescribed in this chapter for depositions taken in actions pending in court.

(c)Perpetuation by action. This Code section does not limit the power of a court to entertain an action to perpetuate testimony.

Section 9-11-28 - Persons before whom depositions may be taken; disqualification for interest; consent of parties

(a)Within the United States and its possessions. Within the United States or within a territory or insular possession subject to the dominion of the United States, depositions shall be taken before an officer authorized to administer oaths by the laws of the United States or by the laws of the place where the examination is held or before a court reporter appointed by the court in which the action is pending or, if within this state, before a certified court reporter or as otherwise provided by the rules of the Board of Court Reporting. A person so appointed has power to administer oaths and take testimony.

(b)In foreign countries. In a foreign state or country depositions shall be taken on notice before a secretary of embassy or legation, consul general, consul, vice-consul, or consular agent of the United States, or before such person or officer as may be appointed by commission or under letters rogatory. A commission or letters rogatory shall be issued only when necessary or convenient, on application and notice, and on such terms and with such directions as are just and appropriate. Officers may be designated in notices or commissions either by name or by descriptive title and letters rogatory may be addressed "To the Appropriate Judicial Authority in (here name the country)."

(c)Disqualification for interest. No deposition shall be taken before a court reporter who is a relative, employee, attorney, or counsel of any of the parties, or who is a relative or employee of such attorney or counsel, or who is financially interested in the action, excepting that a deposition may be taken before a court reporter who is a relative of a party or of an attorney or counsel of a party if all parties represented at the deposition enter their explicit consent to the same upon the record of the deposition.

Section 9-11-29 - Stipulations regarding discovery procedure

Unless the court orders otherwise, the parties may, by written stipulation:

(1) Provide that depositions may be taken before any person, at any time or place, upon any notice, and in any manner and, when so taken, may be used like other depositions; and

(2) Modify the procedures provided by this chapter for other methods of discovery.

Section 9-11-29.1 - When depositions and other discovery material must be filed with court; custodian until filing; retention of depositions and other discovery materials

(a) Depositions and other discovery material otherwise required to be filed with the court under this chapter shall not be required to be so filed unless:

(1) Required by local rule of court;

(2) Ordered by the court;

(3) Requested by any party to the action;

(4) Relief relating to discovery material is sought under this chapter and said material has not previously been filed under some other provision of this chapter, in which event copies of the material in dispute shall be filed by the movant contemporaneously with the motion for relief; or

(5) Such material is to be used at trial or is necessary to a pretrial or posttrial motion and said material has not previously been filed under some other provision of this chapter, in which event the portions to be used shall be filed with the clerk of court at the outset of the trial or at the filing of the motion, insofar as their use can be reasonably anticipated by the parties having custody thereof, but a party attempting to file and use such material which was not filed with the clerk at the outset of the trial or at the filing of the motion shall show to the satisfaction of the court, before the court may authorize such filing and use, that sufficient reasons exist to justify that late filing and use and that the late filing and use will not constitute surprise or manifest injustice to any other party in the proceedings.

(b) Until such time as discovery material is filed under paragraphs (1) through (5) of subsection (a) of this Code section, the original of all depositions shall be retained by the party taking the deposition and the original of all other discovery material shall be retained by the party requesting such material, and the person thus retaining the deposition or other discovery material shall be the custodian thereof.

(c) When depositions and other discovery material are filed with the clerk of court as provided in subsection (a) of this Code section, the clerk of court shall retain such original documents and materials until final disposition, either by verdict or appeal, of the action in which such materials were filed. The clerk of court shall be authorized thereafter to destroy such materials upon microfilming or digitally imaging such materials and maintaining such materials in a manner that facilitates retrieval and reproduction, so long as the microfilm and digital images meet the standards established by the Division of Archives and History of the University System of Georgia; provided, however, that the clerk of court shall not be required to microfilm or digitally image depositions that are not used for evidentiary purposes during the trial of the issues of the case in which such depositions were filed.

Amended by 2013 Ga. Laws 184,§ 2-1, eff. 7/1/2013.

Amended by 2012 Ga. Laws 599,§ 1-1-1, eff. 7/1/2012.

Section 9-11-30 - Depositions upon oral examination

(a)When depositions may be taken. After commencement of the action, any party may take the testimony of any person, including a party, by deposition upon oral examination. Leave of court, granted with or without notice, must be obtained only if the plaintiff seeks to take a deposition prior to the expiration of 30 days after service of the summons and complaint upon any defendant or service made under subsection (f) of Code Section 9-11-4, except that leave is not required if a defendant has served a notice of taking deposition or otherwise sought discovery or if special notice is given as provided in paragraph (2) of subsection (b) of this Code section. The attendance of witnesses may be compelled by subpoena as provided in Code Section 9-11-45. The deposition of a person confined in a penal institution may be taken only by leave of court on such terms as the court prescribes.

(b)Notice of examination.

(1)General requirements. A party desiring to take the deposition of any person upon oral examination shall give reasonable notice in writing to every other party to the action. The notice shall state the time and place for taking the deposition, the means by which the testimony shall be recorded, and the name and address of each person to be examined, if known, and, if the name is not known, a general description sufficient to identify the person to be examined or the particular class or group to which he or she belongs. If a subpoena for the production of documentary and tangible evidence is to be served on the person to be examined, the designation of the materials to be produced, as set forth in the subpoena, shall be attached to, or included in, the notice.

(2)Special notice. Leave of court is not required for the taking of a deposition by plaintiff if the notice:

(A) States that the person to be examined is about to go out of the county where the action is pending and more than 150 miles from the place of trial, or is about to go out of the United States, or is bound on a voyage to sea, and will be unavailable for examination unless the deposition is taken before expiration of the 30 day period; and

(B) Sets forth facts to support the statement.The plaintiff's attorney shall sign the notice, and said attorney's signature constitutes a certification by him or her that, to the best of his or her knowledge, information, and belief, the statement and supporting facts are true. If a party shows that, when he or she was served with notice under this paragraph, he or she was unable through the exercise of diligence to obtain counsel to represent him or her at the taking of the deposition, the deposition may not be used against such party.

(3)Time requirements. The court may, for cause shown, enlarge or shorten the time for taking the deposition.

(4)Recording of deposition. Unless the court orders otherwise, the testimony at a deposition must be recorded by stenographic means, and may also be recorded by sound or sound and visual means in addition to stenographic means, and the party taking the deposition shall bear the costs of the recording. A deposition shall be conducted before an officer appointed or designated under Code Section 9-11-28. Upon motion of a party or upon its own motion, the court may issue an order designating the manner of recording, preserving, and filing of a deposition taken by nonstenographic means, which order may include other provisions to assure that the recorded testimony will be accurate and trustworthy. Any party may arrange for a transcription to be made from the recording of a deposition taken by nonstenographic means. With prior notice to the deponent and other parties, any party may designate another method to record the deponent's testimony in addition to the methods specified by the person taking the deposition. The additional record or transcript shall be made at that party's expense unless the court otherwise orders. The appearance or demeanor of deponents or attorneys shall not be distorted through camera or sound-recording techniques. Notwithstanding the foregoing provisions of this paragraph, a deposition may be taken by telephone or other remote electronic means only upon the stipulation of the parties or by order of the court. For purposes of the requirements of this chapter, a deposition taken by telephone or other remote electronic means is taken in the state and at the place where the deponent is to answer questions.

(5)Production of documents and things. The notice to a party deponent may be accompanied by a request made in compliance with Code Section 9-11-34 for the production of documents and tangible things at the taking of the deposition. The procedure of Code Section 9-11-34 shall apply to the request.

(6)Deposition of organization. A party may, in his or her notice, name as the deponent a public or private corporation or a partnership or association or a governmental agency and designate with reasonable particularity the matters on which examination is requested. The organization so named shall designate one or more officers, directors, or managing agents, or other persons who consent to testify on its behalf, and may set forth, for each person designated, the matters on which he or she will testify. The persons so designated shall testify as to matters known or reasonably available to the organization. This paragraph does not preclude taking a deposition by any other procedure authorized in this chapter.

(c)Examination and cross-examination; record of examination; oath; objections.

(1) Examination and cross-examination of witnesses may proceed as permitted at the trial under the rules of evidence. The authorized officer or court reporter before whom the deposition is to be taken shall put the witness on oath and shall personally, or by someone acting under the direction and in the presence of the authorized officer or court reporter, record the testimony of the witness.

(2) All objections made at the time of the examination to the qualifications of the officer taking the deposition, or to the manner of taking it, or to the evidence presented, or to the conduct of any party, and any other objection to the proceedings shall be noted by the officer upon the deposition. Evidence objected to shall be taken subject to the objections. In lieu of participating in the oral examination, parties may serve written questions in a sealed envelope on the party taking the deposition, and said party shall transmit them to the officer, who shall propound them to the witness and record the answers verbatim.

(3) Unless otherwise ordered by the court or agreed by the parties, the officer shall retain the record of each deposition until the later of (A) five years after the date on which the deposition was taken, or (B) two years after the date of final disposition of the action for which the deposition was taken and any appeals of such action. The officer may preserve the record through storage of the original paper, notes, or recordings or an electronic copy of the notes, recordings, or the transcript on computer disks, cassettes, backup tape systems, optical or laser disk systems, or other retrieval systems.

(d)Motion to terminate or limit examination. At any time during the taking of the deposition, on motion of a party or of the deponent and upon a showing that the examination is being conducted in bad faith or in such manner as unreasonably to annoy, embarrass, or oppress the deponent or party, the court in which the action is pending or the court in the county where the deposition is being taken may order the officer conducting the examination to cease forthwith from taking the deposition or may limit the scope and manner of the taking of the deposition as provided in subsection (c) of Code Section 9-11-26. If the order made terminates the examination, it shall be resumed thereafter only upon the order of the court in which the action is pending. Upon demand of the objecting party or deponent, the taking of the deposition shall be suspended for the time necessary to make a motion for an order. Paragraph (4) of subsection (a) of Code Section 9-11-37 applies to the award of expenses incurred in relation to the motion.

(e)Review by witness; changes; signing. If requested by the deponent or a party before completion of the deposition, the deponent shall have 30 days after being notified by the officer that the transcript or recording is available in which to review the transcript or recording and, if there are changes in form or substance, to sign a statement reciting such changes and the reasons given by the deponent for making them. The officer shall indicate in the certificate prescribed by paragraph (1) of subsection (f) of this Code section whether any review was requested and, if so, shall append any changes made by the deponent during the period allowed. If the deposition is not reviewed and signed by the witness within 30 days of its submission to him or her, the officer shall sign it and state on the record that the deposition was not reviewed and signed by the deponent within 30 days. The deposition may then be used as fully as though signed unless, on a motion to suppress under paragraph (4) of subsection (d) of Code Section 9-11-32, the court holds that the reasons given for the refusal to sign require rejection of the deposition in whole or in part.

(f)Certification and filing by officer; inspection and copying of exhibits; copy of deposition.

(1)

(A) The officer shall certify that the witness was duly sworn by the officer and that the deposition is a true record of the testimony given by the witness. This certificate shall be in writing and accompany the record of the deposition. The officer shall then securely seal the deposition in an envelope marked with the title of the action, the court reporter certification number, and "Deposition of (here insert name of witness)" and shall promptly file it with the court in which the action is pending or deliver it to the party taking the deposition, as the case may be, in accordance with Code Section 9-11-29.1.

(B) Documents and things produced for inspection during the examination of the witness shall, upon the request of a party, be marked for identification and annexed to and returned with the deposition and may be inspected and copied by any party, except that the person producing the materials may substitute copies to be marked for identification, if he or she affords to all parties fair opportunity to verify the copies by comparison with the originals; and, if the person producing the materials requests their return, the officer shall mark them, give each party an opportunity to inspect and copy them, and return them to the person producing them, and the materials may then be used in the same manner as if annexed to and returned with the deposition. Any party may move for an order that the original be annexed to and returned with the deposition to the court, pending final disposition of the case.

(2) Upon payment of reasonable charges therefor, the officer shall furnish a copy of the deposition to any party or to the deponent.

(g)Failure to attend or to serve subpoena; expenses.

(1) If the party giving the notice of the taking of a deposition fails to attend and proceed therewith and another party attends in person or by attorney pursuant to the notice, the court may order the party giving the notice to pay to such other party the reasonable expenses incurred by him and his attorney in attending, including reasonable attorney's fees.

(2) If the party giving the notice of the taking of a deposition of a witness fails to serve a subpoena upon him and the witness, because of such failure, does not attend and if another party attends in person or by attorney because he expects the deposition of that witness to be taken, the court may order the party giving the notice to pay to such other party the reasonable expenses incurred by him and his attorney in attending, including reasonable attorney's fees.

(h)Form of presentation. Except as otherwise directed by the court, a party offering deposition testimony may offer it in stenographic or nonstenographic form, but if in nonstenographic form, the party shall also provide the court with a transcript of the portions so offered. On request of any party in a case tried before a jury, deposition testimony offered other than for impeachment purposes shall be presented in nonstenographic form, if available, unless the court for good cause orders otherwise.

Section 9-11-31 - Depositions upon written questions

(a)Serving questions; notice.

(1) After commencement of the action, any party may take the testimony of any person, including a party, by deposition upon written questions. The attendance of witnesses may be compelled by the use of subpoena as provided in Code Section 9-11-45. The deposition of a person confined in a penal institution may be taken only by leave of court on such terms as the court prescribes.

(2) A party desiring to take a deposition upon written questions shall serve them upon every other party with a notice stating the name and address of the person who is to answer them, if known, and, if the name is not known, a general description sufficient to identify him or the particular class or group to which he belongs and the name or descriptive title and address of the officer before whom the deposition is to be taken. A deposition upon written questions may be taken of a public or private corporation or a partnership or association or governmental agency in accordance with paragraph (6) of subsection (b) of Code Section 9-11-30.

(3) Within 30 days after the notice and written questions are served, a party may serve cross-questions upon all other parties. Within ten days after being served with cross-questions, a party may serve redirect questions upon all other parties. Within ten days after being served with redirect questions, a party may serve recross-questions upon all other parties. The court may, for cause shown, enlarge or shorten the time.

(b)Officer to take responses and prepare record. A copy of the notice and copies of all questions served shall be delivered by the party taking the deposition to the officer designated in the notice, who shall proceed promptly, in the manner provided by subsections (c), (e), and (f) of Code Section 9-11-30, to take the testimony of the witness in response to the questions and to prepare, certify, and file or mail the deposition, attaching thereto the copy of the notice and the questions received by him.

Section 9-11-32 - Use of depositions in court proceedings; effect of errors and irregularities in depositions

(a)Use of depositions. At the trial or upon the hearing of a motion or an interlocutory proceeding, any part or all of a deposition, so far as admissible under the rules of evidence applied as though the witness were then present and testifying, may be used against any party who was present or represented at the taking of the deposition or who had reasonable notice thereof, in accordance with any of the following provisions:

(1) Any deposition may be used by any party for the purpose of contradicting or impeaching the testimony of the deponent as a witness;

(2) The deposition of a party or of anyone who, at the time of taking the deposition, was an officer, director, or managing agent or a person designated under paragraph (6) of subsection (b) of Code Section 9-11-30 or subsection (a) of Code Section 9-11-31 to testify on behalf of a public or private corporation, a partnership or association, or a governmental agency which is a party may be used by an adverse party for any purpose;

(3) The deposition of a witness, whether or not a party, may be used by any party for any purpose if the court finds:

(A) That the witness is dead;

(B) That the witness is out of the county, unless it appears that the absence of the witness was procured by a party offering the deposition;

(C) That the witness is unable to attend or testify because of age, illness, infirmity, or imprisonment;

(D) That the party offering the deposition has been unable to procure the attendance of the witness by subpoena;

(E) That because of the nature of the business or occupation of the witness it is not possible to secure his personal attendance without manifest inconvenience to the public or third persons; or

(F) That the witness will be a member of the General Assembly and that the session of the General Assembly will conflict with the session of the court in which the case is to be tried;

(4) The deposition of a witness, whether or not a party, taken upon oral examination, may be used in the discretion of the trial judge, even though the witness is available to testify in person at the trial. The use of the deposition shall not be a ground for excluding the witness from testifying orally in open court; or

(5) If only part of a deposition is offered in evidence by a party, an adverse party may require him to introduce all of it which is relevant to the part introduced, and any party may introduce any other parts. Substitution of parties does not affect the right to use depositions previously taken; and, when an action in any court of the United States or of any state has been dismissed and another action involving the same subject matter is afterward brought between the same parties or their representatives or successors in interest, all depositions lawfully taken and duly filed in the former action may be used in the latter as if originally taken therefor.

(b)Objections to admissibility. Subject to paragraph (3) of subsection (d) of this Code section, objection may be made at the trial or hearing to receiving in evidence any deposition or part thereof for any reason which would require the exclusion of the evidence if the witness were then present and testifying.

(c)Effect of taking or using depositions. A party does not make a person his own witness for any purpose by taking his deposition. The introduction in evidence of the deposition or any part thereof for any purpose other than that of contradicting or impeaching the deponent makes the deponent the witness of the party introducing the deposition; but this shall not apply to the use by an adverse party of a deposition under paragraph (2) of subsection (a) of this Code section. At the trial or hearing any party may rebut any relevant evidence contained in a deposition whether introduced by him or by any other party.

(d)Effect of errors and irregularities in depositions.

(1)As to notice. All errors and irregularities in the notice for taking a deposition are waived unless written objection is promptly served upon the party giving the notice.

(2)As to disqualification of officer. Objection to taking a deposition because of disqualification of the officer before whom it is to be taken is waived unless made before the taking of the deposition begins or as soon thereafter as the disqualification becomes known or could be discovered with reasonable diligence.

(3)As to taking of deposition.

(A) Objections to the competency of a witness or to the competency, relevancy, or materiality of testimony are not waived by failure to make them before or during the taking of the deposition, unless the ground of the objection is one which might have been obviated or removed if presented at that time.

(B) Errors and irregularities occurring at the oral examination in the manner of taking the deposition, in the form of the questions or answers, in the oath or affirmation, or in the conduct of parties, and errors of any kind which might be obviated, removed, or cured if promptly presented are waived unless seasonable objection thereto is made at the taking of the deposition.

(C) Objections to the form of written questions submitted under Code Section 9-11-31 are waived unless served in writing upon the party propounding them within the time allowed for serving the succeeding cross or other questions and within five days after service of the last questions authorized.

(4)As to completion and return of deposition. Errors and irregularities in the manner in which the testimony is transcribed or the deposition is prepared, signed, certified, sealed, endorsed, transmitted, filed, or otherwise dealt with by the officer under Code Sections 9-11-30 and 9-11-31 are waived unless a motion to suppress the deposition or some part thereof is made with reasonable promptness after such defect is, or with due diligence might have been, ascertained.

Section 9-11-33 - Interrogatories to parties

(a)Availability; procedures for use.

(1) Any party may serve upon any other party written interrogatories to be answered by the party served or, if the party served is a public or private corporation or a partnership or association or a governmental agency, by any officer or agent, who shall furnish such information as is available to the party. Interrogatories may, without leave of court, be served upon the plaintiff after commencement of the action and upon any other party with or after service of the summons and complaint upon that party; provided, however, that no party may serve interrogatories containing more than 50 interrogatories, including subparts, upon any other party without leave of court upon a showing of complex litigation or undue hardship incurred if such additional interrogatories are not permitted.

(2) Each interrogatory shall be answered separately and fully in writing under oath, unless it is objected to, in which event the reasons for objection shall be stated in lieu of an answer. The answers are to be signed by the person making them, and the objections signed by the attorney making them. The party upon whom the interrogatories have been served shall serve a copy of the answers, and objections if any, within 30 days after the service of the interrogatories, except that a defendant may serve answers or objections within 45 days after service of the summons and complaint upon that defendant. The court may allow a shorter or longer time. The party submitting the interrogatories may move for an order under subsection (a) of Code Section 9-11-37 with respect to any objection to or other failure to answer an interrogatory.

(b)Scope; use at trial.

(1) Interrogatories may relate to any matters which can be inquired into under subsection (b) of Code Section 9-11-26, and the answers may be used to the extent permitted by the rules of evidence.

(2) An interrogatory otherwise proper is not necessarily objectionable merely because an answer to the interrogatory involves an opinion or contention that relates to fact or to the application of law to fact; but the court may order that such an interrogatory need not be answered until after designated discovery has been completed or until a pretrial conference or other later time.

(c)Option to produce business records. Where the answer to an interrogatory may be derived or ascertained from the business records of the party upon whom the interrogatory has been served or from an examination, audit, or inspection of such business records, or from a compilation, abstract, or summary based thereon, and the burden of deriving or ascertaining the answer is substantially the same for the party serving the interrogatory as for the party served, it is a sufficient answer to the interrogatory to specify the records from which the answer may be derived or ascertained and to afford to the party serving the interrogatory reasonable opportunity to examine, audit, or inspect such records and to make copies, compilations, abstracts, or summaries.

Section 9-11-34 - Production of documents and things and entry upon land for inspection and other purposes; applicability to nonparties; confidentiality

(a)Scope. Any party may serve on any other party a request:

(1) To produce and permit the party making the request, or someone acting on his behalf, to inspect and copy any designated documents (including writings, drawings, graphs, charts, photographs, phono-records, and other data compilations from which information can be obtained, translated, if necessary, by the respondent through detection devices into reasonably usable form), or to inspect and copy, test, or sample any tangible things which constitute or contain matters within the scope of subsection (b) of Code Section 9-11-26 and which are in the possession, custody, or control of the party upon whom the request is served; or

(2) To permit entry upon designated land or other property in the possession or control of the party upon whom the request is served for the purpose of inspection and measuring, surveying, photographing, testing, or sampling the property or any designated object or operation thereon, within the scope of subsection (b) of Code Section 9-11-26.

(b)Procedure.

(1) The request may, without leave of court, be served upon the plaintiff after commencement of the action and upon any other party with or after service of the summons and complaint upon that party. The request shall set forth the items to be inspected, either by individual item or by category, and describe each item and category with reasonable particularity. The request shall specify a reasonable time, place, and manner of making the inspection and performing the related acts.

(2) The party upon whom the request is served shall serve a written response within 30 days after the service of the request, except that a defendant may serve a response within 45 days after service of the summons and complaint upon that defendant. The court may allow a shorter or longer time. The response shall state, with respect to each item or category, that inspection and related activities will be permitted as requested, unless the request is objected to, in which event the reasons for objection shall be stated. If objection is made to part of an item or category, the part shall be specified. The party submitting the request may move for an order under subsection (a) of Code Section 9-11-37 with respect to any objection to or other failure to respond to the request or any part thereof, or any failure to permit inspection as requested.

(c)Applicability to nonparties.

(1) This Code section shall also be applicable with respect to discovery against persons, firms, or corporations who are not parties, in which event a copy of the request shall be served upon all parties of record; or, upon notice, the party desiring such discovery may proceed by taking the deposition of the person, firm, or corporation on oral examination or upon written questions under Code Section 9-11-30 or 9-11-31. The nonparty or any party may file an objection as provided in subsection (b) of this Code section. If the party desiring such discovery moves for an order under subsection (a) of Code Section 9-11-37 to compel discovery, he or she shall make a showing of good cause to support his or her motion. The party making a request under this Code section shall, upon request from any other party to the action, make all reasonable efforts to cause all information produced in response to the nonparty request to be made available to all parties. A reasonable document copying charge may be required.

(2) This Code section shall also be applicable with respect to discovery against a nonparty who is a practitioner of the healing arts or a hospital or health care facility, including those operated by an agency or bureau of the state or other governmental unit. Where such a request is directed to such a nonparty, a copy of the request shall be served upon the person whose records are sought by certified mail or statutory overnight delivery, return receipt requested, or, if known, that person's counsel, and upon all other parties of record in compliance with Code Section 9-11-5; where such a request to a nonparty seeks the records of a person who is not a party, a copy of the request shall be served upon the person whose records are sought by certified mail or statutory overnight delivery, return receipt requested, or, if known, that person's counsel by certified mail or statutory overnight delivery, return receipt requested, and upon all parties of record in compliance with Code Section 9-11-5; or, upon notice, the party desiring such discovery may proceed by taking the deposition of the person, firm, or corporation on oral examination or upon written questions under Code Section 9-11-30 or 9-11-31. The nonparty, any party, or the person whose records are sought may file an objection with the court in which the action is pending within 20 days of service of the request and shall serve a copy of such objection on the nonparty to whom the request is directed, who shall not furnish the requested materials until further order of the court, and on all other parties to the action. Upon the filing of such objection, the party desiring such discovery may move for an order under subsection (a) of Code Section 9-11-37 to compel discovery and, if he or she shall make a showing of good cause to support his or her motion, discovery shall be allowed. If no objection is filed within 20 days of service of the request, the nonparty to whom the request is directed shall promptly comply therewith.

(3) For any discovery requested from a nonparty pursuant to paragraph (2) of this subsection or a subpoena requesting records from a nonparty pursuant to Code Section 9-11-45, when the nonparty to whom the discovery request is made is not served with an objection and the nonparty produces the requested records, the nonparty shall be immune from regulatory, civil, or criminal liability or damages notwithstanding that the produced documents contained confidential or privileged information.

(d)**Confidentiality.** The provisions of this Code section shall not be deemed to repeal the confidentiality provided by Code Sections 37-3-166 concerning mental illness treatment records, 37-4-125 concerning developmental disability treatment records, 37-7-166 concerning alcohol and drug treatment records, 24-12-20 concerning the confidential nature of AIDS information, and 24-12-21 concerning the disclosure of AIDS information; provided, however, that a person's failure to object to the production of documents as set forth in paragraph (2) of subsection (c) of this Code section shall waive any right of recovery for damages as to the nonparty for disclosure of the requested documents.

Amended by 2015 Ga. Laws 70,§ 4-18, eff. 7/1/2015.

Amended by 2006 Ga. Laws 608,§ 2, eff. 7/1/2006.

Section 9-11-34.1 - Civil actions for evidence seized in criminal proceedings

Notwithstanding the provisions of Code Section 9-11-34, in any civil action based upon evidence seized in a criminal proceeding involving any violation of Part 2 of Article 3 of Chapter 12 of Title 16, a party shall not be permitted to copy any books, papers, documents, photographs, tangible objects, audio and visual tapes, films and recordings, or copies or portions thereof.

Added by 2008 Ga. Laws 722,§ 1, eff. 7/1/2008.

Section 9-11-35 - Physical and mental examination of persons

(a)**Order for examination.** When the mental or physical condition (including the blood group) of a party, or of a person in the custody or under the legal control of a party, is in controversy, the court in which the action is pending may order the party to submit to a physical examination by a physician or to submit to a mental examination by a physician or a licensed psychologist or to produce for examination the person in his custody or legal control. The order may be made only on motion for good cause shown and upon notice to the person to be examined and to all parties and shall specify the time, place, manner, conditions, and scope of the examination and the person or persons by whom it is to be made.

(b)**Report of examining physician or psychologist.**

(1) If requested by the party against whom an order is made under subsection (a) of this Code section or by the person examined, the party causing the examination to be made shall deliver to him a copy of a detailed written report of the examining physician or psychologist setting out his findings, including results of all tests made, diagnoses, and conclusions, together with like reports of all earlier examinations of the same condition.

(2) Any party shall be entitled, upon request, to receive from the party whose physical or mental condition is in issue, or who is in control of, or has legal custody of, a person whose physical or mental condition is in issue, a report of any and every examination, previously or thereafter made, of the condition in issue, unless, in the case of a report of examination of a person not a party, the party shows that he is unable to obtain it.

(3) The court, on motion, may make an order against a party requiring delivery of a report under paragraph (1) or (2) of this subsection on such terms as are just; and, if a physician or psychologist fails or refuses to make a report, the court may exclude his testimony if offered at the trial.

(4) By requesting and obtaining a report of the examination so ordered or by taking the deposition of the examiner, the party examined waives any privilege he may have in that action, or any other action involving the same controversy, regarding the testimony of every other person who has examined or may thereafter examine him in respect to the same mental or physical condition.

(5) Paragraphs (1) through (4) of this subsection apply to examinations made by agreement of the parties, unless the agreement expressly provides otherwise. Paragraphs (1) through (4) of this subsection do not preclude discovery of a report of an examining physician or psychologist or the taking of a deposition of the physician or psychologist in accordance with any other Code section of this chapter.

Amended by 2001 Ga. Laws 256, § 1, eff. 7/1/2001.

Section 9-11-36 - Requests for admission

(a)**Scope; service; answer or objection; motion to determine sufficiency.**

(1) A party may serve upon any other party a written request for the admission, for purposes of the pending action only, of the truth of any matters within the scope of subsection (b) of Code Section 9-11-26 which are set forth in the request and that relate to statements or opinions of fact or of the application of law to fact, including the genuineness of any documents described in the request. Copies of documents shall be served with the request unless they have been or are otherwise furnished or made available for inspection and copying. The request may, without leave of court, be served upon the plaintiff after commencement of the action and upon any other party with or after service of the summons and complaint upon that party.

(2) Each matter of which an admission is requested shall be separately set forth. The matter is admitted unless, within 30 days after service of the request or within such shorter or longer time as the court may allow, the party to whom the request is directed serves upon the party requesting the admission a written answer or objection addressed to the matter, signed by the party or by his attorney; but unless the court shortens the time, a defendant shall not be required to serve answers or objections before the expiration of 45 days after service of the summons and complaint upon him. If objection is made, the reasons therefor shall be stated. The answer shall specifically deny the matter or set forth in detail the reasons why the answering party cannot truthfully admit or deny the matter. A denial shall fairly meet the substance of the requested admission; and, when good faith requires that a party qualify his answer or deny only a part of the matter of which an admission is requested, he shall specify so much of it as is true and qualify or

deny the remainder. An answering party may not give lack of information or knowledge as a reason for failure to admit or deny unless he states that he has made reasonable inquiry and that the information known or readily obtainable by him is insufficient to enable him to admit or deny. A party who considers that a matter of which an admission has been requested presents a genuine issue for trial may not, on that ground alone, object to the request; he may, subject to subsection (c) of Code Section 9-11-37, deny the matter or set forth reasons why he cannot admit or deny it.

(3) The party who has requested the admissions may move to determine the sufficiency of the answers or objections. Unless the court determines that an objection is justified, it shall order that an answer be served. If the court determines that an answer does not comply with the requirements of this subsection, it may order either that the matter is admitted or that an amended answer be served. The court may, in lieu of these orders, determine that final disposition of the request be made at a pretrial conference or at a designated time prior to trial. Paragraph (4) of subsection (a) of Code Section 9-11-37 shall apply to the award of expenses incurred in relation to the motion.

(b)Effect of admission. Any matter admitted under this Code section is conclusively established unless the court, on motion, permits withdrawal or amendment of the admission. Subject to Code Section 9-11-16 governing amendment of a pretrial order, the court may permit withdrawal or amendment when the presentation of the merits of the action will be subserved thereby and the party who obtained the admission fails to satisfy the court that withdrawal or amendment will prejudice him in maintaining his action or defense on the merits. Any admission made by a party under this Code section is for the purpose of the pending action only and is not an admission by him for any other purpose, nor may it be used against him in any other proceeding.

Section 9-11-37 - Failure to make discovery; motion to compel; sanctions; expenses

(a)Motion for order compelling discovery. A party, upon reasonable notice to other parties and all persons affected thereby, may apply for an order compelling discovery as follows:

(1)Appropriate court. An application for an order to a party may be made to the court in which the action is pending or, on matters relating to a deposition, to the court in the county where the deposition is being taken. An application for an order to a deponent who is not a party shall be made to the court in the county where the deposition is being taken;

(2)Motion; protective order. If a deponent fails to answer a question propounded or submitted under Code Section 9-11-30 or 9-11-31, or a corporation or other entity fails to make a designation under paragraph (6) of subsection (b) of Code Section 9-11-30 or subsection (a) of Code Section 9-11-31, or a party fails to answer an interrogatory submitted under Code Section 9-11-33, or if a party, in response to a request for inspection submitted under Code Section 9-11-34, fails to respond that inspection will be permitted as requested or fails to permit inspection as requested, the discovering party may move for an order compelling an answer, or a designation, or an order compelling inspection in accordance with the request. When taking a deposition on oral examination, the proponent of the question may complete or adjourn the examination before he applies for an order. If the court denies the motion in whole or in part, it may make such protective order as it would have been empowered to make on a motion made pursuant to subsection (c) of Code Section 9-11-26;

(3)Evasive or incomplete answer. For purposes of the provisions of this chapter which relate to depositions and discovery, an evasive or incomplete answer is to be treated as a failure to answer; and

(4)Award of expenses of motion.

(A) If the motion is granted, the court shall, after opportunity for hearing, require the party or deponent whose conduct necessitated the motion or the party or attorney advising such conduct or both of them to pay to the moving party the reasonable expenses incurred in obtaining the order, including attorney's fees, unless the court finds that the opposition to the motion was substantially justified or that other circumstances make an award of expenses unjust.

(B) If the motion is denied, the court shall, after opportunity for hearing, require the moving party or the attorney advising the motion or both of them to pay to the party or deponent who opposed the motion the reasonable expenses incurred in opposing the motion, including attorney's fees, unless the court finds that the making of the motion was substantially justified or that other circumstances make an award of expenses unjust.

(C) If the motion is granted in part and denied in part, the court may apportion the reasonable expenses incurred in relation to the motion among the parties and persons in a just manner.

(b)Failure to comply with order.

(1)Sanctions by court in county where deposition is taken. If a deponent fails to be sworn or to answer a question after being directed to do so by the court in the county in which the deposition is being taken, the failure may be considered a contempt of that court.

(2)Sanctions by court in which action is pending. If a party or an officer, director, or managing agent of a party or a person designated under paragraph (6) of subsection (b) of Code Section 9-11-30 or subsection (a) of Code Section 9-11-31 to testify on behalf of a party fails to obey an order to provide or permit discovery, including an order made under subsection (a) of this Code section or Code Section 9-11-35, the court in which the action is pending may make such orders in regard to the failure as are just and, among others, the following:

(A) An order that the matters regarding which the order was made or any other designated facts shall be taken to be established for the purposes of the action in accordance with the claim of the party obtaining the order;

(B) An order refusing to allow the disobedient party to support or oppose designated claims or defenses, or prohibiting him from introducing designated matters in evidence;

(C) An order striking out pleadings or parts thereof, or staying further proceedings until the order is obeyed, or dismissing the action or proceeding or any part thereof, or rendering a judgment by default against the disobedient party;

(D) In lieu of any of the foregoing orders, or in addition thereto, an order treating as a contempt of court the failure to obey any orders except an order to submit to a physical or mental examination; or

(E) Where a party has failed to comply with an order under subsection (a) of Code Section 9-11-35 requiring him to produce another for examination, such orders as are listed in subparagraphs (A), (B), and (C) of this paragraph, unless the party failing to comply shows that he is unable to produce such person for examination.In lieu of any of the foregoing orders, or in addition thereto, the court shall require the party failing to obey the order or the attorney advising him, or both, to pay the reasonable expenses, including attorney's fees, caused by the failure, unless the court finds that the failure was substantially justified or that other circumstances make an award of expenses unjust.

(c)Expenses on failure to admit. If a party fails to admit the genuineness of any document or the truth of any matter as requested under Code Section 9-11-36 and if the party requesting the admissions thereafter proves the genuineness of the document or the truth of the matter, he may apply to the court for an order requiring the other party to pay him the reasonable expenses incurred in making that proof, including reasonable attorney's fees. The court shall make the order unless it finds that the request was held objectionable pursuant to subsection (a) of Code Section 9-11-36, or the admission sought was of no substantial importance, or the party failing to admit had reasonable ground to believe that he might prevail on the matter, or there was other good reason for the failure to admit.

(d)Failure of party to attend at own deposition or serve answers to interrogatories or respond to request for inspection.

(1) If a party or an officer, director, or managing agent of a party or a person designated under paragraph (6) of subsection (b) of Code Section 9-11-30 or subsection (a) of Code Section 9-11-31 to testify on behalf of a party fails to appear before the officer who is to take his deposition, after being served with a proper notice, or fails to serve answers or objections to interrogatories submitted under Code Section 9-11-33, after proper service of the interrogatories, or fails to serve a written response to a request for inspection submitted under Code Section 9-11-34, after proper service of the request, the court in which the action is pending on motion may make such orders in regard to the failure as are just; and, among others, it may take any action authorized under subparagraphs (b)(2)(A) through (b)(2)(C) of this Code section. In lieu of any order, or in addition thereto, the court shall require the party failing to act or the attorney advising him, or both, to pay the reasonable expenses, including attorney's fees, caused by the failure, unless the court finds that the failure was substantially justified or that other circumstances make an award of expenses unjust.

(2) The failure to act described in the provisions of this chapter which relate to depositions and discovery may not be excused on the ground that the discovery sought is objectionable unless the party failing to act has applied for a protective order as provided by subsection (c) of Code Section 9-11-26.

Article 6 - TRIALS

Section 9-11-38 - Right to jury trial
The right of trial by jury as declared by the Constitution of the state or as given by a statute of the state shall be preserved to the parties inviolate.

Section 9-11-39 - Consent to trial by court; jury trial on court order
(a) The parties or their attorneys of record, by written stipulation filed with the court or by an oral stipulation made in open court and entered in the record, may consent to trial by the court sitting without a jury.

(b) In all actions not triable of right by a jury, or where jury trial has been expressly waived, the court may nevertheless order a trial with a jury whose verdict will have the same effect as if trial by jury had been a matter of right or had not been waived.

Section 9-11-40 - Time and place of trial
(a)Time of trial. All civil cases, including divorce and other domestic relations cases, shall be triable any time after the last day upon which defensive pleadings were required to be filed therein; provided, however, that the court shall in all cases afford to the parties reasonable time for discovery procedures, subsequent to the date that defensive pleadings were required to be filed; provided, further, that, in divorce cases involving service by publication, service shall occur on the date of the first publication of notice following the order for service of publication pursuant to subparagraph (f)(1)(C) of Code Section 9-11-4, and such divorce cases shall be triable any time after 60 days have elapsed since the date of the first publication of notice.

(b)Trial in chambers. The judges of any courts of record may, on reasonable notice to the parties, at any time and at chambers in any county in the circuit, hear and determine by interlocutory or final judgment any matter or issue where a jury trial is not required or has been waived. However, nothing in this subsection shall authorize the trial of any divorce case by consent or otherwise until after the last day upon which defensive pleadings were required by law to be filed therein.

(c)Assignment of cases for trial. The courts shall provide for the placing of actions upon the trial calendar:

(1) Without request of the parties but upon notice to the parties; or

(2) Upon request of a party and notice to the other parties.Except for cause, cases shall be placed upon the calendar in chronological order in accordance with filing dates. Precedence shall be given to actions entitled thereto by any statute.

Section 9-11-41 - Dismissal of actions; recommencement within six months
(a)Voluntary dismissal; effect

(1)By plaintiff; by stipulation. Subject to the provisions of subsection (e) of Code Section 9-11-23, Code Section 9-11-66, and any statute, an action may be dismissed by the plaintiff, without order or permission of court:

(A) By filing a written notice of dismissal at any time before the first witness is sworn; or

(B) By filing a stipulation of dismissal signed by all parties who have appeared in the action.

(2)By order of court. Except as provided in paragraph (1) of this subsection, an action shall not be dismissed upon the plaintiff's motion except upon order of the court and upon the terms and conditions as the court deems proper. If a counterclaim has been pleaded by a defendant prior to the service upon him or her of the plaintiff's motion to dismiss, the action shall not be dismissed against the defendant's objection unless the counterclaim can remain pending for independent adjudication by the court.

(3)Effect. A dismissal under this subsection is without prejudice, except that the filing of a second notice of dismissal operates as an adjudication upon the merits.

(b)Involuntary dismissal; effect thereof. For failure of the plaintiff to prosecute or to comply with this chapter or any order of court, a defendant may move for dismissal of an action or of any claim against him. After the plaintiff, in an action tried by the court without a jury, has completed the presentation of his evidence, the defendant, without waiving his right to offer evidence in the event the motion is not granted, may move for dismissal on the ground that upon the facts and the law the plaintiff has shown no right to relief. The court as trier of the facts may then determine the facts and render judgment against the plaintiff or may decline to render any judgment until the close of all the evidence. The effect of dismissals shall be as follows:

(1) A dismissal for failure of the plaintiff to prosecute does not operate as an adjudication upon the merits; and

(2) Any other dismissal under this subsection and any dismissal not provided for in this Code section, other than a dismissal for lack of jurisdiction or for improper venue or for lack of an indispensable party, does operate as an adjudication upon the merits unless the court in its order for dismissal specifies otherwise.

(c)Dismissal of counterclaim, cross-claim, or third-party claim. This Code section also applies to the dismissal of any counterclaim, cross-claim, or third-party claim.

(d)Cost of previously dismissed action. If a plaintiff who has dismissed an action in any court commences an action based upon or including the same claim against the same defendant, the plaintiff shall first pay the court costs of the action previously dismissed.

(e)Dismissal for want of prosecution; recommencement. Any action in which no written order is taken for a period of five years shall automatically stand dismissed, with costs to be taxed against the party plaintiff. For the purposes of this Code section, an order of continuance will be deemed an order. When an action is dismissed under this subsection, if the plaintiff recommences the action within six months following the dismissal then the renewed action shall stand upon the same footing, as to limitation, with the original action.

Amended by 2003 Ga. Laws 363, § 4, eff. 7/1/2003.

Section 9-11-42 - Consolidation; severance

(a)Consolidation. When actions involving a common question of law or fact are pending before the court, if the parties consent, the court may order a joint hearing or trial of any or all the matters in issue in the actions; it may order all the actions consolidated; and it may make such orders concerning proceedings therein as may tend to avoid unnecessary costs or delay.

(b)Separate trials. The court, in furtherance of convenience or to avoid prejudice, may order a separate trial of any claim, cross-claim, counterclaim, or third-party claim, or of any separate issue, or of any number of claims, cross-claims, counterclaims, third-party claims, or issues.

Section 9-11-43 - Evidence

(a)Evidence on trials. In all trials the testimony of witnesses shall be taken orally in open court unless otherwise provided by this chapter or by statute.

(b)Evidence on motions. When a motion is based on facts not appearing of record, the court may hear the matter on affidavits presented by the respective parties, but the court may direct that the matter be heard wholly or partly on oral testimony or depositions; provided, however, that this provision shall not limit the right of parties to use depositions where they would otherwise be entitled to do so.

(c)Determination of the law of other jurisdictions. A party who intends to raise an issue concerning the law of another state or of a foreign country shall give notice in his pleadings or other reasonable written notice. The court, in determining such law, may consider any relevant material or source, including testimony, whether or not submitted by a party or admissible under the rules of evidence. The court's determination shall be treated as a ruling on a question of law.

Section 9-11-44 - [Repealed] Official records

Repealed by 2011 Ga. Laws 52,§ 11, eff. 1/1/2013.

Reserved. Repealed by Ga. L. 2011, p. 99, § 10/HB 24, effective January 1, 2013.

Section 9-11-45 - Subpoena for taking depositions; objections; place of examination

(a)

(1)

(A) The clerk of the superior court of the county in which the action is pending or the clerk of any court of record in the county where the deposition is to be taken shall issue subpoenas for the persons sought to be deposed, upon request.

(B) Upon agreement of the parties, an attorney, as an officer of the court, may issue and sign a subpoena for the person sought to be deposed on behalf of a court in which the attorney is authorized to practice or a court for a venue in which a deposition is compelled by the subpoena, if the deposition pertains to an action pending in a court in which the attorney is authorized to practice.

(C) Subpoenas issued pursuant to this paragraph shall be issued and served in accordance with law governing issuance of subpoenas for attendance at court, except as to issuance by an attorney. The subpoena may command the person to whom it is directed to produce and permit inspection and copying of designated books, papers, documents, or tangible things which constitute or contain matters within the scope of the examination permitted by subsection (b) of Code Section 9-11-26, but in that event the subpoena will be subject to subsection (c) of Code Section 9-11-26; or the court, upon motion made promptly and in any event at or before the time specified in the subpoena for compliance therewith, may quash or modify the subpoena if it is unreasonable and oppressive, or condition denial of the motion upon the advancement by the person in whose behalf the subpoena is issued of the reasonable cost of producing the books, papers, documents, or tangible things.

(2) The person to whom the subpoena is directed may, within ten days after the service thereof or on or before the time specified in the subpoena for compliance, if such time is less than ten days after service, serve upon the attorney designated in the subpoena written objection to inspection or copying of any or all of the designated materials. If objection is made, the party serving the subpoena shall not be entitled to inspect and copy the materials except pursuant to an order of the court from which the subpoena was issued. The party serving the subpoena may, if objection has been made, move, upon notice to the deponent, for an order at any time before or during the taking of the deposition, provided that nothing in this Code section shall be construed as requiring the issuance of a subpoena to compel a party to attend and give his deposition or produce documents at the taking of his deposition where a notice of deposition under Code Section 9-11-30 has been given or a request under Code Section 9-11-34 has been served, such notice or request to a party being enforceable by motion under Code Section 9-11-37.

(b) A person who is to give a deposition may be required to attend an examination:

(1) In the county wherein he resides or is employed or transacts his business in person;

(2) In any county in which he is served with a subpoena while therein; or

(3) At any place which is not more than 30 miles from the county seat of the county wherein the witness resides, is employed, or transacts his business in person.

Section 9-11-46 - Exceptions unnecessary; objections to rulings or orders

(a) Formal exceptions to rulings or orders of the court are unnecessary. For all purposes for which an exception has heretofore been necessary, it is sufficient that a party, at the time the ruling or order of the court is made or sought, makes known to the court the action which he desires the court to take or his objection to the action of the court and his grounds therefor; and, if a party has no opportunity to object to a ruling or order at the time it is made, the absence of an objection does not thereafter prejudice him.

(b) When motion for mistrial or other like relief is made, the question is thereby presented as to whether the moving party is entitled to the relief therein sought or to any lesser relief, and where such motion is denied in whole or in part, it shall not be necessary that the moving party thereafter renew his motion or otherwise seek further ruling by the court.

Section 9-11-47 - Jurors

(a) The parties may by written stipulation, filed of record, stipulate that the jury shall consist of any number less than that fixed by statute.

(b) The court may direct that one or two jurors in addition to the regular panel be called and impaneled to sit as alternate jurors. Alternate jurors in the order in which they are called shall replace jurors who become or are found to be unable or disqualified to perform their duties. Alternate jurors shall be drawn in the same manner, shall have the same qualifications, shall be subject to the same examination and challenges, shall take the same oath, and shall have the same functions, powers, facilities, and privileges as the principal jurors. An alternate juror who does not replace a principal juror may be discharged. However, if the court deems it advisable, it may direct that one or more of the alternate jurors be kept in the custody of one or more court officers, separate and apart from the regular jurors, until the jury has agreed upon a verdict. If one or two alternate jurors are called, each party is entitled to one peremptory challenge in addition to those otherwise allowed by law. The additional peremptory challenge may be used only against an alternate juror, and the other peremptory challenges allowed by law shall not be used against the alternates.

Section 9-11-48 - Reserved

Section 9-11-49 - Special verdicts

(a) The court may require a jury to return only a special verdict in the form of a special written finding upon each issue of fact. In that event the court may submit to the jury written questions susceptible of categorical or other brief answer or may submit written forms of several special findings which might properly be made under the pleadings and evidence; or it may use such other method of submitting the issues and requiring the written findings thereon as it deems most appropriate. The court shall give to the jury such explanation and instruction concerning the matter thus submitted as may be necessary to enable the jury to make its findings upon each issue. If in so doing the court omits any issue of fact raised by the pleadings or by the evidence, each party waives his right to a trial by jury of the issues so omitted unless before the jury retires he demands its submission to the jury. As to an issue omitted without such demand, the court may make a finding; or, if it fails to do so, it shall be deemed to have made a finding in accordance with the judgment on the special verdict.

(b) Upon written request by any party made on or before the call of the case for trial, it shall be the duty of the court to require the jury to return only a special verdict, as provided in subsection (a) of this Code section, in any case involving equitable relief, mandamus, quo warranto, prohibition, a declaratory judgment, and in any other case or proceeding where special verdicts may be specifically required by law. The court shall prescribe the form of the questions for submission to the jury.

Section 9-11-50 - Motions for directed verdict and for judgment notwithstanding the verdict

(a)Motion for directed verdict; when made; effect. A motion for a directed verdict may be made at the close of the evidence offered by an opponent or at the close of the case. A party who moves for a directed verdict at the close of the evidence offered by an opponent may offer evidence in the event that a motion is not granted without having reserved the right to do so and to the same extent as if the motion had not been made. A motion for a directed verdict which is not granted is not a waiver of trial by jury even though all parties to the action have moved for directed verdicts. A motion for a directed verdict shall state the specific grounds therefor. The order of the court granting a motion for a directed verdict is effective without any assent of the jury. If there is no conflict in the evidence as to any material issue and the evidence introduced, with all reasonable deductions therefrom, shall demand a particular verdict, such verdict shall be directed.

(b)Motion for judgment notwithstanding the verdict -- When made; new trial motion. Whenever a motion for a directed verdict made at the close of all the evidence is denied or for any reason is not granted, the court is deemed to have submitted the action to the jury subject to a later determination of the legal questions raised by the motion. Not later than 30 days after entry of judgment, a party who has moved for a directed verdict may move to have the verdict and any judgment entered thereon set aside and to have judgment entered in accordance with his motion for a directed verdict; or, if a verdict was not returned, such party, within 30 days after the jury has been discharged, may move for judgment in accordance with his motion for a directed verdict. A motion for a new trial may be joined with this motion, or a new trial may be prayed for in the alternative. If a verdict was returned, the court may allow the judgment to stand or may reopen the judgment and either order a new trial or direct the entry of judgment as if the requested verdict had been directed. If no verdict was returned, the court may direct the entry of judgment as if the requested verdict had been directed or may order a new trial.

(c)Same -- Conditional rulings on grant of motion; motion for new trial by losing party.

  (1) If the motion for judgment notwithstanding the verdict provided for in subsection (b) of this Code section is granted, the court shall also rule on the motion for a new trial, if any, by determining whether it should be granted if the judgment is thereafter vacated or reversed and shall specify the grounds for granting or denying the motion for the new trial. If the motion for a new trial is thus conditionally granted, the order thereon does not affect the finality of the judgment. In case the motion for a new trial has been conditionally granted and the judgment is reversed on appeal, the new trial shall proceed unless the appellate court has otherwise ordered. In case the motion for a new trial has been conditionally denied, the appellee on appeal may assert error in that denial; and, if the judgment is reversed on appeal, subsequent proceedings shall be in accordance with the order of the appellate court.

(2) The party whose verdict has been set aside on motion for judgment notwithstanding the verdict may serve a motion for a new trial not later than 30 days after entry of the judgment notwithstanding the verdict.

(d)Same -- Denial of motion. If the motion for judgment notwithstanding the verdict is denied, the party who prevailed on that motion may, as appellee, assert grounds entitling him to a new trial in the event the appellate court concludes that the trial court erred in denying the motion for judgment notwithstanding the verdict. If the appellate court reverses the judgment, nothing in this Code section precludes it from determining that the appellee is entitled to a new trial or from directing the trial court to determine whether a new trial shall be granted.

(e)Erroneous denial of directed verdict. Where error is enumerated upon an order denying a motion for directed verdict and the appellate court determines that the motion was erroneously denied, it may direct that judgment be entered below in accordance with the motion or may order that a new trial be had, as the court may determine necessary to meet the ends of justice under the facts of the case.

Section 9-11-51 - Reserved

Section 9-11-52 - Findings by the court

(a) In ruling on interlocutory injunctions and in all nonjury trials in courts of record, the court shall upon request of any party made prior to such ruling, find the facts specially and shall state separately its conclusions of law. If an opinion or memorandum of decision is filed, it will be sufficient if the findings and conclusions appear therein. Findings shall not be set aside unless clearly erroneous, and due regard shall be given to the opportunity of the trial court to judge the credibility of the witnesses.

(b) This Code section shall not apply to actions involving uncontested divorce, alimony, and custody of minors, nor to motions except as provided in subsection (b) of Code Section 9-11-41. The requirements of subsection (a) of this Code section may be waived in writing or on the record by the parties.

(c) Upon motion made not later than 20 days after entry of judgment, the court may make or amend its findings or make additional findings and may amend the judgment accordingly. If the motion is made with a motion for new trial, both motions shall be made within 20 days after entry of judgment. The question of the sufficiency of the evidence to support the findings may be raised on appeal whether or not the party raising the question has made in the trial court an objection to findings or a motion for judgment. When findings or conclusions are not made prior to judgment to the extent necessary for review, failure of the losing party to move therefor after judgment shall constitute a waiver of any ground of appeal which requires consideration thereof.

Section 9-11-53 - Reserved

Article 7 - JUDGMENT

Section 9-11-54 - Judgments

(a)Definition. The term "judgment," as used in this chapter, includes a decree and any order from which an appeal lies.

(b)Judgment upon multiple claims or involving multiple parties. When more than one claim for relief is presented in an action, whether as a claim, counterclaim, cross-claim, or third-party claim, or when multiple parties are involved, the court may direct the entry of a final judgment as to one or more but fewer than all of the claims or parties only upon an express determination that there is no just reason for delay and upon an express direction for the entry of judgment. In the absence of such determination and direction, any order or other form of decision, however designated, which adjudicates fewer than all the claims or the rights and liabilities of fewer than all the parties shall not terminate the action as to any of the claims or parties, and the order or other form of decision is subject to revision at any time before the entry of judgment adjudicating all the claims and the rights and liabilities of all the parties.

(c)Relief granted.

(1) A judgment by default shall not be different in kind from or exceed in amount that prayed for in the demand for judgment. Except as to a party against whom a judgment is entered by default, every final judgment shall grant the relief to which the party in whose favor it is rendered is entitled, even if the party has not demanded such relief in his pleadings; but the court shall not give the successful party relief, though he may be entitled to it, where the propriety of the relief was not litigated and the opposing party had no opportunity to assert defenses to such relief.

(2) As used in this subsection, the term "action for medical malpractice" means any claim for damages resulting from the death of or injury to any person arising out of:

(A) Health, medical, dental, or surgical service, diagnosis, prescription, treatment, or care rendered by a person authorized by law to perform such services or by any person acting under the supervision and control of a lawfully authorized person; or

(B) Care or service rendered by any public or private hospital, nursing home, clinic, hospital authority, facility, or institution, or by any officer, agent, or employee thereof acting within the scope of his employment.

(3) Notwithstanding paragraph (1) of this subsection, where a claim in an action for medical malpractice does not exceed $10,000.00, a judgment by default shall not be different in kind from or exceed in amount that prayed for in the demand for judgment. Where the claim exceeds $10,000.00, a judgment by default may be rendered for the amount determined upon a trial of the issue of damages, provided notice of the trial is served upon the defaulting party at least three days prior to that trial.

(d)Costs. Except where express provision therefor is made in a statute, costs shall be allowed as a matter of course to the prevailing party unless the court otherwise directs; but costs against this state and its officers, agencies, and political subdivisions shall be imposed only to the extent permitted by the law.

Section 9-11-55 - Default judgment

(a)When case in default; opening as matter of right; judgment. If in any case an answer has not been filed within the time required by this chapter, the case shall automatically become in default unless the time for filing the answer has been extended as provided by law. The default may be opened as a matter of right by the filing of such defenses within 15 days of the day of default, upon the payment of costs. If the case is still in default after the expiration of the period of 15 days, the plaintiff at any time thereafter shall be entitled to verdict and judgment by default, in open court or in chambers, as if every item and paragraph of the complaint or other original pleading were supported by proper evidence, without the intervention of a jury, unless the action is one ex delicto or involves unliquidated damages, in which event the plaintiff shall be required to introduce evidence and establish the amount of damages before the court without a jury, with the right of the defendant to introduce evidence as to damages and the right of either to move for a new trial in respect of such damages; provided, however, in the event a defendant, though in default, has placed damages in issue by filing a pleading raising such issue, either party shall be entitled, upon demand, to a jury trial of the issue as to damages. An action based upon open account shall not be considered one for unliquidated damages within the meaning of this Code section.

(b)Opening default. At any time before final judgment, the court, in its discretion, upon payment of costs, may allow the default to be opened for providential cause preventing the filing of required pleadings or for excusable neglect or where the judge, from all the facts, shall determine that a proper case has been made for the default to be opened, on terms to be fixed by the court. In order to allow the default to be thus opened, the showing shall be made under oath, shall set up a meritorious defense, shall offer to plead instanter, and shall announce ready to proceed with the trial.

Section 9-11-56 - Summary judgment

(a)For claimant. A party seeking to recover upon a claim, counterclaim, or cross-claim or to obtain a declaratory judgment may, at any time after the expiration of 30 days from the commencement of the action or after service of a motion for summary judgment by the adverse party, move with or without supporting affidavits for a summary judgment in his favor upon all or any part thereof.

(b)For defending party. A party against whom a claim, counterclaim, or cross-claim is asserted or a declaratory judgment is sought may, at any time, move with or without supporting affidavits for a summary judgment in his favor as to all or any part thereof.

(c)Motion and proceedings thereon. The motion shall be served at least 30 days before the time fixed for the hearing. The adverse party prior to the day of hearing may serve opposing affidavits. The judgment sought shall be rendered forthwith if the pleadings, depositions, answers to interrogatories, and admissions on file, together with the affidavits, if any, show that there is no genuine issue as to any material fact and that the moving party is entitled to a judgment as a matter of law; but nothing in this Code section shall be construed as denying to any party the right to trial by jury where there are substantial issues of fact to be determined. A summary judgment may be rendered on the issue of liability alone although there is a genuine issue as to the amount of damage.

(d)Case not fully adjudicated on motion. If on motion under this Code section judgment is not rendered upon the whole case or for all the relief asked and a trial is necessary, the court at the hearing of the motion, by examining the pleadings and the evidence before it and by interrogating counsel shall, if practicable, ascertain what material facts exist without substantial controversy and what material facts are actually and in good faith controverted. It shall thereupon make an order specifying the facts that appear without substantial controversy, including the extent to which the amount of damages or other relief is not in controversy, and directing such proceedings in the action as are just. Upon the trial of the action the facts so specified shall be deemed established, and the trial shall be conducted accordingly.

(e)Form of affidavits; further testimony; defense required. Supporting and opposing affidavits shall be made on personal knowledge, shall set forth such facts as would be admissible in the evidence, and shall show affirmatively that the affiant is competent to testify to the matters stated therein. Sworn or certified copies of all papers or parts thereof referred to in an affidavit shall be attached thereto or served therewith. The court may permit affidavits to be supplemented or opposed by depositions, answers to interrogatories, or further affidavits. All affidavits shall be filed with the court and copies thereof shall be served on the opposing parties. When a motion for summary judgment is made and supported as provided in this Code section, an adverse party may not rest upon the mere allegations or denials of his pleading, but his response, by affidavits or as otherwise provided in this Code section, must set forth specific facts showing that there is a genuine issue for trial. If he does not so respond, summary judgment, if appropriate, shall be entered against him.

(f)When affidavits are unavailable. Should it appear from the affidavits of a party opposing the motion that he cannot, for reasons stated, present by affidavits facts essential to justify his opposition, the court may refuse the application for judgment, or may order a continuance to permit affidavits to be obtained or depositions to be taken or discovery to be had, or may make such other order as is just.

(g)Affidavits made in bad faith. Should it appear to the satisfaction of the court at any time that any of the affidavits presented pursuant to this Code section are presented in bad faith or solely for the purpose of delay, the court shall forthwith order the party employing them to pay to the other party the amount of the reasonable expenses which the filing of the affidavits caused him to incur, including reasonable attorney's fees, and any offending party may be adjudged guilty of contempt.

(h)Appeal. An order granting summary judgment on any issue or as to any party shall be subject to review by appeal. An order denying summary judgment shall be subject to review by direct appeal in accordance with subsection (b) of Code Section 5-6-34.

Section 9-11-57 - Reserved

Section 9-11-58 - Entry of judgment; judge's name to be typed, printed, or stamped after signature; filing of civil case disposition form

(a)Signing. Except when otherwise specifically provided by statute, all judgments shall be signed by the judge and filed with the clerk. The signature of the judge shall be followed by the spelling of the judge's name and title legibly typed, printed, or stamped. The failure of the judgment to have the typed, printed, or stamped name of the judge shall not invalidate the judgment.

(b)When judgment entered. The filing with the clerk of a judgment, signed by the judge, with the fully completed civil case disposition form constitutes the entry of the judgment, and, unless the court otherwise directs, no judgment shall be effective for any purpose until the entry of the same, as provided in this subsection. As part of the filing of the final judgment, a civil case disposition form shall be filed by the prevailing party or by the plaintiff if the case is settled, dismissed, or otherwise disposed of without a prevailing party; provided, however, that the amount of a sealed or otherwise confidential settlement agreement shall not be disclosed on the civil case disposition form. The form shall be substantially in the form prescribed by the Judicial Council of Georgia. If any of the information required by the form is sealed by the court, the form shall state that fact and the information under seal shall not be provided. The entry of the judgment shall not be made by the clerk of the court until the civil case disposition form is filed. The entry of the judgment shall not be delayed for the taxing of costs. This subsection shall not apply to actions brought pursuant to Article 3 of Chapter 7 of Title 44, relating to landlord and tenant dispossessory proceedings.

Amended by 2017 Ga. Laws 240,§ 2-2, eff. 1/1/2018.

Amended by 2006 Ga. Laws 660,§ 2, eff. 7/1/2006.

Section 9-11-59 - Reserved

Section 9-11-60 - Relief from judgments

(a)Collateral attack. A judgment void on its face may be attacked in any court by any person. In all other instances, judgments shall be subject to attack only by a direct proceeding brought for that purpose in one of the methods prescribed in this Code section.

(b)Methods of direct attack. A judgment may be attacked by motion for a new trial or motion to set aside. Judgments may be attacked by motion only in the court of rendition.

(c)Motion for new trial. A motion for new trial must be predicated upon some intrinsic defect which does not appear upon the face of the record or pleadings.

(d)Motion to set aside. A motion to set aside may be brought to set aside a judgment based upon:

(1) Lack of jurisdiction over the person or the subject matter;

(2) Fraud, accident, or mistake or the acts of the adverse party unmixed with the negligence or fault of the movant; or

(3) A nonamendable defect which appears upon the face of the record or pleadings. Under this paragraph, it is not sufficient that the complaint or other pleading fails to state a claim upon which relief can be granted, but the pleadings must affirmatively show no claim in fact existed.

(e)Complaint in equity. The use of a complaint in equity to set aside a judgment is prohibited.

(f)Procedure; time of relief. Reasonable notice shall be afforded the parties on all motions. Motions to set aside judgments may be served by any means by which an original complaint may be legally served if it cannot be legally served as any other motion. A judgment void because of lack of jurisdiction of the person or subject matter may be attacked at any time. Motions for new trial must be brought within the time prescribed by law. In all other instances, all motions to set aside judgments shall be brought within three years from entry of the judgment complained of.

(g)Clerical mistakes. Clerical mistakes in judgments, orders, or other parts of the record and errors therein arising from oversight or omission may be corrected by the court at any time of its own initiative or on the motion of any party and after such notice, if any, as the court orders.

(h)Law of the case rule. The law of the case rule is abolished; but generally judgments and orders shall not be set aside or modified without just cause and, in setting aside or otherwise modifying judgments and orders, the court shall consider whether rights have vested thereunder and whether or not innocent parties would be injured thereby; provided, however, that any ruling by the Supreme Court or the Court of Appeals in a case shall be binding in all subsequent proceedings in that case in the lower court and in the Supreme Court or the Court of Appeals as the case may be.

Section 9-11-61 - Harmless error

No error in either the admission or the exclusion of evidence and no error or defect in any ruling or order or in anything done or omitted by the court or by any of the parties is ground for granting a new trial or for setting aside a verdict or for vacating, modifying, or otherwise disturbing a judgment or order, unless refusal to take such action appears to the court inconsistent with substantial justice. The court at every stage of the proceeding must disregard any error or defect in the proceeding which does not affect the substantial rights of the parties.

Section 9-11-62 - Stay of proceedings to enforce a judgment

(a)Stay upon entry of judgment. No execution shall issue upon a judgment nor shall proceedings be taken for its enforcement until the expiration of ten days after its entry, except that, in the case of a default judgment, execution may issue and enforcement proceedings may be taken at any time after entry of judgment and except that, in any case in which both the plaintiff or plaintiffs and the defendant or defendants agree, in writing, and file a copy of such agreement with the clerk of the court, execution may issue and enforcement proceedings may be taken at any time after entry of judgment. Unless otherwise ordered by the court, an interlocutory or final judgment in an action for an injunction or in a receivership action shall not be stayed during the period after its entry and until an appeal is taken or during the pendency of an appeal. Subsection (c) of this Code section governs the suspending, modifying, restoring, or granting of an injunction during the pendency of an appeal.

(b)Stay on motion for new trial or for judgment. The filing of a motion for a new trial or motion for judgment notwithstanding the verdict shall act as supersedeas unless otherwise ordered by the court; but the court may condition supersedeas upon the giving of bond with good security in such amounts as the court may order.

(c)Injunction pending appeal. When an appeal is taken from an interlocutory or final judgment granting, dissolving, or denying an injunction, the court in its discretion may suspend, modify, restore, or grant an injunction during the pendency of the appeal upon such terms as to bond or otherwise as it considers proper for the security of the rights of the adverse party.

(d)Stay in favor of the state or agency thereof. When an appeal is taken by the state or by any county, city, or town within the state, or an officer or agency thereof, and the operation or enforcement of the judgment is stayed, no bond, obligation, or other security shall be required from the appellant.

(e)Power of appellate court not limited. The provisions in this Code section do not limit any power of an appellate court or of a judge or justice thereof to stay proceedings during the pendency of an appeal or to suspend, modify, restore, or grant an injunction during the pendency of an appeal or to make any order appropriate to preserve that status quo or the effectiveness of the judgment subsequently to be entered.

(f)Stay of judgment as to multiple claims or multiple parties. When a court has ordered a final judgment under the conditions stated in subsection (b) of Code Section 9-11-54, the court may stay enforcement of that judgment until the entering of a subsequent judgment or judgments and may prescribe such conditions as are necessary to secure the benefit thereof to the party in whose favor the judgment is entered.

Article 8 - PROVISIONAL AND FINAL REMEDIES AND SPECIAL PROCEEDINGS

Section 9-11-63 - Reserved

Section 9-11-64 - Reserved

Section 9-11-65 - Injunctions and restraining orders

(a)Interlocutory injunction.

(1)Notice. No interlocutory injunction shall be issued without notice to the adverse party.

(2)Consolidation of hearing with trial on merits. Before or after the commencement of the hearing of an application for an interlocutory injunction, the court may order the trial of the action on the merits to be advanced and consolidated with the hearing of the application. Even when this consolidation is not ordered, any evidence received upon an application for an interlocutory injunction which would be admissible upon the trial on the merits shall become a part of the record on the trial and need not be repeated upon the trial. This paragraph shall be construed and applied so as to save any rights of the parties which they may have to trial by jury.

(b)Temporary restraining order; when granted without notice; duration; hearing; application to dissolve or modify. A temporary restraining order may be granted without written or oral notice to the adverse party or his attorney only if:

(1) It clearly appears from specific facts shown by affidavit or by the verified complaint that immediate and irreparable injury, loss, or damage will result to the applicant before the adverse party or his attorney can be heard in opposition; and

(2) The applicant's attorney certifies to the court, in writing, the efforts, if any, which have been made to give the notice and the reasons supporting the party's claim that notice should not be required.Every temporary restraining order granted without notice shall be endorsed with the date and hour of issuance, shall be filed forthwith in the clerk's office and entered of record, and shall expire by its terms within such time after entry, not to exceed 30 days, as the court fixes, unless the party against whom the order is directed consents that it may be extended for a longer period. In case a temporary restraining order is granted without notice, the motion for an interlocutory injunction shall be set down for hearing at the earliest possible time and shall take precedence over all matters except older matters of the same character; when the motion comes on for hearing, the party who obtained the temporary restraining order shall proceed with the application for an interlocutory injunction; and, if he does not do so, the court shall dissolve the temporary restraining order. On two days' notice to the party who obtained the temporary restraining order without notice or on such shorter notice to that party as the court may prescribe, the adverse party may appear and move its dissolution or modification; and in that event the court shall proceed to hear and determine the motion as expeditiously as the ends of justice require.

(c)Security. As a prerequisite to the issuance of a restraining order or an interlocutory injunction, the court may require the giving of security by the applicant, in such sum as the court deems proper, for the payment of such costs and damages as may be incurred or suffered by any party who is found to have been enjoined or restrained wrongfully. A surety upon a bond or undertaking under this Code section submits himself to the jurisdiction of the court and irrevocably appoints the clerk of the court as his agent upon whom any papers affecting his liability on the bond or undertaking may be served. His liability may be enforced on motion without the necessity of an independent action. The motion and such notice of the motion as the court prescribes may be served on the clerk of the court, who shall forthwith mail copies to the persons giving the security if their addresses are known.

(d)Form and scope of injunction or restraining order. Every order granting an injunction and every restraining order shall be specific in terms; shall describe in reasonable detail, and not by reference to the complaint or other document, the act or acts sought to be restrained; and is binding only upon the parties to the action, their officers, agents, servants, employees, and attorneys, and upon those persons in active concert or participation with them who receive notice of the order by personal service or otherwise.

(e)When inapplicable. This Code section is not applicable to actions for divorce, alimony, separate maintenance, or custody of children. In such actions, the court may make prohibitive or mandatory orders, with or without notice or bond, and upon such terms and conditions as the court may deem just.

Section 9-11-66 - Receivers

An action wherein a receiver has been appointed shall not be dismissed except by order of the court.

Section 9-11-67 - Deposit in court

In an action in which any part of the relief sought is a judgment for a sum of money or the disposition of any other thing capable of delivery, a party, upon notice to every other party, and by leave of court, may deposit with the court all or any part of such sum or thing to be held by the clerk of the court, subject to withdrawal, in whole or in part, at any time thereafter upon order of the court, upon posting of sufficient security. Where the thing deposited is money, interest thereupon shall abate.

Section 9-11-67.1 - Settlement offers and agreements for personal injury, bodily injury, and death from motor vehicle; payment methods

(a) Prior to the filing of an answer, any offer to settle a tort claim for personal injury, bodily injury, or death arising from the use of a motor vehicle and prepared by or with the assistance of an attorney on behalf of a claimant or claimants shall be in writing and:

(1) Shall contain the following material terms:

(A) The time period within which such offer must be accepted, which shall be not less than 30 days from receipt of the offer;

(B) Amount of monetary payment;

(C) The party or parties the claimant or claimants will release if such offer is accepted;

(D) For any type of release, whether the release is full or limited and an itemization of what the claimant or claimants will provide to each releasee; and

(E) The claims to be released;

(2) Shall include medical or other records in the offeror's possession incurred as a result of the subject claim that are sufficient to allow the recipient to evaluate the claim; and

(3) May include a term requiring that in order to settle the claim the recipient shall provide the offeror a statement, under oath, regarding whether all liability and casualty insurance issued by the recipient that provides coverage or that may provide coverage for the claim at issue has been disclosed to the offeror.

(b)

(1) Unless otherwise agreed by both the offeror and the recipients in writing, the terms outlined in subsection (a) of this Code section shall be the only terms which can be included in an offer to settle made under this Code section.

(2) The recipients of an offer to settle made under this Code section may accept the same by providing written acceptance of the material terms outlined in subsection (a) of this Code section in their entirety.

(c) Nothing in this Code section is intended to prohibit parties from reaching a settlement agreement in a manner and under terms otherwise agreeable to both the offeror and recipient of the offer.

(d) Upon receipt of an offer to settle set forth in subsection (a) of this Code section, the recipients shall have the right to seek clarification regarding the terms, the terms of the release, liens, subrogation claims, standing to release claims, medical bills, medical records, and other relevant facts. An attempt to seek reasonable clarification shall be in writing and shall not be deemed a counteroffer. In addition, if a release is not provided with an offer to settle, a recipient's providing of a proposed release shall not be deemed a counteroffer.

(e) An offer to settle made pursuant to this Code section shall be sent by certified mail or statutory overnight delivery, return receipt requested, shall specifically reference this Code section, and shall include an address or a facsimile number or email address to which a written acceptance pursuant to subsection (b) of this Code section may be provided.

(f) The person or entity providing payment to satisfy the material term set forth in subparagraph (a)(1)(B) of this Code section may elect to provide payment by any one or more of the following means:

(1) Cash;

(2) Money order;

(3) Wire transfer;

(4) A cashier's check issued by a bank or other financial institution;

(5) A draft or bank check issued by an insurance company; or

(6) Electronic funds transfer or other method of electronic payment.

(g) Nothing in this Code section shall prohibit a party making an offer to settle from requiring payment within a specified period; provided, however, that such date shall not be less than 40 days from the receipt of the offer.

(h) This Code section shall apply to causes of action for personal injury, bodily injury, and death arising from the use of a motor vehicle on or after July 1, 2021.

Amended by 2021 Ga. Laws 203,§ 1, eff. 7/1/2021.

Added by 2013 Ga. Laws 271,§ 1, eff. 7/1/2013.

Section 9-11-68 - Offers of settlement; damages for frivolous claims or defenses

(a) At any time more than 30 days after the service of a summons and complaint on a party but not less than 30 days (or 20 days if it is a counteroffer) before trial, either party may serve upon the other party, but shall not file with the court, a written offer, denominated as an offer under this Code section, to settle a tort claim for the money specified in the offer and to enter into an agreement dismissing the claim or to allow judgment to be entered accordingly. Any offer under this Code section must:

(1) Be in writing and state that it is being made pursuant to this Code section;

(2) Identify the party or parties making the proposal and the party or parties to whom the proposal is being made;

(3) Identify generally the claim or claims the proposal is attempting to resolve;

(4) State with particularity any relevant conditions;

(5) State the total amount of the proposal;

(6) State with particularity the amount proposed to settle a claim for punitive damages, if any;

(7) State whether the proposal includes attorney's fees or other expenses and whether attorney's fees or other expenses are part of the legal claim; and

(8) Include a certificate of service and be served by certified mail or statutory overnight delivery in the form required by Code Section 9-11-5.

(b)

(1) If a defendant makes an offer of settlement which is rejected by the plaintiff, the defendant shall be entitled to recover reasonable attorney's fees and expenses of litigation incurred by the defendant or on the defendant's behalf from the date of the rejection of the offer of settlement through the entry of judgment if the final judgment is one of no liability or the final judgment obtained by the plaintiff is less than 75 percent of such offer of settlement.

(2) If a plaintiff makes an offer of settlement which is rejected by the defendant and the plaintiff recovers a final judgment in an amount greater than 125 percent of such offer of settlement, the plaintiff shall be entitled to recover reasonable attorney's fees and expenses of litigation incurred by the plaintiff or on the plaintiff's behalf from the date of the rejection of the offer of settlement through the entry of judgment.

(c) Any offer made under this Code section shall remain open for 30 days unless sooner withdrawn by a writing served on the offeree prior to acceptance by the offeree, but an offeror shall not be entitled to attorney's fees and costs under subsection (b) of this Code section to the extent an offer is not open for at least 30 days (unless it is rejected during that 30 day period). A counteroffer shall be deemed a rejection but may serve as an offer under this Code section if it is specifically denominated as an offer under this Code section. Acceptance or rejection of the offer by the offeree must be in writing and served upon the offeror. An offer that is neither withdrawn nor accepted within 30 days shall be deemed rejected. The fact that an offer is made but not accepted does not preclude a subsequent offer. Evidence of an offer is not admissible except in proceedings to enforce a settlement or to determine reasonable attorney's fees and costs under this Code section.

(d)

(1) The court shall order the payment of attorney's fees and expenses of litigation upon receipt of proof that the judgment is one to which the provisions of either paragraph (1) or paragraph (2) of subsection (b) of this Code section apply; provided, however, that if an appeal is taken from such judgment, the court shall order payment of such attorney's fees and expenses of litigation only upon remittitur affirming such judgment.

(2) If a party is entitled to costs and fees pursuant to the provisions of this Code section, the court may determine that an offer was not made in good faith in an order setting forth the basis for such a determination. In such case, the court may disallow an award of attorney's fees and costs.

(e) Upon motion by the prevailing party at the time that the verdict or judgment is rendered, the moving party may request that the finder of fact determine whether the opposing party presented a frivolous claim or defense. In such event, the court shall hold a separate bifurcated hearing at which the finder of fact shall make a determination of whether such frivolous claims or defenses were asserted and to award damages, if any, against the party presenting such frivolous claims or defenses. Under this subsection:

(1) Frivolous claims shall include, but are not limited to, the following:

(A) A claim, defense, or other position that lacks substantial justification or that is not made in good faith or that is made with malice or a wrongful purpose, as those terms are defined in Code Section 51-7-80;

(B) A claim, defense, or other position with respect to which there existed such a complete absence of any justiciable issue of law or fact that it could not be reasonably believed that a court would accept the asserted claim, defense, or other position; and

(C) A claim, defense, or other position that was interposed for delay or harassment;

(2) Damages awarded may include reasonable and necessary attorney's fees and expenses of litigation; and

(3) A party may elect to pursue either the procedure specified in this subsection or the procedure specified in Code Section 9-15-14, but not both.

Amended by 2006 Ga. Laws 589,§ 1, eff. 4/27/2006.

Added by 2005 Ga. Laws 1,§ 5, eff. 2/16/2005.

Section 9-11-69 - Execution; discovery in aid thereof

Process to enforce a judgment for the payment of money shall be a writ of execution unless the court directs otherwise. In aid of the judgment or execution, the judgment creditor, or his successor in interest when that interest appears of record, may do any or all of the following:

(1) Examine any person, including the judgment debtor by taking depositions or propounding interrogatories;

(2) Compel the production of documents or things; and

(3) Upon a showing of reasonable necessity, obtain permission from a court of competent jurisdiction to enter upon that part of real property belonging to or lawfully occupied by the debtor which is not used as a residence and which property is not bona fide in the lawful possession of another; in the manner provided in this chapter for such discovery measures prior to judgment.

Section 9-11-70 - Judgment for specific acts; vesting title

A decree for specific performance shall operate as a deed to convey land or other property without any conveyance being executed by the vendor. The decree, certified by the clerk, shall be recorded in the registry of deeds in the county where the land lies and shall stand in the place of a deed. In all other cases where a judgment directs a party to perform other specific acts and the party fails to comply within the time specified, the court may direct the acts to be done at the cost of the disobedient party by some other person appointed by the court; and acts when so done have like effect as if done by the party. The court may also in proper cases adjudge the party in contempt. If real or personal property is within the state, the court in lieu of directing a conveyance thereof may enter a judgment divesting the title of any party and vesting it in others; and the judgment has the effect of a conveyance executed in due form of law. When any order or judgment is for the delivery of possession, the party in whose favor it is entered is entitled to a writ of execution upon oral or written application to the clerk.

Article 9 - GENERAL PROVISIONS

Section 9-11-71 through 9-11-77 - Reserved

Section 9-11-78 - Motion days

Unless local conditions make it impracticable, each court shall establish regular times and places, at intervals sufficiently frequent for the prompt dispatch of business, at which motions requiring notice and hearing may be heard and disposed of; but the judge at any time or place and on such notice, if any, as is reasonable may make orders for the advancement, conduct, and hearing of actions.

Section 9-11-79 - Reserved

Section 9-11-80 - Reserved

Section 9-11-81 - Applicability

This chapter shall apply to all special statutory proceedings except to the extent that specific rules of practice and procedure in conflict herewith are expressly prescribed by law; but, in any event, the provisions of this chapter governing the sufficiency of pleadings, defenses, amendments, counterclaims, cross-claims, third-party practice, joinder of parties and causes, making parties, discovery and depositions, interpleader, intervention, evidence, motions, summary judgment, relief from judgments, and the effect of judgments shall apply to all such proceedings.

Section 9-11-82 - Jurisdiction and venue unaffected

This chapter shall not be construed to extend or limit the jurisdiction of the courts or the venue of actions therein.

Section 9-11-83 - Local court rules

Each court by action of a majority of the judges thereof may from time to time make and amend rules governing its practice not inconsistent with this chapter or any other statute.

Section 9-11-84 - Forms

The forms contained in Code Sections 9-11-101 through 9-11-132 are sufficient under this chapter and are intended to indicate the simplicity and brevity of statement which this chapter contemplates.

Section 9-11-85 - Short title

This chapter may be known and cited as the "Georgia Civil Practice Act."

Article 10 - FORMS

Section 9-11-100 - Reserved

Section 9-11-101 - Form of summons

IN THE COURT OF COUNTY STATE OF GEORGIA A.B.,) Plaintiff)) v.) Civil action) File no. C.D.,) (Clerk will insert Defendant) number.) SUMMONS To the above-named defendant: You are hereby summoned and required to file with the clerk of said court and serve upon , plaintiff's attorney, whose address is , an answer to the complaint which is herewith served upon you, within 30 days after service of this summons upon you, exclusive of the day of service. If you fail to do so, judgment by default will be taken against you for the relief demanded in the complaint. Clerk of court

Section 9-11-102 - Reserved

Section 9-11-103 - Form of complaint on a promissory note

IN THE COURT OF COUNTY STATE OF GEORGIA A.B.,) Plaintiff)) v.) Civil action) File no. C.D.,) (Clerk will insert Defendant) number.) COMPLAINT The defendant C.D., herein named, is a resident of (street), (city), County, Georgia, and is subject to the jurisdiction of this court.

1. Defendant on or about June 1, 1965, executed and delivered to plaintiff a promissory note in the following words and figures: (here set out the note verbatim); (a copy of which is hereto annexed as Exhibit A); whereby defendant promised to pay to plaintiff or order on June 1, 1966, the sum of $10,000.00 with interest thereon at the rate of 6 percent per annum.

2. Defendant owes to plaintiff the amount of said note and interest. Wherefore, plaintiff demands judgment against defendant for the sum of $10,000.00, interest, costs, and attorney fees (where applicable). Attorney for plaintiff Address

Section 9-11-104 - Form of complaint on an account

IN THE COURT OF COUNTY STATE OF GEORGIA A.B.,) Plaintiff)) v.) Civil action) File no. C.D.,) (Clerk will insert Defendant) number.) COMPLAINT The defendant C.D., herein named, is a resident of (street), (city), County, Georgia, and is subject to the jurisdiction of this court. Defendant owes plaintiff $10,000.00 according to the account hereto annexed as Exhibit A. Wherefore, plaintiff demands judgment against defendant for the sum of $10,000.00, interest, costs, and attorney fees (where applicable). Attorney for plaintiff Address

Section 9-11-105 - Form of complaint for goods sold and delivered

IN THE COURT OF COUNTY STATE OF GEORGIA A.B.,) Plaintiff)) v.) Civil action) File no. C.D.,) (Clerk will insert Defendant) number.) COMPLAINT The defendant C.D., herein named, is a resident of (street), (city), County, Georgia, and is subject to the jurisdiction of this court. Defendant owes plaintiff $10,000.00 for goods sold and delivered by plaintiff to defendant between June 1, 1966, and December 1, 1966. Wherefore, plaintiff demands judgment against defendant for the sum of $10,000.00, interest, costs, and attorney fees (where applicable). Attorney for plaintiff Address

Section 9-11-106 - Form of complaint for money lent

IN THE COURT OF COUNTY STATE OF GEORGIA A.B.,) Plaintiff)) v.) Civil action) File no. C.D.,) (Clerk will insert Defendant) number.) COMPLAINT The defendant C.D., herein named, is a resident of (street), (city), County, Georgia, and is subject to the jurisdiction of this court. Defendant owes plaintiff $10,000.00 for money lent by plaintiff to defendant on June 1, 1966. Wherefore, plaintiff demands judgment against defendant for the sum of $10,000.00, interest, costs, and attorney fees (where applicable). Attorney for plaintiff Address

Section 9-11-107 - Form of complaint for money paid by mistake

IN THE COURT OF COUNTY STATE OF GEORGIA A.B.,) Plaintiff)) v.) Civil action) File no. C.D.,) (Clerk will insert Defendant) number.) COMPLAINT The defendant C.D., herein named, is a resident of (street), (city), County, Georgia, and is subject to the jurisdiction of this court. Defendant owes plaintiff $10,000.00 for money paid by plaintiff to defendant by mistake on June 1, 1966, under the following circumstances: (Here state the circumstances with particularity). Wherefore, plaintiff demands judgment against defendant for the sum of $10,000.00, interest, costs, and attorney fees (where applicable). Attorney for plaintiff Address

Section 9-11-108 - Form of complaint for money had and received

IN THE COURT OF COUNTY STATE OF GEORGIA A.B.,) Plaintiff)) v.) Civil action) File no. C.D.,) (Clerk will insert Defendant) number.) COMPLAINT The defendant C.D., herein named, is a resident of (street), (city), County, Georgia, and is subject to the jurisdiction of this court. Defendant owes plaintiff $10,000.00 for money had and received from one G.H. on June 1, 1966, to be paid by defendant to plaintiff. Wherefore, plaintiff demands judgment against defendant for the sum of $10,000.00, interest, costs, and attorney fees (where applicable). Attorney for plaintiff Address

Section 9-11-109 - Form of complaint for negligence

IN THE COURT OF COUNTY STATE OF GEORGIA A.B.,) Plaintiff)) v.) Civil action) File no. C.D.,) (Clerk will insert Defendant) number.) COMPLAINT The defendant C.D., herein named, is a resident of (street), (city), County, Georgia, and is subject to the jurisdiction of this court.

1. On June 1, 1966, on a public highway called Broad Street in Athens, Georgia, defendant negligently drove a motor vehicle against plaintiff who was then crossing said highway.

2. As a result plaintiff was thrown down and had his leg broken and was otherwise injured, was prevented from transacting his business, suffered great pain of body and mind, and incurred expenses for medical attention and hospitalization in the sum of $1,000.00. Wherefore, plaintiff demands judgment against defendant in the sum of $10,000.00 and costs. Attorney for plaintiff Address

Section 9-11-110 - Form of complaint for negligence when plaintiff is unable to determine responsible person

IN THE COURT OF COUNTY STATE OF GEORGIA A.B.,) Plaintiff)) v.) Civil action) File no. C.D. and E.F.,) (Clerk will insert Defendants) number.) COMPLAINT The defendant C.D., herein named, is a resident of (street), (city), County, Georgia, and is subject to the jurisdiction of this court. (Add appropriate statement about domicile of defendant E.F.)

1. On June 1, 1966, on a public highway called Broad Street in Athens, Georgia, defendant C.D. or defendant E.F., or both defendants C.D. and E.F., willfully or recklessly or negligently drove or caused to be driven a motor vehicle against plaintiff who was then crossing said highway.

2. As a result plaintiff was thrown down and had his leg broken and was otherwise injured, was prevented from transacting his business, suffered great pain of body and mind, and incurred expenses for medical attention and hospitalization in the sum of $1,000.00. Wherefore, plaintiff demands judgment against C.D. or against E.F. or against both in the sum of $10,000.00 and costs. Attorney for plaintiff Address

Section 9-11-111 - Form of complaint for conversion

IN THE COURT OF COUNTY STATE OF GEORGIA A.B.,) Plaintiff)) v.) Civil action) File no. C.D.,) (Clerk will insert Defendant) number.) COMPLAINT The defendant C.D., herein named, is a resident of (street), (city), County, Georgia, and is subject to the jurisdiction of this court. On or about December 1, 1966, defendant converted to his own use ten bonds of the Company (here insert brief identification as by number and issue) of the value of $10,000.00, the property of plaintiff. Wherefore, plaintiff demands judgment against defendant in the sum of $10,000.00, interest, and costs. Attorney for plaintiff Address

Section 9-11-112 - Form of complaint for specific performance of contract to convey land

IN THE COURT OF COUNTY STATE OF GEORGIA A.B.,) Plaintiff)) v.) Civil action) File no. C.D.,) (Clerk will insert Defendant) number.) COMPLAINT The defendant C.D., herein named, is a resident of (street), (city), County, Georgia, and is subject to the jurisdiction of this court.

1. On or about December 1, 1966, plaintiff and defendant entered into an agreement in writing, a copy of which is hereto annexed as Exhibit A.

2. In accordance with said agreement, plaintiff tendered to defendant the purchase price and requested a conveyance of the land, but defendant refused to accept the tender and refused to make the conveyance.

3. Plaintiff now offers to pay the purchase price. Wherefore, plaintiff demands:

(1) That defendant be required specifically to perform said agreement,

(2) Damages in the sum of $1,000.00, and

(3) That, if specific performance is not granted, plaintiff have judgment against defendant in the sum of $10,000.00 Attorney for plaintiff Address

Section 9-11-113 - Form of complaint on claim for debt and to set aside fraudulent conveyance under Code Section 9-11-18

IN THE COURT OF COUNTY STATE OF GEORGIA A.B.,) Plaintiff)) v.) Civil action) File no. C.D. and E.F.,) (Clerk will insert Defendants) number.) COMPLAINT The defendant C.D., herein named, is a resident of (street), (city), County, Georgia, and is subject to the jurisdiction of this court. (Add appropriate statement about domicile of defendant E.F.)

1. Defendant C.D. on or about executed and delivered to plaintiff a promissory note in the following words and figures: (here set out the note verbatim); (a copy of which is hereto annexed as Exhibit A); whereby defendant C.D. promised to pay to plaintiff or order on the sum of $5,000.00 with interest thereon at the rate of percent per annum.

2. Defendant C.D. owes to plaintiff the amount of said note and interest.

3. Defendant C.D. on or about conveyed all his property, real and personal (or specify and describe), to defendant E.F. for the purpose of defrauding plaintiff and hindering and delaying the collection of the indebtedness evidenced by the note above-referred to. Wherefore, plaintiff demands:

(1) That plaintiff have judgment against defendant C.D. for $10,000.00 and interest;

(2) That the aforesaid conveyance to defendant E.F. be declared void and the judgment herein be declared a lien on said property;

(3) That plaintiff have judgment against the defendants for costs. Attorney for plaintiff Address

Section 9-11-114 - Form of complaint for negligence under Federal Employers' Liability Act

IN THE COURT OF COUNTY STATE OF GEORGIA A.B.,) Plaintiff)) v.) Civil action) File no. C.D.,) (Clerk will insert Defendant) number.) COMPLAINT The defendant C.D., herein named, is a resident of (street), (city), County, Georgia, and is subject to the jurisdiction of this court.

1. During all the times herein mentioned defendant owned and operated in interstate commerce a railroad which passed through a tunnel located at and known as Tunnel No. .

2. On or about June 1, 1966, defendant was repairing and enlarging the tunnel in order to protect interstate trains and passengers and freight from injury and in order to make the tunnel more conveniently usable for interstate commerce.

3. In the course of thus repairing and enlarging the tunnel on said day, defendant employed plaintiff as one of its workmen and negligently put plaintiff to work in a portion of the tunnel which defendant had left unprotected and unsupported.

4. By reason of defendant's negligence in thus putting plaintiff to work in that portion of the tunnel, plaintiff was, while so working pursuant to the defendant's orders, struck and crushed by a rock which fell from the unsupported portion of the tunnel and was (here describe plaintiff's injuries).

5. Prior to these injuries, plaintiff was a strong, able-bodied man, capable of earning $ per day. By these injuries he has been made incapable of any gainful activity, has suffered great physical and mental pain, and has incurred expense in the amount of $ for medicine, medical attendance, and hospitalization. Wherefore, plaintiff demands judgment against defendant in the sum of $ and costs. Attorney for plaintiff Address

Section 9-11-115 through 9-11-117 - Reserved

Section 9-11-118 - Form of complaint for interpleader and declaratory relief

IN THE COURT OF COUNTY STATE OF GEORGIA A.B.,) Plaintiff)) v.) Civil action) File no. C.D., E.F., and X.Y.,) (Clerk will insert Defendants) number.) COMPLAINT The defendant C.D., herein named, is a resident of (street), (city), County, Georgia, and is subject to the jurisdiction of this court. (Add appropriate statement about domicile of remaining defendants.)

1. On or about June 1, 1965, plaintiff issued to G.H. a policy of life insurance whereby plaintiff promised to pay to K.L. as beneficiary the sum of $10,000.00 upon the death of G.H. The policy required the payment by G.H. of a stipulated premium on June 1, 1966, and annually thereafter as a condition precedent to its continuance in force.

2. No part of the premium due June 1, 1966, was ever paid and the policy ceased to have any force or effect after July 1, 1966.

3. Thereafter, on September 1, 1966, G.H. and K.L. died as the result of a collision between a locomotive and the automobile in which G.H. and K.L. were riding.

4. Defendant C.D. is the duly appointed and acting executor of the will of G.H., defendant E.F. is the duly appointed and acting executor of the will of K.L., and defendant X.Y. claims to have been duly designated as beneficiary of said policy in place of K.L.

5. Each of the defendants, C.D., E.F., and X.Y., is claiming that the above-mentioned policy was in full force and effect at the time of the death of G.H.; each of them is claiming to be the only person entitled to receive payment of the amount of the policy and has made demand for payment thereof.

6. By reason of these conflicting claims of the defendants, plaintiff is in great doubt as to which defendant is entitled to be paid the amount of the policy if it was in force at the time of death of G.H. Wherefore, plaintiff demands that the court adjudge:

(1) That none of the defendants is entitled to recover from plaintiff the amount of said policy or any part thereof.

(2) That each of the defendants be restrained from instituting any action against plaintiff for the recovery of the amount of said policy or any part thereof.

(3) That, if the court shall determine that said policy was in force at the death of G.H., the defendants be required to interplead and settle between themselves their rights to the money due under said policy and that plaintiff be discharged from all liability in the premises except to the person whom the court shall adjudge entitled to the amount of said policy.

(4) That plaintiff recover its costs. Attorney for plaintiff Address

Amended by 2006 Ga. Laws 453,§ 9, eff. 4/14/2006.

Section 9-11-119 - Form of motion to dismiss, presenting defense of failure to state a claim

IN THE COURT OF COUNTY STATE OF GEORGIA A.B.,) Plaintiff)) v.) Civil action) File no. C.D.,) Defendant) MOTION TO DISMISS The defendant moves the court as follows:

1. To dismiss the action because the complaint fails to state a claim against defendant upon which relief can be granted.

2. (Additional defenses under subsection (b) of Code Section 9-11-12.) Attorney for defendant Address NOTICE OF MOTION To: Attorney for plaintiff Please take notice that the undersigned will bring the above motion on for hearing before this court at , on the day of , , at :]].M. or as soon thereafter as counsel can be heard. Attorney for defendant Address

Section 9-11-120 - Form of answer presenting defenses under subsection (b) of Code Section 9-11-12

IN THE COURT OF COUNTY STATE OF GEORGIA A.B.,) Plaintiff)) v.) Civil action) File no. C.D.,) Defendant) ANSWER First Defense The complaint fails to state a claim against defendant upon which relief can be granted. Second Defense If defendant is indebted to plaintiff for the goods mentioned in the complaint, he is indebted to him jointly with G.H. G.H. is alive, is subject to the jurisdiction of the court, and has not been made a party. Third Defense Defendant admits the allegations contained in paragraphs 1 and 4 of the complaint, alleges that he is without knowledge or information sufficient to form a belief as to the truth of the allegations contained in paragraph 2 of the complaint, and denies each and every other allegation contained in the complaint. Fourth Defense The right of action set forth in the complaint did not accrue within six years next before the commencement of this action. COUNTERCLAIM (Here set forth any claim as a counterclaim in the manner in which a claim is pleaded in a complaint.) CROSS-CLAIM AGAINST DEFENDANT M.N. (Here set forth the claim constituting a cross-claim against defendant M.N. in the manner in which a claim is pleaded in a complaint.) Attorney for defendant Address

Section 9-11-121 - Form of answer to complaint set forth in Code Section 9-11-108, with counterclaim for interpleader

IN THE COURT OF COUNTY STATE OF GEORGIA A.B.,) Plaintiff)) v.) Civil action) File no. C.D.,) Defendant) ANSWER Defense Defendant denies the allegations stated to the extent set forth in the counterclaim herein. COUNTERCLAIM FOR INTERPLEADER

1. Defendant received the sum of $10,000.00 as a deposit from E.F.

2. Plaintiff has demanded the payment of such deposit to him by virtue of an assignment of it which he claims to have received from E.F.

3. E.F. has notified the defendant that he claims such deposit, that the purported assignment is not valid, and that he holds the defendant responsible for the deposit. Wherefore, defendant demands:

(1) That the court order E.F. to be made a party defendant to respond to the complaint and to this counterclaim.

(2) That the court order the plaintiff and E.F. to interplead their respective claims.

(3) That the court adjudge whether the plaintiff or E.F. is entitled to the sum of money.

(4) That the court discharge defendant from all liability in the premises except to the person it shall adjudge entitled to the sum of money.

(5) That the court award to the defendant its costs and attorney's fees. Attorney for defendant Address

Section 9-11-122 - Form of summons and complaint against third-party defendant

IN THE COURT OF COUNTY STATE OF GEORGIA A.B.,) Plaintiff)) v.) Civil action) File no. C.D.,) Defendant and Third-) Party Plaintiff) v.)) E.F.,) Third-Party Defendant) SUMMONS To the above-named third-party defendant: You are hereby summoned and required to file with the clerk of said court and serve upon , plaintiff's attorney whose address is , and upon , who is attorney for C.D., defendant and third-party plaintiff, and whose address is , an answer to the third-party complaint which is herewith served upon you, within 30 days after the service of this summons upon you exclusive of the day of service. If you fail to do so, judgment by default will be taken against you for the relief demanded in the third-party complaint. There is also served upon you herewith a copy of the complaint of the plaintiff which you may but are not required to answer. Clerk of court IN THE COURT OF COUNTY STATE OF GEORGIA A.B.,) Plaintiff)) v.) Civil action) File no. C.D.,) Defendant and Third-) Party Plaintiff)) v.)) E.F.,) Third-Party Defendant) THIRD-PARTY COMPLAINT

1. Plaintiff, A.B., has filed against defendant, C.D., a complaint, a copy of which is hereto attached as "Exhibit A." A copy of all other pleadings filed prior to the filing of this third-party complaint is hereto attached as "Exhibit B."

2. (Here state the grounds upon which C.D. is entitled to recover from E.F. all or part of what A.B. may recover from C.D. The statements should be framed as in an original complaint.) Wherefore, C.D. demands judgment against third-party defendant E.F. for all sums that may be adjudged against defendant C.D. in favor of plaintiff A.B. Attorney for C.D., third-party plaintiff Address

Section 9-11-123 - Form of motion to intervene as a defendant under Code Section 9-11-24

IN THE COURT OF COUNTY STATE OF GEORGIA A.B.,) Plaintiff) v.) Civil action C.D.,) File no. Defendant) E.F.,) Applicant for Intervention) MOTION TO INTERVENE AS A DEFENDANT E.F. moves for leave to intervene as a defendant in this action, in order to assert the defenses set forth in his proposed answer, of which a copy is hereto attached, on the ground that . Attorney for E.F., applicant for intervention Address NOTICE OF MOTION (Contents the same as in Code Section 9-11-119) IN THE COURT OF COUNTY STATE OF GEORGIA A.B.,) Plaintiff) v.) Civil action C.D.,) File no. Defendant) E.F.,) Intervenor) INTERVENOR'S ANSWER First Defense Intervenor admits the allegations stated in paragraphs 1 and 4 of the complaint, denies the allegations in paragraph 3, and denies the allegations in paragraph 2 insofar as they assert the . Second Defense (Set forth defenses) Attorney for E.F., intervenor Address (Like form if intervention is as plaintiff).

Section 9-11-124 - Form of motion for production of documents under Code Section 9-11-34

IN THE COURT OF COUNTY STATE OF GEORGIA A.B.,) Plaintiff)) v.) Civil action) File no. C.D.,) Defendant) MOTION FOR PRODUCTION OF DOCUMENTS Plaintiff A.B. moves the court for an order requiring defendant C.D.:

1. To produce and to permit plaintiff to inspect and to copy each of the following documents: (Here list the documents and describe each of them).

2. To produce and to permit plaintiff to inspect and to photograph each of the following objects: (Here list the objects and describe each of them).

3. To permit plaintiff to enter (here describe property to be entered) and to inspect and to photograph (here describe the portion of the real property and the objects to be inspected and photographed). Defendant C.D. has the possession, custody, or control of each of the foregoing documents and objects and of the above-mentioned real estate. Each of them constitutes or contains evidence relevant and material to a matter involved in this action, as is more fully shown in Exhibit A hereto attached. Attorney for plaintiff Address NOTICE OF MOTION (Contents the same as in Code Section 9-11-119)

EXHIBIT A AFFIDAVIT State of , County of A.B., being first duly sworn says:

1. (Here set forth all that plaintiff knows which shows that defendant has the papers or objects in his possession or control.)

2. (Here set forth all that plaintiff knows which shows that each of the above-mentioned items is relevant to some issue in the action.) Sworn to and subscribed before me this A.B. day of , . Address

Amended by 2015 Ga. Laws 9,§ 9, eff. 3/13/2015.

Section 9-11-125 - Form of request for admission under Code Section 9-11-36

IN THE COURT OF COUNTY STATE OF GEORGIA A.B.,) Plaintiff)) v.) Civil action) File no. C.D.,) Defendant) REQUEST FOR ADMISSION OF FACTS AND GENUINENESS OF DOCUMENTS Plaintiff A.B. requests defendant C.D. within days after service of this request to make the following admissions for the purpose of this action only and subject to all pertinent objections to admissibility which may be interposed at the trial:

1. That each of the following documents exhibited with this request is genuine: (Here list the documents and describe each document).

2. That each of the following statements is true: (Here list the statements). Attorney for plaintiff Address

Section 9-11-126 through 9-11-130 - Reserved

Section 9-11-131 - Form of judgment on jury verdict

IN THE COURT OF COUNTY STATE OF GEORGIA A.B.,) Plaintiff)) v.) Civil action) File no. C.D.,) Defendant) JUDGMENT This action came on for trial before the court and a jury, Honorable John Marshall, presiding, and the issue having been duly tried and the jury having duly rendered its verdict, It Is Ordered and Adjudged (That the plaintiff A.B. recover of the defendant C.D. the sum of $, with interest thereon at the rate of percent as provided by law, and his costs of action.) or (That the plaintiff take nothing, that the action be dismissed on the merits, and that the defendant C.D. recover of the plaintiff A.B. his costs of action.) Dated at , Georgia, this day of , . Judge

Section 9-11-132 - Form of judgment on decision by the court

IN THE COURT OF COUNTY STATE OF GEORGIA A.B.,) Plaintiff)) v.) Civil action) File no. C.D.,) Defendant) JUDGMENT This action came on for (trial) (hearing) before the court, Honorable John Marshall, presiding, and the issues having been duly (tried) (heard) and a decision having been duly rendered, It Is Ordered and Adjudged (That the plaintiff A.B. recover of the defendant C.D. the sum of $, with interest thereon at the rate of percent as provided by law, and his costs of action.) or (That the plaintiff take nothing, that the action be dismissed on the merits, and that the defendant C.D. recover of the plaintiff A.B. his costs of action.) Dated at , Georgia, this day of , . Judge

Section 9-11-133 - Forms meeting requirements for civil case filing and disposition information

The Judicial Council of Georgia, with the approval of the Supreme Court, shall promulgate forms to be used for civil case filing and disposition information; provided, however, that the general civil case filing information form and domestic relations case filing information form shall be required to contain an acknowledgment by the filer that the complaint and any exhibits or other attachments satisfy the redaction requirements of Code Section 9-11-7.1.

Amended by 2017 Ga. Laws 240,§ 1-1, eff. 1/1/2018.

Amended by 2014 Ga. Laws 586,§ 3, eff. 7/1/2014.

Amended by 2013 Ga. Laws 33,§ 9, eff. 4/24/2013.

Amended by 2010 Ga. Laws 624,§ 9, eff. 6/3/2010.

Amended by 2007 Ga. Laws 264,§ 4, eff. 1/1/2008.

Chapter 12 - VERDICT AND JUDGMENT

Article 1 - GENERAL PROVISIONS

Section 9-12-1 - What verdict to cover

The verdict shall cover the issues made by the pleadings and shall be for the plaintiff or for the defendant.

Section 9-12-2 - Instructions on form of verdict

In the trial of all civil cases, the judge upon request of the jury shall furnish the jury with written instructions as to the form of their verdict.

Section 9-12-3 - How verdict received

Verdicts shall be received only in open court in the absence of agreement of the parties.

Section 9-12-4 - Construction of verdicts

Verdicts shall have a reasonable intendment and shall receive a reasonable construction. They shall not be avoided unless from necessity.

Section 9-12-5 - Verdict may be molded

In a proper case, the superior court may mold the verdict so as to do full justice to the parties in the same manner as a decree in equity.

Section 9-12-6 - Amendment of verdict - To conform to pleadings

A verdict may be so amended as to make it conform to the pleadings if the error plainly appears upon the face of the record.

Section 9-12-7 - Amendment of verdict - After dispersal of jury

A verdict may be amended in mere matter of form after the jury has dispersed. However, after a verdict has been received and recorded and the jury has dispersed, it may not be amended in matter of substance either by what the jurors say they intended to find or otherwise.

Section 9-12-8 - Amendment of verdict - When part illegal

If a part of a verdict is legal and a part illegal, the court will construe the verdict and order it amended by entering a remittitur as to that part which is illegal and giving judgment for the balance.

Section 9-12-9 - Judgment to conform to verdict

Judgment and execution shall conform to the verdict.

Section 9-12-10 - Judgment for principal and interest

In all cases where judgment is obtained, the judgment shall be entered for the principal sum due, with interest, provided the claim upon which it was obtained draws interest. No part of the judgment shall bear interest except the principal which is due on the original debt.

Section 9-12-11 - Sureties and endorsers to be identified in judgment

In all judgments against sureties or endorsers on any draft, promissory note, or other instrument in writing, the plaintiff or his attorney shall designate and identify the relation of the parties under the contract on which the judgment is rendered.

Section 9-12-12 - Judgment for costs against fiduciary

When the verdict of a jury is against an executor, administrator, or other trustee in his representative character, a judgment for costs shall be entered against him in the same character.

Section 9-12-13 - Amount of judgment on bond

All judgments entered against the obligors on any bond, whether official or voluntary, shall be for the amount of damages found by the verdict of the jury and not for the penalty thereof.

Section 9-12-14 - Amendment of judgment to conform to verdict

A judgment may be amended by order of the court to conform to the verdict upon which it is predicated, even after an execution issues.

Section 9-12-15 - Judgment aided by verdict or amendable not set aside

A judgment may not be set aside for any defect in the pleadings or the record that is aided by verdict or amendable as a matter of form.

Section 9-12-16 - Validity of judgment when court does not have jurisdiction

The judgment of a court having no jurisdiction of the person or the subject matter or which is void for any other cause is a mere nullity and may be so held in any court when it becomes material to the interest of the parties to consider it.

Section 9-12-17 - When creditors or purchasers may attack judgment

Creditors or bona fide purchasers may attack a judgment for any defect appearing on the face of the record or the pleadings or for fraud or collusion, whenever and wherever it interferes with their rights, either at law or in equity.

Section 9-12-18 - Right to confess judgment and appeal; where and when entered

(a) Either party has a right to confess judgment without the consent of his adversary and to appeal from such confession without reserving the right to do so in cases where an appeal is allowed by law.

(b) No confession of judgment shall be entered except in the county where the defendant resided at the commencement of the action unless expressly provided for by law. The action must have been regularly filed and docketed as in other cases. However, a judge of a superior court or a magistrate may confess judgment in his own court.

Section 9-12-19 - Judgment suspended by appeal

Where a judgment is entered and, within the time allowed for entering an appeal, an appeal is entered, the judgment shall be suspended.

Section 9-12-20 - Judgment when security given on appeal

In all cases of appeal where security has been given, the plaintiff or his attorney may enter judgment against the principal and his surety jointly and severally.

Section 9-12-21 - Judgments transferable; status of transferee

A person in whose favor a judgment has been entered or a person to whom a judgment has been transferred may bona fide and for a valuable consideration transfer any judgment to a third person. In all such cases the transferee of any judgment shall have the same rights and shall be subject to the same equities and to the same defenses as was the original holder of the judgment.

Section 9-12-22 - Effect of transfer by attorney; ratification

The transfer of a judgment by the attorney of record of the person in whose favor the judgment was entered shall be good to pass the title thereto as against every person except the person in whose favor judgment was entered or his assignee without notice. Ratification by the plaintiff shall estop him also from denying the transfer. Receipt of the money from the transfer shall be such a ratification.

Section 9-12-23 - Effect of consent judgment

The consent of the parties to a judgment has the effect of removing any issuable defenses previously filed. After such a consent the court may render judgment without the verdict of a jury.

Article 2 - EFFECT OF JUDGMENTS

Section 9-12-40 - Judgment conclusive between which persons and on what issues

A judgment of a court of competent jurisdiction shall be conclusive between the same parties and their privies as to all matters put in issue or which under the rules of law might have been put in issue in the cause wherein the judgment was rendered until the judgment is reversed or set aside.

Section 9-12-41 - Effect of judgment in rem

A judgment in rem is conclusive upon everyone.

Section 9-12-42 - Judgment no bar absent decision on merits

Where the merits were not and could not have been in question, a former recovery on purely technical grounds shall not be a bar to a subsequent action brought so as to avoid the objection fatal to the first. For a former judgment to be a bar to subsequent action, the merits of the case must have been adjudicated.

Section 9-12-43 - Parol evidence admissible

Parol evidence shall be admissible to show that a matter apparently covered by a judgment was not really passed upon by the court.

Article 3 - DORMANCY AND REVIVAL OF JUDGMENTS

Section 9-12-60 - When judgment becomes dormant; how dormancy prevented; docketing; applicability

(a) A judgment shall become dormant and shall not be enforced:

(1) When seven years shall elapse after the rendition of the judgment before execution is issued thereon and is entered on the general execution docket of the county in which the judgment was rendered;

(2) Unless entry is made on the execution by an officer authorized to levy and return the same and the entry and the date thereof are entered by the clerk on the general execution docket within seven years after issuance of the execution and its record; or

(3) Unless a bona fide public effort on the part of the plaintiff in execution to enforce the execution in the courts is made and due written notice of such effort specifying the time of the institution of the action or proceedings, the nature thereof, the names of the parties thereto, and the name of the court in which it is pending is filed by the plaintiff in execution or his attorney at law with the clerk and is entered by the clerk on the general execution docket, all at such times and periods that seven years will not elapse between such entries of such notices or between such an entry and a proper entry made as prescribed in paragraph (2) of this subsection.

(b) The record of the execution made as prescribed in paragraph (1) of subsection (a) of this Code section or of every entry as prescribed in paragraph (2) or (3) of subsection (a) of this Code section shall institute a new seven-year period within which the judgment shall not become dormant, provided that when an entry on the execution or a written notice of public effort is filed for record, the execution shall be recorded or rerecorded on the general execution docket with all entries thereon. It shall not be necessary in order to prevent dormancy that such execution be entered or such entry be recorded on any other docket.

(c) When an entry on an execution or a written notice of public effort is filed for record and the original execution is recorded in a general execution docket other than the current general execution docket, the original execution shall be rerecorded in the current general execution docket with all entries thereon. When an original execution is so rerecorded, a notation shall be made upon the original execution which states that it has been rerecorded and gives the book and page number where the execution has been rerecorded. When an original execution is so rerecorded in the current general execution docket, it shall be indexed in the current general execution docket in the same manner as if it were an original execution. Nothing in this subsection shall affect the priority of any judgment or lien; and no judgment or lien shall lose any priority because an execution is rerecorded.

(d) The provisions of subsection (a) of this Code section shall not apply to judgments or orders for child support or spousal support.

Section 9-12-61 - Dormant judgments renewed by action or scire facias; time of renewal

When any judgment obtained in any court becomes dormant, the same may be renewed or revived by an action or by scire facias, at the option of the holder of the judgment, within three years from the time it becomes dormant.

Section 9-12-62 - Nature of scire facias

Scire facias to revive a judgment is not an original action but is the continuation of the action in which the judgment was obtained.

Section 9-12-63 - Issuance of scire facias; copies; service; return

A scire facias to revive a dormant judgment in the courts must issue from and be returnable to the court of the county in which the judgment was obtained. It shall be directed to all and singular the sheriffs of this state and shall be signed by the clerk of such court who shall make out copies thereof. An original and a copy shall issue for each county in which any party to be notified resides. A copy shall be served by the sheriff of the county in which the party to be notified resides 20 days before the sitting of the court to which the scire facias is made returnable and the original shall be returned to the clerk of the court from which it issued.

Section 9-12-64 - Revival on motion after service of scire facias; when defendant entitled to jury trial

In all cases of scire facias to revive a judgment, when service has been perfected, the judgment may be revived on motion at the first term without the intervention of a jury unless the person against whom judgment was entered files an issuable defense under oath, in which case the defendant in judgment shall be entitled to a trial by jury as in other cases.

Section 9-12-65 - Scire facias when judgment transferred

When a judgment has been transferred, the scire facias shall issue in the name of the original holder of the judgment for the use of the transferee.

Section 9-12-66 - Venue of action to renew judgment

An action to renew a dormant judgment shall be brought in the county where the defendant in judgment resides at the commencement of the action.

Section 9-12-67 - Revival of judgment against nonresident; service by publication

If the defendant in judgment or other party to be notified resides outside this state, a dormant judgment may be revived against such defendant or his representative by such process as is issued in cases in which the defendant resides in this state, provided that the defendant in judgment or other party to be notified shall be served with scire facias by publication in the newspaper in which the official advertisements of the county are published, twice a month for two months previous to the term of the court at which it is intended to revive the judgment, which service shall be as effectual in all cases as if the defendant or person to be notified had been personally served.

Section 9-12-68 - Revival of dormant decrees for payment of money

Decrees for the payment of money shall become dormant like other judgments when not enforced and may be revived as provided by law for other judgments.

Article 4 - JUDGMENT LIENS

Section 9-12-80 - Equal dignity and binding effect of judgments

All judgments obtained in the superior courts, magistrate courts, or other courts of this state shall be of equal dignity and shall bind all the property of the defendant in judgment, both real and personal, from the date of such judgments except as otherwise provided in this Code.

Section 9-12-81 - General execution docket; when money judgment in county of defendant's residence creates lien against third parties without notice

(a) The clerk of superior court of each county shall be required to keep a general execution docket in paper or electronic data base form.

(b) As against the interest of third parties acting in good faith and without notice who have acquired a transfer or lien binding the property of the defendant in judgment, no money judgment obtained within the county of the defendant's residence in any court of this state or federal court in this state shall create a lien upon the property of the defendant unless the execution issuing thereon is entered upon the execution docket. When the execution has been entered upon the docket, the lien shall date from such entry.
Amended by 2012 Ga. Laws 599,§ I-1-2, eff. 7/1/2012.

Section 9-12-82 - When money judgment outside county of defendant's residence creates lien against third parties without notice

As against bona fide purchasers for value without actual notice of a judgment or other third parties acting in good faith and without notice who have acquired a transfer or lien binding the defendant's property, no money judgment obtained in any court of this state or federal court in this state outside the county of the defendant's residence shall create a lien upon the property of the defendant located in any county other than that where obtained unless the execution issuing thereon is entered upon the general execution docket of the county of the defendant's residence within 30 days from the date of the judgment. When the execution is entered upon the docket after the 30 days, the lien shall date from such entry.

Section 9-12-83 - When money judgment creates lien on land located outside county in which obtained against third parties without notice

No money judgment obtained in any court of this state or federal court in this state shall create any lien on land in any county other than that in which it was obtained as against the interests of third parties acting in good faith and without notice who have acquired a transfer or lien binding defendant's property unless at the time of the transfer or the acquisition of the lien the execution was recorded on the general execution docket in the county in which such land is located.

Section 9-12-84 - When money judgment against nonresident creates lien on land within state against third parties without notice

(a) As against the interests of third parties acting in good faith and without notice who have acquired a transfer or lien binding any real estate situated in this state owned by a nonresident, no money judgment obtained in any court of this state or federal court in this state against the nonresident shall create a lien upon the real estate of the nonresident unless the execution issuing thereon is entered upon the general execution docket of the county in which the real estate is situated. When the execution is entered upon the docket, the lien shall date from such entry.

(b) Nothing in this Code section shall be construed to affect the validity or force of any judgment as between the parties thereto.

Section 9-12-85 - Deeds, mortgages, judgments, or liens between parties not affected by money judgments

Nothing in Code Sections 9-12-81 and 9-12-82 shall be construed to affect the validity or force of any deed, mortgage, judgment, or other lien of any kind as between the parties thereto.

Section 9-12-86 - Recordation in county where property located prerequisite to lien on land

(a) For purposes of this Code section, the term "applicable records" shall include deed books, lis pendens dockets, federal tax lien dockets, general execution dockets, and attachment dockets.

(b) No judgment, decree, or order or any writ of fieri facias issued pursuant to any judgment, decree, or order of any superior court, city court, magistrate court, municipal court, or any federal court shall in any way affect or become a lien upon the title to real property until the judgment, decree, order, or writ of fieri facias is recorded in the office of the clerk of the superior court of the county in which the real property is located and is entered in the indexes to the applicable records in the office of the clerk. Such entries and recordings must be requested and paid for by the plaintiff or the defendant, or his attorney at law.

(c) The recording and indexing required by this Code section shall be in addition to and supplemental to all other recording of judgments, decrees, and orders required by law.

(d) This Code section shall only apply to judgments, decrees, or orders rendered after March 25, 1958.

Section 9-12-87 - Judgments from same term considered of equal date

(a) All judgments signed on verdicts rendered at the same term of court shall be considered, held, and taken to be of equal date.

(b) In the case of judgments signed on verdicts rendered at the same term of the court, no execution shall be entitled to any preference by reason of being first placed in the hands of the levying officer.

Section 9-12-88 - Extent property affected by judgment pending appeal

In all cases in which a judgment is rendered and an appeal is entered from the judgment, the property of the defendant in judgment shall not be bound by the judgment except so far as to prevent the alienation by the defendant of his property between its signing and the signing of the judgment on the appeal, but the property shall be bound from the signing of the judgment on the appeal.

Section 9-12-89 - Effect of appellate proceeding on lien

A judgment in the trial court which is taken to the Supreme Court or the Court of Appeals and is affirmed loses no lien or priority by the proceeding in the appellate court.

Section 9-12-90 - Judgments relating to common disaster

(a) Liens of all judgments obtained in actions for damages growing out of a common disaster or occurrence shall be equal in rank or priority regardless of the date of the rendition of the verdict or the entering of the judgment. However, this Code section shall apply only to judgments obtained in actions which are filed within 12 months from the date of the happening of the disaster or occurrence giving rise to the cause of action.

(b) This Code section applies to all actions filed in the courts of this state in which damages are sought to be recovered on account of injuries sustained in or death resulting from a common disaster or occurrence.

Section 9-12-91 - Effect of judgment on promissory notes

A judgment creates no lien upon promissory notes in the hands of the defendant.

Section 9-12-92 - Effect of judgment lien on personalty removed to another state, sold, and returned

When a judgment lien has attached to personal property which is removed to another state and sold, the property shall be subject to the judgment lien if brought back to this state.

Section 9-12-93 - When purchased property discharged from lien

When any person has bona fide and for a valuable consideration purchased real or personal property and has been in the possession of the real property for four years or of the personal property for two years, such property shall be discharged from the lien of any judgment against the person from whom it was purchased or against any predecessor in title of real or personal property. Nothing contained herein shall be construed to otherwise affect the validity or enforceability of such judgment, except to discharge such property from any such lien of judgment.

Section 9-12-94 - Clerk's fees

For entering an execution upon the general execution docket, the clerk shall be entitled to the fees enumerated in Code Section 15-6-77.

Article 5 - UNIFORM FOREIGN-COUNTRY FOREIGN MONEY JUDGMENTS RECOGNITION ACT

Section 9-12-110 - Short title

This article shall be known and may be cited as the "Uniform Foreign-Country Money Judgments Recognition Act."

Amended by 2015 Ga. Laws 167,§ 2-1, eff. 7/1/2015.

Section 9-12-111 - Definitions

As used in this article, the term:

(1) "Foreign country" means a government other than:

    (A) The United States;

    (B) Any state, district, commonwealth, territory, or insular possession of the United States; or

    (C) Any other government with regard to which the decision in this state as to whether to recognize a judgment of such government's court is initially subject to determination under the Full Faith and Credit Clause of the United States Constitution.

(2) "Foreign-country judgment" means any judgment of a court of a foreign country.

Amended by 2015 Ga. Laws 167,§ 2-1, eff. 7/1/2015.

Section 9-12-112 - Applicability; burden of proof

(a) Except as otherwise provided in subsection (b) of this Code section, this article applies to any foreign-country judgment to the extent that such judgment:

    (1) Grants or denies recovery of a sum of money; and

    (2) Under the law of the foreign country where rendered, is final, conclusive, and enforceable.

(b) This article shall not apply to a foreign-country judgment, even if such judgment grants or denies recovery of a sum of money, to the extent that such judgment is:

    (1) A judgment for taxes;

(2) A fine or other penalty; or

(3) A judgment for divorce, support, or maintenance, or any other judgment rendered in connection with domestic relations.

(c) A party seeking recognition of a foreign-country judgment has the burden of establishing that this article applies to such foreign-country judgment.

Amended by 2015 Ga. Laws 167,§ 2-1, eff. 7/1/2015.

Section 9-12-113 - Recognition and enforcement of foreign-country judgments

(a) Except as otherwise provided in subsection (b) of this Code section, a court of this state shall recognize a foreign-country judgment meeting the requirements of Code Section 9-12-112.

(b) A court of this state shall not recognize a foreign-country judgment if:

(1) The judgment was rendered under a judicial system that does not provide impartial tribunals or procedures compatible with the requirements of due process of law;

(2) The foreign court did not have personal jurisdiction over the defendant;

(3) The foreign court did not have jurisdiction over the subject matter;

(4) The defendant in the proceedings in the foreign court did not receive notice of the proceedings in sufficient time to enable the defendant to defend;

(5) The judgment was obtained by fraud that deprived the losing party of an adequate opportunity to present its case;

(6) The judgment or cause of action on which the judgment is based is repugnant to the public policy of this state or of the United States;

(7) The judgment conflicts with another final and conclusive judgment;

(8) The proceedings in the foreign court were contrary to an agreement between the parties under which the dispute in question was to be determined otherwise than by proceedings in such foreign court;

(9) In the case of jurisdiction based only on personal service, the foreign court was a seriously inconvenient forum for the trial of the action;

(10) The judgment was rendered in circumstances that raise substantial doubt about the integrity of the rendering court with respect to such judgment; or

(11) The specific proceeding in the foreign court leading to the judgment was not compatible with the requirements of due process of law.

(c) A party resisting recognition of a foreign-country judgment has the burden of establishing that a ground for nonrecognition stated in subsection (b) of this Code section exists.

Amended by 2016 Ga. Laws 625,§ 9, eff. 5/3/2016.

Amended by 2015 Ga. Laws 167,§ 2-1, eff. 7/1/2015.

Section 9-12-114 - Recognition of personal jurisdiction

(a) A foreign-country judgment shall not be refused recognition for lack of personal jurisdiction if:

(1) The defendant was served personally in the foreign country;

(2) The defendant voluntarily appeared in the proceedings other than for the purpose of protecting property seized or threatened with seizure in the proceedings or of contesting the jurisdiction of the court over the defendant;

(3) Prior to the commencement of the proceedings, the defendant had agreed to submit to the jurisdiction of the foreign court, with respect to the subject matter involved;

(4) The defendant was domiciled in the foreign country when the proceedings were instituted or was a corporation or other form of business organization that had its principal place of business in or was organized under the laws of the foreign country;

(5) The defendant had a business office in the foreign country and the proceedings in the foreign court involved a cause of action arising out of business done by the defendant through that office in the foreign country; or

(6) The defendant operated a motor vehicle or airplane in the foreign country and the proceedings involved a cause of action arising out of such operation.

(b) The courts of this state may recognize other bases of personal jurisdiction other than those listed in subsection (a) of this Code section.

Amended by 2015 Ga. Laws 167,§ 2-1, eff. 7/1/2015.

Section 9-12-115 - Procedure for recognition

(a) If recognition of a foreign-country judgment is sought as an original matter, the issue of recognition shall be raised by filing an action seeking recognition of such foreign-country judgment.

(b) If recognition of a foreign-country judgment is sought in a pending action, the issue of recognition may be raised by counterclaim, cross-claim, or third-party claim.

(c) Chapter 11 of this title shall apply to any claim, counterclaim, cross-claim, or third-party claim for recognition of a foreign-country judgment.

Amended by 2015 Ga. Laws 167,§ 2-1, eff. 7/1/2015.

Section 9-12-116 - Effect of recognition of foreign-country judgments

If the court in a proceeding under Code Section 9-12-115 finds that the foreign-country judgment is entitled to recognition under this article then, to the extent that the foreign-country judgment grants or denies recovery of a sum of money, the foreign-country judgment is:

(1) Conclusive between the parties to the same extent as the judgment of a sister state entitled to full faith and credit in this state would be conclusive; and

(2) Enforceable in the same manner and to the same extent as a judgment rendered in this state.

Amended by 2015 Ga. Laws 167,§ 2-1, eff. 7/1/2015.

Section 9-12-117 - Stay pending appeal

If a party establishes that an appeal from a foreign-country judgment is pending or will be taken, the court may stay the proceedings with regard to the foreign-country judgment until the time for appeal expires or the appellant has had sufficient time to prosecute the appeal and has failed to do so.

Amended by 2015 Ga. Laws 167,§ 2-1, eff. 7/1/2015.

Section 9-12-118 - Uniform construction

In applying and construing this article, consideration shall be given to the need to promote uniformity of the law with respect to its subject matter among states that enact the "Uniform Foreign-Country Money Judgments Recognition Act."

Amended by 2015 Ga. Laws 167,§ 2-1, eff. 7/1/2015.

Section 9-12-119 - Situations not covered by article

This article does not prevent the recognition under principles of comity or otherwise of a foreign-country judgment not within the scope of this article.

Amended by 2015 Ga. Laws 167,§ 2-1, eff. 7/1/2015.

Article 6 - ENFORCEMENT OF FOREIGN JUDGMENTS

Section 9-12-130 - Short title

This article may be cited as the "Uniform Enforcement of Foreign Judgments Law."

Section 9-12-131 - "Foreign judgment" defined

As used in this article, the term "foreign judgment" means a judgment, decree, or order of a court of the United States or of any other court that is entitled to full faith and credit in this state.

Section 9-12-132 - Filing of judgment; force and effect following filing

A copy of any foreign judgment authenticated in accordance with an act of Congress or statutes of this state may be filed in the office of the clerk of any court of competent jurisdiction of this state. The clerk shall treat the foreign judgment in the same manner as a judgment of the court in which the foreign judgment is filed. A filed foreign judgment has the same effect and is subject to the same procedures, defenses, and proceedings for reopening, vacating, staying, enforcing, or satisfying as a judgment of the court in which it is filed and may be enforced or satisfied in like manner.

Section 9-12-133 - Filing of foreign judgment; notice to judgment debtor; Code Section 9-11-4 inapplicable to article

(a) At the time a foreign judgment is filed, the judgment creditor or the judgment creditor's attorney shall make and file with the clerk of the court an affidavit showing the name and last known post office address of the judgment debtor and the judgment creditor.

(b) The clerk shall promptly mail notice of the filing of the foreign judgment to the judgment debtor at the address given and shall note the mailing in the docket. The notice must include the name and post office address of the judgment creditor and, if the judgment creditor has an attorney in this state, the attorney's name and address. The judgment creditor may mail a notice of the filing of the judgment to the judgment debtor and may file proof of mailing with the clerk. Lack of mailing notice of filing by the clerk does not affect the enforcement proceedings if proof of mailing by the judgment creditor has been filed.

(c) The provisions of Code Section 9-11-4 shall not apply to this article.

(d) The provisions of subsections (a) and (b) of this Code section shall not apply to the registration of a guardianship order or conservatorship order from another state under Article 4 of Chapter 11 of Title 29.

Amended by 2019 Ga. Laws 233,§ 35, eff. 1/1/2020.

Amended by 2015 Ga. Laws 167,§ 5-1, eff. 7/1/2015.

Section 9-12-134 - Appeal or stay of foreign judgment; security for satisfaction

(a) If the judgment debtor shows the court that an appeal from the foreign judgment is pending or will be taken or that a stay of execution has been granted and proves that the judgment debtor has furnished the security for the satisfaction of the judgment required by the state in which it was rendered, the court shall stay enforcement of the foreign judgment until the appeal is concluded, the time for appeal expires, or the stay of execution expires or is vacated.

(b) If the judgment debtor shows the court any ground on which enforcement of a judgment of the court of this state would be stayed, including the ground that an appeal from the foreign judgment is pending or will be taken or that the time for taking such an appeal has not yet expired, the court shall stay enforcement of the foreign judgment for an appropriate period until all available appeals are concluded or the time for taking all appeals has expired and require the same security for satisfaction of the judgment that is required in this state, subject to the provisions of subsections (b) and (f) of Code Section 5-6-46.

(c) With respect to a guardianship order or conservatorship order from another state registered and recorded under Article 4 of Chapter 11 of Title 29, nothing in subsection (a) or (b) of this Code section shall prevent an appropriate court from taking any action permitted by subsection (d) of Code Section 29-4-70, subsection (d) of Code Section 29-5-110, or Articles 1 and 2 of Chapter 11 of Title 29.

Amended by 2019 Ga. Laws 233,§ 36, eff. 1/1/2020.

Amended by 2004 Ga. Laws 778, § 2, eff. 5/19/2004.

Section 9-12-135 - Clerk's fees

(a) A person filing a foreign judgment shall pay to the clerk of court the same sums as in civil cases in superior court as provided in Code Section 15-6-77; provided, however, that a person registering a guardianship order or conservatorship order from another state under Article 4 of Chapter 11 of Title 29 shall pay to the probate court in which such order is registered the same sums as in adult guardianship matters in probate court as provided in paragraph (1) of subsection (g) of Code Section 15-9-60.

(b) Fees for other enforcement proceedings shall be as otherwise provided by law.

Amended by 2019 Ga. Laws 233,§ 37, eff. 1/1/2020.

Section 9-12-136 - Actions to enforce judgments preserved

The judgment creditor retains the right to bring an action to enforce a judgment instead of proceeding under this article.

Section 9-12-137 - Uniform construction

This article shall be interpreted and construed to achieve its general purposes to make the law of those states which enact it uniform.

Section 9-12-138 - Judgments to which article applies

This article shall apply to foreign judgments of other states only if those states have adopted the "Uniform Enforcement of Foreign Judgments Act" in substantially the same form as this article.

Chapter 13 - EXECUTIONS AND JUDICIAL SALES

Article 1 - GENERAL PROVISIONS

Section 9-13-1 - Entry and signing of judgment prerequisite to execution

No execution shall issue until judgment is entered and signed by the party in whose favor verdict was rendered or by his attorney, or by the presiding judge or justice.

Section 9-13-2 - Execution suspended by appeal

If execution is issued before the expiration of the time allowed for entering an appeal, the execution will be suspended on the entering of an appeal by either party.

Section 9-13-3 - Execution to follow judgment

Every execution shall follow the judgment upon which it issued and shall describe the parties thereto as described in the judgment.

Section 9-13-4 - Judge may frame executions

The judge of any superior court may frame and cause to be issued by the clerk thereof any writ of execution to carry into effect any lawful judgment or decree rendered in his court.

Section 9-13-5 - Amendment of execution - To conform to judgment or time of return

A writ of fieri facias may be amended so as to conform to the judgment upon which it issued and to the time of its return; and such amendments shall in no manner affect the validity of the writ of fieri facias, nor shall the levy of the writ fall or be in any manner invalidated thereby.

Section 9-13-6 - Amendment of execution - To conform to amended judgment

Where a judgment has been amended by order of the court in conformity to the verdict upon which it is predicated and execution has previously issued thereon, the clerk of the court in which the judgment was rendered shall have power to amend the execution at any time so as to make it conform to the amended judgment; and such amendment shall not cause any levy on the execution to fall.

Section 9-13-7 - Amendment of execution - To correct mistake in issuance; alias execution

(a) When the clerk of any court has made any mistake in issuing an execution, the clerk or any of his successors in office may correct the mistake by amending the execution and shall note and certify on the execution the fact that the amendment was made by him.

(b) Alternatively, the clerk may issue an alias execution to be signed and dated by him at the time it is issued instead of the execution in which the mistake was made. The clerk shall note the fact of the issuing of the alias on the original, which original shall remain on file in his office, and shall likewise make a memorandum thereof on the execution docket; he shall also transcribe upon the alias all the entries and credits from the original. No order of court shall be necessary in the cases contemplated by this Code section.

Section 9-13-8 - Issuance of alias execution to replace lost original

(a) When an execution which was regularly issued from a court is lost or destroyed, the judge or justice of the court from which the same was issued may at any time, upon proper application and proof of the facts by the affidavit of the applicant, his agent, or his attorney or by any other satisfactory proof, grant an order for the issuing of an alias execution in lieu of the lost original execution. The alias execution shall have all the legal force and effect of the lost or destroyed original execution.

(b) When an execution which was regularly issued by an officer of the state as authorized by law is lost or destroyed, the state officer or the successor to the state officer by whom the same was issued may at any time issue an alias execution in lieu of the lost original execution. The alias execution shall be dated the same date as the original execution and the officer shall endorse the word "alias" on the alias execution. The alias execution shall have all the legal force and effect of the lost or destroyed original execution.

(c) When an execution which was regularly issued by an officer of a county or local government as authorized by law is lost or destroyed, the judge of the probate court of the county in which the original execution was issued may issue an alias execution upon the filing by the party having the right to control the original execution of a statement under oath of the loss or destruction of such original execution. The judge shall endorse the word "alias" on the alias execution. The alias execution shall have all the legal force and effect of the lost or destroyed original execution.

Section 9-13-9 - When execution returnable

All executions, except as otherwise provided by this Code, shall be made returnable to the next term of the court from which they issued.

Section 9-13-10 - Issuance of execution; to whom directed; on what property levied

Except as otherwise provided by law, executions shall be issued by the clerk of the court in which judgment is obtained, shall bear teste in the name of the judge of such court, shall bear date from the time of their issuing, shall be directed "To all and singular the sheriffs of this state and their lawful deputies," and may be levied on all the estate of the defendant, both real and personal, which is subject to levy and sale.

Section 9-13-11 - Direction, levy, service, and return of execution when sheriff a party

All executions, orders, decrees, attachments for contempt, and final process issued by the clerks of the courts in favor of or against any sheriff shall be directed to the coroner of the county in which the sheriff resides and to all and singular the sheriffs of the state, except the sheriff of the county in which the interested sheriff resides, and may be levied, served, and returned by the coroner, other sheriff, or constable of the county at the option of the plaintiff or the party seeking the remedy.

Section 9-13-12 - Entry of levy on process

The officer making a levy shall enter the same on the process by virtue of which levy is made and in the entry shall plainly describe the property levied on and the amount of the interest of defendant therein.

Section 9-13-13 - Written notice of levy on land

(a) In all cases of levying on land, written notice of the levy must be given personally or delivered by certified mail or statutory overnight delivery to the tenant in possession and to the defendant if not in possession.

(b) The officer levying on land under an execution, within five days thereafter, shall leave a written notice of the levy with the tenant in possession of the land, if any; and, if the defendant is not in possession, the officer shall also leave a written notice with the defendant if he is in the county or shall transmit the notice by mail to the defendant within the time aforesaid.

Section 9-13-14 - Bonds taken by executing officers valid; rights of plaintiffs not affected

(a) All bonds taken by sheriffs or other executing officers from defendants in execution for the delivery of property, on the day of sale or any other time, which they may have levied on by virtue of any fi. fa. or other legal process from any court shall be good and valid in law and recoverable in any court having jurisdiction thereof.

(b) No bond taken in conformity with subsection (a) of this Code section shall in any case prejudice or affect the rights of the plaintiff in execution; the bond shall relate to and have effect solely between the officer to whom it is given and the defendant in execution. The officer shall in no case excuse himself for not having made the money on an execution by having taken the bond but shall be liable to be ruled as prescribed by law.

Section 9-13-15 - Measure of damages on forthcoming bond

Whenever personal property is levied upon under any judicial process from the courts of this state and a forthcoming bond is given for the same, the measure of damages to be recovered upon the bond shall be the value of the property at the time of its delivery under the bond, with interest thereon; and, if the property deteriorates in value by reason of being used by the person giving the bond or otherwise and is then delivered to the officer making the seizure, the officer or the plaintiff in execution may recover on the bond the difference between the value at the time of the delivery of the property under the bond and its value when turned over to the officer making the levy, with interest thereon. The amount of damages shall in no case exceed the amount due on the execution levied.

Section 9-13-16 - Penalty for fraudulent levy

Any person who fraudulently causes any process, attachment, distress, or execution to be levied on any estrayed animal, lot of land, or other property, knowing that the same is not subject to the process or writ, shall, for the first offense, be guilty of a misdemeanor. For any subsequent conviction, the person shall be sentenced to confinement for not less than two nor more than four years.

Article 2 - PARTIES IN EXECUTION

Section 9-13-30 - Execution against sureties and endorsers

When, in a judgment against sureties or endorsers on a draft, promissory note, or other instrument in writing, the plaintiff or his attorney has designated and identified the relation of the parties under the contract on which the judgment was rendered, execution shall issue accordingly.

Section 9-13-31 - Execution against principal and his surety on appeal

In all cases of appeal where security has been given and judgment has been entered against the principal and surety, jointly and severally, execution shall issue accordingly and shall proceed against either or both at the option of the plaintiff until his debt is satisfied.

Section 9-13-32 - Execution following death of defendant

On the death of a defendant after final judgment when no execution has been issued prior to such death, execution may issue as though the death had not taken place.

Section 9-13-33 - Executions using partnership name valid

Executions issued in favor of or against partners, where the partnership style is used therein instead of the individual names of the persons composing the firm, shall be valid.

Section 9-13-34 - Right to transfer execution; status of transferee

Any plaintiff in judgment or transferee may in good faith and for a valuable consideration transfer any execution to a third person. In all cases the transferee of any execution shall have the same rights and shall be subject to the same equities and the same defenses as was the original plaintiff in judgment.

Section 9-13-35 - Effect of transfer by attorney; ratification

The transfer of an execution by the attorney of record shall be good to pass the title thereto as against every person except the plaintiff in execution or his assignee without notice. Ratification by the plaintiff shall estop him also from denying the transfer. Receipt of the money from the transfer shall be such a ratification.

Section 9-13-36 - Transfer of execution upon payment; status of transferee; recording necessary to preserve lien; exception for tax executions

(a) Except as otherwise provided for in subsection (b) of this Code section, whenever any person other than the person against whom the same has issued pays any execution, issued without the judgment of a court, under any law, the officer whose duty it is to enforce the execution, upon the request of the party paying the same, shall transfer the execution to the party. The transferee shall have the same rights as to enforcing the execution and priority of payment as might have been exercised or claimed before the transfer, provided that the transferee shall have the execution entered on the general execution docket of the superior court of the county in which the same was issued and, if the person against whom the same was issued resides in a different county, also in the county of such person's residence within 30 days from the transfer; in default thereof the execution shall lose its lien upon any property which has been transferred bona fide and for a valuable consideration before the recordation and without notice of the existence of the execution.

(b) This Code section shall not be applicable to tax executions. Tax executions shall be governed exclusively by Chapters 3 and 4 of Title 48.

Amended by 2006 Ga. Laws 759,§ 1, eff. 7/1/2006.

Article 3 - PROPERTY AGAINST WHICH EXECUTION LEVIED

Section 9-13-50 - Designation by defendant of property to be levied on; when sheriff bound thereby

(a) The defendant in execution shall be at liberty to point out what part of his property he may think proper to be levied on, which property the sheriff or other officer shall be bound to take and sell first if the same is, in the opinion of the levying officer, sufficient to satisfy the judgment and costs.

(b) When a defendant in execution shall point out property on which to levy the execution which is in the possession of a person not a party to the judgment from which the execution issued, the sheriff or other officer shall not levy thereon but shall proceed to levy on such property as may be found in the possession of the defendant.

Section 9-13-51 - Sale of property subject to lien; order of application to payment

Where property is subject to a lien and part of it is sold by the debtor, the part remaining shall be first applied to the payment of the lien. If the property subject to the lien is sold in several parcels at different times, the parcels shall be charged in the inverse order of their alienation.

Section 9-13-52 - When sheriff may levy on and sell land outside county

A sheriff or other levying officer shall not sell land outside the county in which he is sheriff or such officer except when the defendant in execution owns a tract or tracts of land divided by the line of the county of his residence, in which case the land may be sold in the county of his residence; if such tract of land is in a county other than that of the defendant's residence, it may be levied on and sold in either county.

Section 9-13-53 - When constable may levy on land; sale by sheriff

No constable, except as provided by this Code, shall be authorized to levy on any real estate unless there is no personal property to be found sufficient to satisfy the debt or unless the real estate, being in the possession of the defendant, was pointed out by the defendant. In such event the constable is authorized to levy on such real estate, if in his county, and to deliver over the execution to the sheriff of the county a return of the property levied upon; and the sheriff shall proceed to advertise and sell the same as in case of levies made by himself.

Section 9-13-54 - When growing crop levied on and sold

No sheriff or other officer shall levy on any growing crop of corn, wheat, oats, rye, rice, cotton, potatoes, or any other crop usually raised or cultivated by planters or farmers nor sell the same until the crop has matured and is fit to be gathered. However, this Code section shall not prevent any levying officer from levying on and selling crops in cases where the defendant in execution absconds or removes himself from the county or state, or from selling growing crops with the land.

Section 9-13-55 - Seizure prerequisite to sale of personalty

To authorize a sale of personal property there shall be an actual or constructive seizure.

Section 9-13-56 - Future interests in personalty

A future interest in personalty may not be seized and sold but the lien of judgments shall attach thereto so as to prevent alienation before the right to present possession accrues.

Section 9-13-57 - Choses in action

Choses in action are not liable to be seized and sold under execution, unless made so specially by statute.

Section 9-13-58 - Corporation's disclosure of worth of defendant's shares mandated; refusal treated as contempt

Upon demand by any sheriff, constable, or other levying officer having in his hands any execution against any person who is the owner of any shares of stock of a bank or corporation upon the president, superintendent, manager, or other officer having access to the books of the bank or corporation, the president, superintendent, manager, or other officer aforesaid shall disclose to the levying officer the number of shares and the par value thereof owned by the defendant in execution and, on refusal to do so, shall be considered in contempt of court and punished accordingly.

Section 9-13-59 - What property liable to execution in action against joint contractors or partners when not all served

Where, in an action against two or more joint contractors, joint and several contractors, or partners, service is perfected on only part of the contractors or partners and the officer serving the writ returns that the others are not to be found, the judgment obtained shall bind, and execution may be levied on, the joint or partnership property as well as the individual property, real and personal, of the defendant or defendants who have been served with a copy of the process. However, the judgment shall not bind nor shall execution be levied on the individual property of the defendant or defendants not served with process.

Section 9-13-60 - Taking up of debt to give defendant legal title to property; notice of levy and sale; application of proceeds

(a) Where any person other than the vendor or other than the holder or assignee of the purchase money or secured debt has a judgment against a defendant in execution who does not hold legal title to property but has an interest or equity therein, such plaintiff in execution may take up the debt necessary to be paid by the defendant in order to give the defendant legal title to the property by paying the debt with interest to date if due and interest to maturity if not due; and thereupon a conveyance to the defendant in execution or, if he is dead, to his executor or administrator shall be made by the vendor or holder of title given to secure the debt or, if dead, by the executor or administrator thereof. When the conveyance has been filed and recorded, the property may be levied on and sold as property of the defendant.

(b) In all cases provided for in subsection (a) of this Code section, notice of the levy and time of sale shall be given by the levying officer to the vendor or holder of the title given to secure the debt, if known, and also to the defendant in execution and, in case of death, to their legal representatives. Depositing a properly addressed and stamped letter into the United States mail shall be deemed sufficient notice under this subsection.

(c) The proceeds of the sale shall be applied first to the payment of liens superior to the claims taken up by the plaintiff in execution, next to the payment of principal advanced by the plaintiff in execution to put title in defendant, with interest to date of sale, and the balance to the execution under which the property was sold, and to other liens according to priority, to be determined as provided by law.

Article 4 - SATISFACTION OR DISCHARGE OF JUDGMENT AND EXECUTION

Section 9-13-70 - Suspension of execution for 60 days pending payment; bond

(a) In all cases in which a verdict or judgment is rendered, the party against whom the same is entered may, either in open court or in the clerk's office, within four days after the adjournment of court, enter into bond with good and sufficient security for the payment of the verdict or judgment and costs within 60 days.

(b) When bond and security have been given as provided in this Code section, the verdict and judgment, or the execution thereon, shall be suspended for the 60 days. If the party fails to pay the verdict or judgment within that time, execution shall issue against the party and his security without further proceedings thereon.

Section 9-13-71 - Sufficient levy on personalty prima-facie satisfaction; effect of dismissal

A levy upon personal property sufficient to pay the debt, which levy is unaccounted for, shall be prima-facie evidence of satisfaction to the extent of the value of the property. The unexplained dismissal of the levy shall be an abandonment of the lien so far as third persons are concerned.

Section 9-13-72 - Release of property subject to execution

If the plaintiff in execution, for a valuable consideration, releases property which is subject to execution, the release shall be a satisfaction of the execution to the extent of the value of the property so released insofar as purchasers and creditors are concerned. However, nothing in this Code section shall apply to any such release made by the transferee of any execution issued for taxes due the state or any county or municipality therein or of any execution issued by any municipality on account of assessments made against real estate for street or other improvements. In all such cases the execution shall be discharged or satisfied only to the extent of the amount of taxes or other assessments owing by the parcel released.

Section 9-13-73 - Application of fund to younger lien with senior lienholder's consent

If an execution creditor having the older lien on a fund in the hands of the sheriff or other officer allows the fund by his consent to be applied to a younger writ of execution, it shall be considered an extinguishment pro tanto of the creditor's lien insofar as third persons may be concerned.

Section 9-13-74 - Release by agreement

An agreement for a valuable consideration never to enforce a judgment or execution shall release the judgment or execution.

Section 9-13-75 - Setoff of judgments; collection of balance

One judgment may be set off against another, on motion, whether in the hands of an original party or an assignee. The balance on the larger is collectable under execution. The rights of an assignee shall not be interfered with if bona fide and for value.

Section 9-13-76 - Execution by defendant after setoff

In all cases of mutual debts and setoffs where the jury finds a balance for the defendant, the defendant may enter judgment for the amount and take out execution in the manner as plaintiffs may do by this Code, provided that the defendant at the time of filing his answer files therewith a true copy or copies of the subject matter of such setoffs.

Section 9-13-77 - Control of execution after payment - By security

The security paying off an execution shall have control thereof.

Section 9-13-78 - Control of execution after payment - By joint debtor

When judgments have been obtained against several persons and one of them has paid more than his just proportion of the same, he may have full power to control and use the execution as securities in execution control the same against principals or cosureties by having this payment entered on the execution issued to enforce the judgment, and he shall not be compelled to bring an action against the codebtors for the excess of payment on the judgment.

Section 9-13-79 - Partial payments to be entered

When a payment on an execution is made which does not entirely satisfy the judgment upon which the execution has been issued, the plaintiff in execution or his attorney shall authorize the clerk to enter the amount of the payments upon the execution.

Section 9-13-80 - Execution to be canceled when satisfied; private right of action; damages

(a) Upon the satisfaction of the entire debt upon which an execution has been issued, the plaintiff in execution or his or her attorney shall timely direct the clerk to cancel the execution and mark the judgment satisfied. Such direction shall be delivered to the clerk not later than 30 days following the date upon which the execution was fully satisfied.

(b)

(1) A private right of action shall be granted to a judgment debtor upon the failure of such plaintiff or counsel to comply with the provisions of subsection (a) of this Code section.

(2) Failure to direct cancellation and satisfaction within 60 days after satisfaction of the entire debt shall be prima-facie evidence of untimeliness.

(3) Recovery may be had by way of motion in the action precipitating the judgment and execution or by separate action in any court of competent jurisdiction.

(4) Damages shall be presumed in the amount of $100.00 and the court may award reasonable attorney's fees. Actual damages may be recovered, but in no event shall recovery exceed $500.00; provided, however, the court may also award reasonable attorney's fees.

(c) In order to authorize the clerk of superior court to make an entry of satisfaction with respect to an execution on the general execution docket, there shall be presented for filing on the general execution docket:

(1) A satisfaction upon the original execution or alias execution itself;

(2) A satisfaction as provided in subsection (d) of this Code section; or

(3) A satisfaction as provided in subsection (e) of this Code section.Any clerk of superior court who cancels of record any execution in the manner authorized in this subsection shall be immune from any civil liability, either in such clerk's official capacity or personally, for so canceling of record such security deed.

(d) Proof of satisfaction of an execution, the original of which has been lost, stolen, or otherwise mislaid, may be made based upon an affidavit executed by the plaintiff in execution or owner or holder of record of such execution and who so swears in such affidavit, which affidavit shall be recorded in the execution docket and shall be in the following form:County, Georgia

Affidavit for Satisfaction of Execution

The original execution having been lost or destroyed and the indebtedness, penalties, and interest referred to in that certain writ of fi. fa. styled v. , dated , and of record in General Execution Docket Book , Page , in the office of the clerk of the Superior Court of County, Georgia, having been satisfied in full and the undersigned being the present owner of such writ of fi. fa. by virtue of being the plaintiff in fi. fa. or the heir, assign, transferee, or devisee of the original plaintiff in

fi. fa., the clerk of such superior court is authorized and directed to make an entry of satisfaction with respect to such writ of fi. fa.

In witness whereof, the undersigned has set his or her hand and seal, this day of , .

(SEAL)

Signature

Signed, sealed, and

delivered on the

date above shown

Notary Public

(SEAL)

My commission expires: .

(e) In the event that a plaintiff in execution or any person that owns or holds an execution has failed to properly transmit a legally sufficient satisfaction or cancellation to authorize and direct the clerk or clerks to cancel the execution of record within 60 days after a written notice mailed to such plaintiff in execution or owner or holder of record by registered or certified mail or statutory overnight delivery, return receipt requested, the clerk or clerks are authorized and directed to cancel the execution upon recording an affidavit by the attorney for the judgment debtor against whom the execution was issued or any attorney who has caused the indebtedness and other obligations under the execution to be paid in full or any attorney who has actual knowledge that the indebtedness has been paid in full. The notice shall be mailed to the plaintiff in execution or owner or holder of record, shall identify the execution, and shall include a recital or explanation of this subsection. The affidavit shall include a recital of actions taken to comply with this subsection. Such affidavit shall include as attachments the following items:

(1) A written verification which was given at the time of payment by the plaintiff in execution or owner or holder of record of the amount necessary to pay off such obligations; and

(2) Any one of the following:

(A) Copies of the front and back of a canceled check to the plaintiff in execution or owner or holder of record showing payment of such obligations;

(B) Confirmation of a wire transfer to the owner or holder of record showing payment of such obligations; or

(C) A bank receipt showing payment to the plaintiff in execution or owner or holder of record of such obligations.

(f) Any person who files an affidavit in accordance with subsection (d) or (e) of this Code section which affidavit is fraudulent shall be guilty of a felony and shall be punished by imprisonment for not less than one year nor more than three years or by a fine of not less than $1,000.00 nor more than $5,000.00, or both.

Amended by 2004 Ga. Laws 494, § 1, eff. 7/1/2004.

Article 5 - CLAIMS

Section 9-13-90 - Claims authorized; to be on oath

When any sheriff or other officer shall levy an execution or other process on property claimed by a third person not a party to the execution, the person, his agent, or his attorney may make oath claiming the property.

Section 9-13-91 - Bond and security for damages; how damages determined

The person claiming the property levied on, or his agent or attorney, shall give bond to the sheriff or other levying officer, with good and sufficient security in a sum not larger than double the amount of the execution levied, made payable to the plaintiff in execution. Where the property levied on is of less value than the execution, the amount of the bond shall be double the value of the property levied upon, at a reasonable valuation to be judged by the levying officer, conditioned to pay the plaintiff in execution all damages which the jury on the trial of the claim may assess against the person claiming the property in case it appears that the claim was made for the purpose of delay only.

Section 9-13-92 - Affidavit of indigence

In all claim cases where claimants are unable to give bond and security as required in this article, the claimants may file, in addition to the oath required in Code Section 9-13-90, an affidavit as follows:

"I, A.B., do swear that I do not interpose this claim for delay only; that I bona fide claim the right and title to the same; that I am advised and believe that the claim will be sustained; and that because of my indigence I am unable to give bond and security as required by law."

When the affidavit has been made and delivered to the levying officer, it shall suspend the sale in the same manner as if bond and security had been given.

Section 9-13-93 - Postponement of sale

When affidavit and bond have been made and delivered as required in Code Sections 9-13-90 and 9-13-91, it shall be the duty of the sheriff or other levying officer to postpone the sale of the property until otherwise ordered.

Section 9-13-94 - Forthcoming bond for possession of property; amount and condition; not authorized for realty; when and where recoverable

(a) In all cases where a levy is made upon property that is claimed by a third person and the person desires the possession thereof, it shall be the duty of the sheriff or other levying officer to take bond, made payable to the sheriff with good security for a sum equal to double the value of the property levied on to be estimated by the levying officer, for the delivery of the property at the time and place of sale, provided the property so levied upon shall be found subject to the execution. However, it shall not be lawful to require or take a forthcoming bond for real estate.

(b) When bond and security have been given as provided in this Code section, it shall be the duty of the sheriff or other levying officer to leave the property in the possession of the claimant. In the event that the claimant or his security fails to deliver the property after it has been found to be subject to execution, the bond shall be made recoverable in any court having cognizance of the same.

Section 9-13-95 - Execution of affidavit and bond by partner or joint owner

One of several partners or persons jointly interested may make the affidavit and execute the bond in the name of the firm or persons jointly interested, who shall be bound thereby as though each individual had signed it himself.

Section 9-13-96 - When plaintiff in execution may give forthcoming bond

If the claimant to personal property levied on is unable to give a forthcoming bond, it shall be the privilege of the plaintiff in execution to give the bond, to be approved by the levying officer, and, upon the bond being given and approved, it shall be the duty of the levying officer to deliver the property to the plaintiff. However, in no event shall the plaintiff be allowed any compensation for keeping the property.

Section 9-13-97 - Sale of property on claimants' application; order; advertisement; disposition of proceeds

In the event the claimant is unable, and the plaintiff neglects or refuses, to give bond for the forthcoming of the property, the claimant may apply to the judge of the probate court and procure an order for the sale of the same; and, when the order has been granted, it shall be the duty of the levying officer to advertise the time and place of sale at not less than three public places, to be selected in different parts of the county in which the sale is to take place, for 15 days immediately preceding the time of sale. On the day of sale, between the hours of 10:00 A.M. and 4:00 P.M., the property shall be sold; and the money arising from the sale shall remain in the hands of the levying officer subject to the order of court upon the final hearing of the claim.

Section 9-13-98 - When and where claim, levy, and execution to be returned

When an execution issued from a court is levied upon personal property and claimed by a person not a party to the execution, it shall be the duty of the levying officer to return the same, together with the execution, to the next term of the court from which the execution issued. Where an execution is levied upon real property and the same is claimed in the manner aforesaid, it shall be the duty of the officer making the levy to return the same, together with the execution and claim, to the next term of the superior court of the county in which the land so levied upon lies.

Section 9-13-99 - Return of claim or illegality against execution from probate court

Whenever an execution issued from a probate court is levied upon personal property and a claim to the property or an affidavit of illegality is interposed, it shall be the duty of the sheriff or other levying officer to return the same, together with the execution and all the other papers, to the next term of the superior court of the county from which the execution was issued. If the levy has been made upon realty, the execution, with the claim or illegality papers, shall be returned by the levying officer to the next term of the superior court of the county where the land lies and the issue shall be tried as is provided for the trial of claim and illegality cases.

Section 9-13-100 - Claim to be tried by jury

The court to which a claim is returned shall cause the right of property to be decided by a jury at the first term thereof, unless continued in the same manner as other cases.

Section 9-13-101 - Additional oath of jurors; damages and costs when claim made for delay

Every juror on the trial of the claim of property either real or personal shall be sworn, in addition to the oath usually administered, to give such damages as may seem reasonable and just, in an amount not less than 10 percent of the amount due upon the execution when the value of the property in dispute exceeds the amount of the execution, or of the value of the property when the value of the property is less than the execution levied, to the plaintiff against the claimant in case it shall be shown that the claim was made for delay only. The jury may give a verdict in the manner aforesaid and judgment may be entered thereon against the claimant and his security for the damages so assessed and the costs of the trial.

Section 9-13-102 - Burden of proof

Upon the trial of all claims provided for in this article, the burden of proof shall lie upon the plaintiff in execution in all cases where the property levied on is not in possession of the defendant in execution at the time of the levy.

Section 9-13-103 - Withdrawal or discontinuance of claim limited

Whenever a claim of property is made in terms of this article and is returned to the proper court by the sheriff or other levying officer, the claimant shall not be permitted to withdraw or discontinue his claim more than once without the consent of the plaintiff in execution or some person duly authorized to represent the plaintiff; rather, the court shall proceed to the trial of the claim of the property and it shall be the duty of the jury to assess damages accordingly.

Section 9-13-104 - Trial of damage issue where claim dismissed or withdrawn

Whenever a claim is dismissed for insufficiency or is withdrawn, the plaintiff in execution may have a case made up and submitted to the jury charging that the claim was filed for the purpose of delay. Upon proof of the same, defendant and claimant having the same power to resist the case as in claim cases where damages are claimed, the jury, under instructions from the court, may give damages as in cases where the claim is not withdrawn but is submitted for trial to the jury. The cases so submitted shall be tried at the time of the disposal of the claim if the parties are ready, but continuances shall be granted as in other cases.

Section 9-13-105 - How damages assessed

Upon the trial of claims to property which may be pending in the court, when damages are found by the jury, the damages shall be assessed upon the whole amount then due upon the execution when the value of the property in dispute exceeds the amount of the execution and upon the value of the property when the value of the property is less than the execution levied.

Section 9-13-106 - Withdrawal of original execution and filing of copy

The plaintiff in execution in all claim cases shall have the right to withdraw the original execution from the files of the court by making application therefor, in person or by attorney, to the clerk of the court if there is a clerk or to the court if there is no clerk. Upon application being made, the clerk or court shall make a true copy of the execution with all the entries thereon and shall certify the same to be true, which certified copy shall be filed with the claim papers in lieu of the original execution; and an entry of the filing shall be made thereon.

Article 6 - ILLEGALITY

Section 9-13-120 - Affidavit of illegality - When authorized; bond and security

When an execution against the property of any person issues illegally, or is proceeding illegally, and the execution is levied on such property, the person may make oath in writing, stating the cause of the illegality, and deliver the same to the sheriff or other executing officer together with bond and good security for the forthcoming of the property, as provided by this article.

Section 9-13-121 - Affidavit of illegality - To show lack of service; not available to go behind judgment

If the defendant was not served and did not appear, he may take advantage of the defect by affidavit of illegality. However, if he has had his day in court, he may not go behind the judgment by an affidavit of illegality.

Section 9-13-122 - Affidavit of illegality - Not available for excessive levy generally

An affidavit of illegality shall not be a remedy for an excessive levy except where authorized by statute.

Section 9-13-123 - Affidavit of illegality - By whom filed

An affidavit of illegality may be filed by an attorney in fact or by an executor, administrator, or other trustee.

Section 9-13-124 - Affidavit of illegality - When received

No affidavit of illegality shall be received by any sheriff or other executing officer until a levy has been made.

Section 9-13-125 - Affidavit of illegality - When and how amendable

Affidavits of illegality are, upon motion and leave of court, amendable instanter by the insertion of new and independent grounds, provided that the defendant shall swear that he did not know of such grounds when the original affidavit was filed.

Section 9-13-126 - Amount and condition of forthcoming bond

When an execution is levied on personal property and an affidavit of illegality is filed thereto and the party filing the illegality desires to take or keep possession of the property, he shall deliver to the sheriff or other levying officer a bond payable to the levying officer, with good security in a sum equal to double the value of the property so levied upon, to be judged of by the levying officer, conditioned for the delivery of the property levied upon at the time and place of sale in the event that the illegality is dismissed by the court or withdrawn, which bond shall be recoverable in any court having cognizance thereof.

Section 9-13-127 - Suspension of execution; return of execution, affidavit, and bond; determination by court; issue tried by jury

When levy has been made and affidavit and bond delivered to the levying officer, it shall be the duty of the officer to suspend further proceedings on the execution and to return the execution, affidavit, and bond to the next term of the court from which the execution issued. It shall be the duty of the court to make a determination thereon at the first term thereof unless the plaintiff or his attorney desires to controvert the facts contained in the affidavit, in which case an issue shall be joined and tried by a jury at the same term unless good cause is shown for a continuance.

Section 9-13-128 - Damages for delay; procedure following dismissal or withdrawal of illegality

Upon the trial of an issue formed on an affidavit of illegality, the jury trying the case shall have power to assess such damages as may seem reasonable and just, not exceeding 25 percent of the principal debt, where it is made to appear that the illegality was interposed for delay only. Whenever an illegality is dismissed for insufficiency or informality or is withdrawn, plaintiff in execution may proceed as is provided in cases where claims are dismissed or withdrawn.

Section 9-13-129 - Property subject to other executions; retention of sale proceeds to satisfy first execution; release of bond pro tanto

When an execution has been levied on property and an affidavit of illegality has been filed to stay proceedings thereon, the property so levied on shall be subject to levy and sale under other executions. The officer making the first levy shall claim, receive, hold, and retain the amount of the proceeds of the sale as the court deems sufficient to pay the execution first levied, including interest up to the time of the court at which the illegality shall be determined. Any bond given by the defendant on filing the affidavit shall be released and discharged so far as relates to the property sold.

Article 7 - JUDICIAL SALES

Part 1 - ADVERTISEMENT

Section 9-13-140 - How judicial sales advertised; description of property; advertisement and sale of livestock

(a) The sheriff, coroner, or other officer shall publish weekly for four weeks in the legal organ for the county, or if there is no newspaper designated as such, then in the nearest newspaper having the largest general circulation in such county, notice of all sales of land and other property executed by the officer. In the advertisement the officer shall give a full and complete description of the property to be sold, making known the names of the plaintiff, the defendant, and any person who may be in the possession of the property. In the case of real property, such advertisement shall include the legal description of such real property and may include the street address of such real property, if available, but provided that no foreclosure shall be invalidated by the failure to include a street address or by the insertion of an erroneous street address.

(b) However, horses, hogs, and cattle may be sold at any time by the consent of the defendant, in which case it shall be the duty of the officer to give the plaintiff ten days' notice thereof and also to advertise the same at three or more public places in the county where the property may be at least ten days before the sale.

Section 9-13-141 - Timing of advertisements

In all cases where the law requires citations, notices, or advertisements by probate court judges, clerks, sheriffs, county bailiffs, administrators, executors, guardians, trustees, or others to be published in a newspaper for 30 days or for four weeks or once a week for four weeks, it shall be sufficient and legal to publish the same once a week for four weeks, that is, one insertion each week for each of the four weeks, immediately preceding the term or day when the order is to be granted or the sale is to take place. The number of days between the date of the first publication and the term or day when the order is to be granted or the sale is to take place, whether more or less than 30 days, shall not in any manner invalidate or render irregular the notice, citation, advertisement, order, or sale.

Section 9-13-142 - Requirements for official organ of publication; designation where no journal or newspaper qualifies; how official organ changed; notice to Secretary of State

(a) No journal or newspaper published in this state shall be declared, made, or maintained as the official organ of any county for the publication of sheriff's sales, citations of probate court judges, or any other advertising commonly known in terms of "official or legal advertising" and required by law to be published in such county official newspaper unless the newspaper shall meet and maintain the following qualifications:

(1) "Newspaper" as used in this Code section means a printed product of multiple pages containing not greater than 75 percent advertising content in no more than one-half of its issues during the previous 12 months, excluding separate advertising supplements inserted into but separately identifiable from any regular issue or issues of the newspaper;

(2) The newspaper shall be published within the county and continuously at least weekly for a period of two years or is the direct successor of such a newspaper. Failure to publish for not more than two weeks in any calendar year shall not disqualify a newspaper otherwise qualified;

(3) For a period of two years prior to designation and thereafter, the newspaper shall have and maintain at least 75 percent paid circulation as established by an independent audit. Paid circulation shall not include newspapers that are distributed free or in connection with a service or promotion at no additional charge to the ultimate recipient. For circulation to be considered paid, the recipient of the newspaper or such recipient's employer or household must pay reasonable and adequate consideration for the newspaper. No rules of circulation of audit companies, the United States Postal Service, or accounting principles may be considered in determining paid circulation if they are inconsistent with the provisions of this subsection;

(4) Based on the published results of the 1990 United States decennial census or any future such census, the newspaper shall have and maintain at least the following paid circulation within the county for which it is designated as the legal organ newspaper:

    (A) Five hundred copies per issue in counties having a population of less than 20,000;

    (B) Seven hundred fifty copies per issue in counties having a population of at least 20,000 but less than 100,000; or

    (C) One thousand five hundred copies per issue in counties having a population of 100,000 or greater; and

(5) For purposes of this Code section, paid circulation shall include home or mail delivery subscription sales, counter, vendor and newsrack sales, and sales to independent newspaper contract carriers for resale. Paid circulation shall not include multiple copies purchased by one entity unless the multiple copies are purchased for and distributed to the purchaser's officers, employees, or agents, or within the purchaser's household.

(b) However, in counties where no journal or newspaper meets the qualifications set forth in subsection (a) of this Code section, the official organ may be designated by the judge of the probate court, the sheriff, and the clerk of the superior court, a majority of these officers governing from among newspapers otherwise qualified to be a legal organ that meet the minimum circulation in the preceding subsection for the county, or if there is no such newspaper, then the newspaper having the greatest general paid circulation in the county.

(c) Any selection or change in the official organ of any county shall be made upon the concurrent action of the judge of the probate court, the sheriff, and the clerk of the superior court of the county or a majority of the officers. No change in the official legal organ shall be effective without the publication for four weeks of notice of the decision to make a change in the newspaper in which legal advertisements have previously been published. All changes in the official legal organ shall be made effective on January 1 unless a change has to be made where there is no other qualified newspaper.

(d) Notwithstanding the other provisions of this Code section, an official organ of any county meeting the qualifications under the statute in force at the time of its appointment and which was appointed prior to July 1, 1999, may remain the official organ of that county until a majority of the judge of the probate court, the sheriff, and the clerk of the superior court determine to appoint a new official organ for the county.

(e) During the month of December in each year, the judge of the probate court of each county shall notify the Secretary of State, on a form supplied by the Secretary of State, of the name and mailing address of the journal or newspaper currently serving as the official organ of the county. The judge of the probate court shall also likewise notify the Secretary of State of any change in the official organ of the county at the time that such change is made. The Secretary of State shall maintain at all times a current listing of the names and addresses of all county organs and shall make such list available to any person upon request.

Section 9-13-143 - Rates for legal advertisements

(a) The rates to be allowed to publishers for publishing legal advertisements shall be as follows:

    (1) For each 100 words, not more than the sum of $10.00 for each insertion for the first four insertions; and

    (2) For each subsequent insertion, not more than the sum of $9.00 per 100 words. In all cases fractional parts shall be charged for at the same rates.

(b) For the purpose of the computation in subsection (a) of this Code section, a block of numbers or a block of letters and numbers shall be counted as one word. If the block of numbers or letters or any combination thereof contains a hyphen, a semicolon, a colon, or other similar character or punctuation mark, the block shall still be counted as one word, provided there are no intervening spaces. When an intervening space does occur, this space shall mark the start of a new word.

(c) No judge of the probate court, sheriff, coroner, clerk, marshal, or other officer shall receive or collect from the parties, plaintiff or defendant, other or greater rates than set forth in this Code section.

Section 9-13-144 - Alternate advertising when rates not agreed on

(a) If the judge of the probate court, the sheriff, or other officer is unable to procure advertisements at the rate prescribed in Code Section 9-13-143 in a newspaper published at the county site of the county, he may have the advertisements published in any newspaper in this state having the largest general circulation in the county, provided that any paper published in the county shall be next entitled to the public advertisements and provided, further, that the rates shall be agreed upon.

(b) If contracts cannot be made with newspapers at the rates prescribed, then the sheriff and the judge of the probate court or other advertising officers shall post their advertisements at the courthouse and in a public place in each militia district in the county for the length of time required by law for advertising in newspapers.

Section 9-13-145 - Advertising costs paid in advance; exception when affidavit of indigence filed

No sheriff or deputy sheriff shall be required to advertise the property of any defendant in execution for sale until the cost of the advertisement shall have been first paid by the plaintiff in execution, his agent, or his attorney, provided that when any such party plaintiff, or his agent or attorney for him, shall make and file an affidavit in writing that because of his indigence he is unable to pay such cost, it shall be the duty of the sheriff or his deputy to proceed as required by law.

Part 2 - CONDUCT AND EFFECT

Section 9-13-160 - Time of conducting public sale

(a) For the purposes of this Code section, the term "public sale" means any sale, the notice of which must by law in any manner be given to the public.

(b) All public sales conducted within this state shall be between the hours of 10:00 A.M. and 4:00 P.M. eastern standard time or eastern daylight time, whichever is applicable, on the date fixed for the sale.

Section 9-13-161 - Where and when sales under execution held; change of place of public sales by court order

(a) Unless otherwise provided, sales of property taken under execution shall be made by the sheriffs or coroners only at the courthouse of the county where the levy was made on the first Tuesday in each month, between the hours of 10:00 A.M. and 4:00 P.M., and at public outcry; provided, however, that, should the first Tuesday of the month fall on New Year's Day or Independence Day, such sales shall take place on the immediately following Wednesday. A change in the time of such sales from the first Tuesday of the month to the first Wednesday of the month as provided in this subsection shall also apply to all public sales within the county required to be conducted at the time of the sheriff's sales.

(b) In all cases where any sheriff, coroner, or other levying officer shall levy any execution or other legal process upon any corn, lumber, timber of any kind, bricks, machinery, or other articles difficult and expensive to transport, the officer may sell the property without carrying and exposing the same at the courthouse door on the day of sale, but the levying officer shall give a full description of the property and the place where it is located in the advertisement of the sale.

(c) By general order of the presiding judge of the superior court of the county, published in the official newspaper of the county and entered on the minutes of the court, all sales of property under execution within a county may be held at a place other than at the courthouse when, in the opinion of the judge, the holding of such sales before the courthouse door would create an undue traffic hazard or unnecessarily endanger the person or property of persons using the public streets. However, no such property shall be sold at a place different from that shown in the advertisement of the sale. Any change in the place of such sales within any county, as provided in this Code section, shall also apply to all public sales within the county required to be conducted in the manner of sheriff's sales.

Section 9-13-161.1 - Holding of sales of personal property at place other than courthouse; advertisement of general order as to sale location

(a) In any county of this state having a population of 600,000 or more according to the United States decennial census of 1990 or any future such census, the chief judge of the superior court shall be authorized and empowered to provide, by general order published in the official newspaper of the county and also in two other newspapers having general circulation in such county and entered upon the minutes of the court, that all sales of personal property by the sheriff of such county may be held at a place other than at the courthouse where, in the opinion of the chief judge, the holding of such sales before the courthouse door would create an undue traffic hazard or unnecessarily endanger the person or property of persons using the public streets.

(b) No such property shall be sold at a place different from that shown in the advertisement of the sale.

(c) After the issuance of the first general order as provided in subsection (a) of this Code section, the chief judge may from time to time change the place of holding such sales by another general order published as provided in subsection (a) of this Code section.

(d) This Code section shall be supplemental to other provisions of law, with a view towards efficient and orderly handling of sheriff's sales.

(e) Nothing in this Code section shall be construed to affect the time, manner, or place of any sale not made by the sheriff but required to be made at the same time, manner, or place as sheriff's sales.

Section 9-13-162 - Continuance of sale from day to day

Any sheriff, coroner, constable, tax collector, guardian, trustee, or any other officer of this state, when selling property at public sale by virtue of any law of this state, may continue the sale from day to day until the sale is completed, provided that the trustee or other officer has given notice of the intended continuance in the advertisement of the sale.

Section 9-13-163 - Sale of perishable property - When and by whom ordered; where held

Whenever any personal property which is of a perishable nature or liable to deteriorate from keeping or the keeping of which is attended by expense is levied on by virtue of any fi. fa., attachment, or other process, and the defendant fails to recover possession of the same and it remains in the hands of the levying officer, upon the facts being made plainly to appear to the judge of the court from which the process has issued or to the judge of the superior court of the county or to the judge of the probate court of the county in which the levy has been made during the absence of the judge of the superior court, it shall be the duty of the judge to order a sale of the property. The sale shall be at the usual place of holding sheriff's sales for the county where the property is located.

Section 9-13-164 - Sale of perishable property - Advertisement; notice; disposition of proceeds

(a) The time and place of holding a sale under Code Section 9-13-163 shall be advertised at the courthouse and at two other public places at least ten days before the day of sale.

(b) The judge or judge of the probate court may order a sale of livestock, fruit, or other personal property in a perishable condition, after three days' notice.

(c) No judicial officer shall grant any order for the sale of personal property where the defendant in execution or other process or his attorney has not had at least two days' notice of applicant's intention to apply for such order, which notice shall specify the time and place of hearing. In cases of attachment for purchase money falling within this Code section, like notice shall be furnished the plaintiff or his attorney. In no case shall the notice be dispensed with, except where it is made to appear that it is impracticable to have the notice perfected or where the case is an urgent one, in which latter event the court may, in the exercise of a sound discretion, grant the order without notice.

(d) The money arising from the sale shall be held by the officer making the same, subject to the order of the court having jurisdiction of the same.

Section 9-13-165 - Sale of perishable property - Under tax executions

Whenever a tax fi. fa. is levied on property which is of a perishable nature or is liable to deteriorate in value from keeping or which is attended with expense in keeping, the same may be sold under Code Sections 9-13-163 and 9-13-164.

Section 9-13-166 - Form of tender

Purchasers at judicial sales need not tender cash but, as an alternative, may tender a cashier's or certified check which is drawn for the amount of the purchase price and which is issued by or certified by any financial institution insured by the Federal Deposit Insurance Corporation or the Federal Savings and Loan Insurance Corporation.

Section 9-13-167 - Purchaser to ascertain title and condition; under what conditions officer personally liable

(a) The purchaser shall look for himself as to the title and soundness of all property sold under judicial process.

(b) Actual fraud or misrepresentation by the officer or his agent may bind the officer personally. No covenant of warranty shall bind him individually unless made with that intention and for a valuable consideration.

Section 9-13-168 - Obligations of purchaser

The purchaser at a judicial sale shall not be bound to look to the appropriation of the proceeds of the sale nor to the returns made by the officer, nor shall he be required to see that the officer has complied fully with all regulations prescribed in such cases. All such irregularities shall create questions and liabilities between the officer and the parties interested in the sale. An innocent purchaser shall be bound only to see that the officer has competent authority to sell and that he is apparently proceeding to sell under the prescribed forms.

Section 9-13-169 - Note or memorandum unnecessary

No note or memorandum in writing shall be necessary to charge any person at a judicial sale.

Section 9-13-170 - Liability for purchase money; officer's collection options

(a) Any person who becomes the purchaser of any real or personal property at any sale made at public outcry by any executor, administrator, or guardian or by any sheriff or other officer under and by virtue of any execution or other legal process, who fails or refuses to comply with the terms of the sale when requested to do so, shall be liable for the amount of the purchase money. It shall be at the option of the sheriff or other officer either to proceed against the purchaser for the full amount of the purchase money or to resell the real or personal property and then proceed against the first purchaser for any deficiency arising from the sale.

(b) The action provided for in subsection (a) of this Code section may be brought in the name of the sheriff or other officer making the sale for the use of the plaintiff or defendant in execution or any other person in interest, as the case may be.

Section 9-13-171 - When defendant bound by sale under void process

Where property is sold under void process and the proceeds are applied to valid liens against the defendant or the defendant receives the benefit thereof, he shall be bound thereby if he is present and does not object to the sale.

Section 9-13-172.1 - "Eligible sale" defined; recision of sale; damages

(a) As used in this Code section, "eligible sale" means a judicial or nonjudicial sale that was conducted in the usual manner of a sheriff's sale and that was rescinded by the seller within 30 days after the sale but before the deed or deed under power has been delivered to the purchaser.

(b) Upon rescission of an eligible sale, the seller shall return to the purchaser, within five days of the rescission, all bid funds paid by the purchaser.

(c) Where the eligible sale was rescinded due to an automatic stay pursuant to the filing of bankruptcy by a person with an interest in the property, the damages that may be awarded to the purchaser in any civil action shall be limited to the amount of the bid funds tendered at the sale.

(d) Where the eligible sale was rescinded due to:

(1) The statutory requirements for the sale not being fulfilled;

(2) The default leading to the sale being cured prior to the sale; or

(3) The plaintiff in execution and the defendant in execution having agreed prior to the sale to cancel the sale based upon an enforceable promise by the defendant to cure the default, the damages that may be awarded to the purchaser in any civil action shall be limited solely to the amount of the bid funds tendered at the sale plus interest on the funds at the rate of 18 percent annually, calculated daily. Notwithstanding any other provision of law, specific performance shall not be a remedy available under this Code section.

Amended by 2021 Ga. Laws 307,§ 9, eff. 5/10/2021.

Added by 2003 Ga. Laws 173, § 1, eff. 7/1/2003.

Section 9-13-172 - When execution sale set aside

Courts shall have full power over their officers making execution sales. Whenever the court is satisfied that a sale made under process is infected with fraud, irregularity, or error to the injury of either party, the court shall set aside the sale.

Section 9-13-173 - Effect of judicial sale on title

A sale regularly made by virtue of judicial process issuing from a court of competent jurisdiction shall convey the title as effectually as if the sale were made by the person against whom the process was issued.

Section 9-13-174 - When sheriff's successor empowered to make titles

If a sheriff fails to make titles to a purchaser, his successor in office may make them in the same manner as if he had sold the property.

Section 9-13-175 - Duty of officer to place purchaser in possession; which persons officer may dispossess

When any sheriff or other officer sells any real estate or present interest in land by virtue of and under any execution or otherwise, it shall be his duty, upon application, to place the purchaser or his agent or attorney in possession of the real estate. To this end, the officer may dispossess the defendant, his heirs, his tenants, or his lessees, vendees, or assignees since the judgment. However, he may not dispossess other persons claiming under an independent title.

Section 9-13-176 - How possession obtained after expiration of court term or replacement of officer

If the purchaser of real estate at sheriff's and other sales under execution fails to make application for possession thereof until the next term of the superior court after the sale has taken place or until the officer making the sale has gone out of office, the possession may be obtained only under an order of the superior court.

Section 9-13-177 - Right to enforce covenants

The purchaser at a judicial sale may enforce any covenants of warranty running with the land which are incorporated in the previous title deeds.

Section 9-13-178 - When title deeds prior to purchase must be proved

In all controversies in the courts of this state, the purchaser at a judicial sale shall not be required to show title deeds prior to his purchase unless it is necessary for his case to show good title in the person whose interest he purchased.

Chapter 14 - HABEAS CORPUS

Article 1 - GENERAL PROVISIONS

Section 9-14-1 - Who may seek writ

(a) Any person restrained of his liberty under any pretext whatsoever, except under sentence of a state court of record, may seek a writ of habeas corpus to inquire into the legality of the restraint.

(b) Any person alleging that another person in whom for any cause he is interested is kept illegally from the custody of the applicant may seek a writ of habeas corpus to inquire into the legality of the restraint.

(c) Any person restrained of his liberty as a result of a sentence imposed by any state court of record may seek a writ of habeas corpus to inquire into the legality of the restraint.

Section 9-14-2 - Habeas corpus on account of detention of spouse or child

In all writs of habeas corpus sought on account of the detention of a spouse or child, the court on hearing all the facts may exercise its discretion as to whom the custody of the spouse or child shall be given and shall have the power to give the custody of a child to a third person.

Section 9-14-3 - Petition for writ - Contents

The application for the writ of habeas corpus shall be by petition in writing, signed by the applicant, his attorney or agent, or some other person in his behalf, and shall state:

(1) The name or description of the person whose liberty is restrained;

(2) The person restraining, the mode of restraint, and the place of detention as nearly as practicable;

(3) The cause or pretense of the restraint. If the restraint is under the pretext of legal process, a copy of the process must be annexed to the petition if this is within the power of the applicant;

(4) A distinct averment of the alleged illegality in the restraint or of any other reason why the writ of habeas corpus is sought; and

(5) A prayer for the writ of habeas corpus.

Section 9-14-4 - Petition for writ - Verification; to whom presented

The petition for the writ of habeas corpus must be verified by the oath of the applicant or some other person in his behalf. It may be presented to the judge of the superior court of the circuit in which the illegal detention exists who may order the party restrained of his liberty to be brought before him from any county in his circuit, or it may be presented to the judge of the probate court of the county, except in cases of capital felonies or in which a person is held for extradition under warrant of the Governor.

Section 9-14-5 - When writ granted

When upon examination of the petition for a writ of habeas corpus it appears to the judge that the restraint of liberty is illegal, he shall grant the writ, requiring the person restraining the liberty of another or illegally detaining such person in his custody to bring the person before him at a time and place to be specified in the writ for the purpose of an examination into the cause of the detention.

Section 9-14-6 - Form of writ

The writ of habeas corpus may be substantially as follows:

IN THE COURT OF COUNTY STATE OF GEORGIA A.B.,) Petitioner)) v.) Civil action) C.D.,) File no. Respondent) WRIT OF HABEAS CORPUS To C.D.: You are hereby commanded to produce the body of , alleged to be illegally detained by you, together with the cause of the detention, before me on the day of , , at]:]].M., then and there to be disposed of as the law directs. Given under my hand and official signature, this day of , . Judge

Section 9-14-7 - Return day for writ

The return day of the writ of habeas corpus in civil cases shall always be within 20 days after the presentation of the petition therefor. The return day of the writ in criminal cases shall always be within eight days after the presentation of the petition therefor.

Section 9-14-8 - Service of writ

The writ of habeas corpus shall be served by delivery of a copy thereof by any officer authorized to make a return of any process or by any other citizen. The entry of the officer or the affidavit of the citizen serving the writ shall be sufficient evidence of the service. The person serving the writ shall exhibit the original if required to do so. If personal service cannot be effected, the writ may be served by leaving a copy at the house, jail, or other place in which the party in whose behalf the writ issues is detained.

Section 9-14-9 - When warrant for arrest of person detained to be issued along with writ

If the affidavit of the applicant to the effect that he has reason to apprehend that the party detaining or holding another in custody will remove him beyond the limits of the county or conceal him from the officers of the law is filed with the petition, the judge granting the writ shall at the same time issue his warrant directed to the sheriff, deputy sheriff, coroner, or any lawful constable of the county requiring the officers to search for and arrest the body of the person detained and to bring him before the judge to be disposed of as he may direct.

Section 9-14-10 - Respondent's return to writ - When and where made

The return of the party served with the writ shall be made at the time and place specified by the court. Two days from the time of service shall be allowed for every 20 miles which the party has to travel from the place of detention to the place appointed for the hearing. If service has not been made a sufficient time before the hearing to cover the time allowed in this Code section to reach the place of hearing, the return shall be made within the time so allowed immediately after the service.

Section 9-14-11 - Respondent's return to writ - Verification; production of person detained

Every return to a writ of habeas corpus shall be under oath. If the custody or detention of the party on whose behalf the writ issues is admitted, his body shall be produced unless prevented by providential cause or prohibited by law.

Section 9-14-12 - Respondent's return to writ - Statement of transfer of custody; procedure when transfer made to avoid writ

If the return denies the custody or detention of the person in question, it shall further state distinctly the latest date, if ever, at which custody was had and when and to whom custody was transferred. If it appears that a transfer of custody was made to avoid the writ of habeas corpus, the party making the return may be imprisoned, in the discretion of the judge hearing the case, until the body of the party kept or detained is produced.

Section 9-14-13 - Production of legal process

In every case in which detention is justified under legal process, the legal process shall be produced and submitted to the judge at the hearing of the return.

Section 9-14-14 - Hearing of issue

If the return denies any of the material facts stated in the petition or alleges other facts upon which issue is taken, the judge hearing the return may in a summary manner hear testimony as to the issue. To that end, he may compel the attendance of witnesses and the production of papers, may adjourn the examination of the question, or may exercise any other power of a court which the principles of justice may require.

Section 9-14-15 - To whom notice of hearing given

If the person who is the subject of a petition for the writ of habeas corpus is detained upon a criminal charge and the district attorney is in the county, he shall be notified of the hearing. If he is not, the notice shall be given to the prosecutor of the criminal charge.

Section 9-14-16 - When person not to be discharged

No person shall be discharged upon the hearing of a writ of habeas corpus in the following cases:

(1) When he is imprisoned under lawful process issued from a court of competent jurisdiction unless his case is one in which bail is allowed and proper bail is tendered;

(2) By reason of any irregularity in the warrant or commitment where the same substantially conforms to the requirements of law;

(3) For want of bond to prosecute;

(4) When the person is imprisoned under a bench warrant which is regular upon its face;

(5) By reason of any misnomer in the warrant or commitment when the court is satisfied that the person detained is the party charged with the offense;

(6) When the person is in custody for a contempt of court and the court has not exceeded its jurisdiction in the length of the imprisonment imposed; or

(7) In any other case in which it appears that the detention is authorized by law.

Section 9-14-17 - Discharge for defect in affidavit, warrant, or commitment

If the person in question is detained upon a criminal charge and it appears to the court that there is probable cause for his detention, he shall not be discharged for any defect in the affidavit, warrant, or commitment until a reasonable time has been given to the prosecutor to remedy the defect by a new proceeding.

Section 9-14-18 - Discharge after arrest for offense committed in another state

If a person is arrested on suspicion of the commission of an offense in another state and the suspicion is reasonable, the person shall not be discharged until a sufficient time has been given for a demand to be made on the Governor for his rendition.

Section 9-14-19 - Powers of court in cases not covered by Code Sections 9-14-16 through 9-14-18

In cases other than those specified in Code Sections 9-14-16, 9-14-17, and 9-14-18, the judge hearing the return shall discharge, remand, or admit the person in question to bail or shall deliver him to the custody of the officer or person entitled thereto, as the principles of law and justice may require.

Section 9-14-20 - Recordation of proceedings by clerk of court; fees

In all habeas corpus cases, the proceedings shall be returned to the clerk of the superior court of the county the judge of which heard the same or to the probate court if the case was heard by the judge of the probate court and shall be recorded by such officer as are other cases. For such services, the officer shall receive the fees provided by Code Section 15-6-77.

Section 9-14-21 - Costs of proceedings

The judge hearing the return to a writ of habeas corpus may in his discretion award the costs of the proceeding against either party and may order execution to issue therefor by the clerk.

Section 9-14-22 - Appeals; speedy hearing; transmittal of remittitur

(a) Appeals in habeas corpus cases shall be governed, in all respects where applicable, by the laws in reference to appeals in other cases regarding the practice in the lower courts and in the Supreme Court relating to the time and manner of signing, filing, serving, transmitting, and hearing.

(b) It shall be the duty of the Supreme Court to give a speedy hearing and determination in habeas corpus cases either under existing rules or under special rules to be formulated by the court for such purpose.

(c) If the judgment of the court below is affirmed by the Supreme Court, the clerk of the Supreme Court shall promptly transmit the remittitur to the clerk of the court from which the appeal was taken. Upon the receipt of the remittitur, the clerk shall notify the judge of the court who shall have full power to pass an order, sentence, or judgment necessary to carry into execution the judgment of the court.

Section 9-14-23 - Attachment for contempt for disobedience of writ

Any person disregarding the writ of habeas corpus in any manner whatever shall be liable to attachment for contempt, issued by the judge granting the writ, under which attachment the person may be imprisoned until he complies with the legal requirements of the writ.

Article 2 - PROCEDURE FOR PERSONS UNDER SENTENCE OF STATE COURT OF RECORD

Section 9-14-40 - Legislative intent

(a) The General Assembly finds that:

(1) Expansion of the scope of habeas corpus in federal court by decisions of the United States Supreme Court together with other decisions of the court substantially curtailing the doctrine of waiver of constitutional rights by an accused and limiting the requirement of exhaustion of state remedies to those currently available have resulted in an increasingly large number of convictions of the courts of this state being collaterally attacked by federal habeas corpus based upon issues and contentions not previously presented to or passed upon by courts of this state;

(2) The increased reliance upon federal courts tends to weaken state courts as instruments for the vindication of constitutional rights with a resultant deterioration of the federal system and federal-state relations; and

(3) To alleviate such problems, it is necessary that the scope of state habeas corpus be expanded and the state doctrine of waiver of rights be modified.

(b) The General Assembly further finds that expansion of state habeas corpus to include many sharply contested issues of a factual nature requires that only the superior courts have jurisdiction of such cases.

Section 9-14-41 - Article as exclusive procedure

Notwithstanding the other provisions of this chapter, this article provides the exclusive procedure for seeking a writ of habeas corpus for persons whose liberty is being restrained by virtue of a sentence imposed against them by a state court of record.

Section 9-14-42 - Grounds for writ; waiver of objection to jury composition

(a) Any person imprisoned by virtue of a sentence imposed by a state court of record who asserts that in the proceedings which resulted in his conviction there was a substantial denial of his rights under the Constitution of the United States or of this state may institute a proceeding under this article.

(b) The right to object to the composition of the grand or trial jury will be deemed waived under this Code section unless the person challenging the sentence shows in the petition and satisfies the court that cause exists for his being allowed to pursue the objection after the conviction and sentence have otherwise become final.

(c) Any action brought pursuant to this article shall be filed within one year in the case of a misdemeanor, except as otherwise provided in Code Section 40-13-33, or within four years in the case of a felony, other than one challenging a conviction for which a death sentence has been imposed or challenging a sentence of death, from:

(1) The judgment of conviction becoming final by the conclusion of direct review or the expiration of the time for seeking such review; provided, however, that any person whose conviction has become final as of July 1, 2004, regardless of the date of conviction, shall have until July 1, 2005, in the case of a misdemeanor or until July 1, 2008, in the case of a felony to bring an action pursuant to this Code section;

(2) The date on which an impediment to filing a petition which was created by state action in violation of the Constitution or laws of the United States or of this state is removed, if the petitioner was prevented from filing such state action;

(3) The date on which the right asserted was initially recognized by the Supreme Court of the United States or the Supreme Court of Georgia, if that right was newly recognized by said courts and made retroactively applicable to cases on collateral review; or

(4) The date on which the facts supporting the claims presented could have been discovered through the exercise of due diligence.

(d) At the time of sentencing, the court shall inform the defendant of the periods of limitation set forth in subsection (c) of this Code section.

Amended by 2004 Ga. Laws 661, § 1, eff. 7/1/2004.

Section 9-14-43 - Jurisdiction and venue

A petition brought under this article must be filed in the superior court of the county in which the petitioner is being detained. The superior courts of such counties shall have exclusive jurisdiction of habeas corpus actions arising under this article. If the petitioner is not in custody or is being detained under the authority of the United States, any of the several states other than Georgia, or any foreign state, the petition must be filed in the superior court of the county in which the conviction and sentence which is being challenged was imposed.

Amended by 2004 Ga. Laws 661, § 2, eff. 7/1/2004.

Section 9-14-44 - Petition - Contents and verification

A petition brought under this article shall identify the proceeding in which the petitioner was convicted, give the date of rendition of the final judgment complained of, clearly set forth the respects in which the petitioner's rights were violated, and state with specificity which claims were raised at trial or on direct appeal, providing appropriate citations to the trial or appellate record. The petition shall have attached thereto affidavits, records, or other evidence supporting its allegations or shall state why the same are not attached. The petition shall identify any previous proceedings that the petitioner may have taken to secure relief from his or her conviction and, in the case of prior habeas corpus petitions, shall state which claims were previously raised. Argument and citations of authorities shall be omitted from the petition; however, a brief may be submitted in support of the petition setting forth any applicable argument. The petition must be verified by the oath of the applicant or of some other person in his or her behalf.

Section 9-14-45 - Petition - Service

Service of a petition brought under this article shall be made upon the person having custody of the petitioner. If the petitioner is being detained under the custody of the Department of Corrections, an additional copy of the petition shall be served on the Attorney General. If the petitioner is being detained under the custody of some authority other than the Department of Corrections, an additional copy of the petition shall be served upon the district attorney of the county in which the petition is filed. Service upon the Attorney General or the district attorney may be had by mailing a copy of the petition and a proper certificate of service.

Section 9-14-46 - Custody and production of petitioner

Custody and control of the petitioner shall be retained by the Department of Corrections or other authority having custody of the petitioner. It shall be the duty of the department or authority to produce the petitioner at such times and places as the court may direct.

Section 9-14-47 - Time for answer and hearing

Except as otherwise provided in Code Section 9-14-47.1 with respect to petitions challenging for the first time state court proceedings resulting in a sentence of death, within 20 days after the filing and docketing of a petition under this article or within such further time as the court may set, the respondent shall answer or move to dismiss the petition. The court shall set the case for a hearing on the issues within a reasonable time after the filing of defensive pleadings.

Section 9-14-47.1 - Petitions challenging for the first time state court proceedings resulting in a death sentence

(a) In petitions filed under this article challenging for the first time state court proceedings resulting in a death sentence, the provisions of this article shall apply except as specifically provided otherwise in this Code section.

(b) Within ten days of the filing of a petition challenging for the first time state court proceedings resulting in a death sentence, the superior court clerk of the county where the petition is filed shall give written notice to The Council of Superior Court Judges of Georgia of the filing of the petition which shall serve as a request for judicial assistance under paragraph (3) of subsection (b) of Code Section 15-1-9.1. Within 30 days of receipt of such notice, the president of the council shall, under guidelines promulgated by the executive committee of the council, assign the case to a judge of a circuit other than the circuit in which the conviction and sentence were imposed.

(c) The Council of Superior Court Judges of Georgia shall establish, by uniform court rules, appropriate time periods and schedules applicable to petitions filed on or after January 1, 1996, challenging for the first time state court proceedings resulting in a sentence of death. Such rules shall be adopted by the Supreme Court of Georgia on or before December 31, 1995. Such new time periods and schedules shall include, but specifically not be limited to, the following:

(1) Respondent's filing of an answer or motion to dismiss the petition;

(2) Petitioner's filing of any amendments to the petition;

(3) Filing by either party of motions and responses to motions;

(4) Scheduling and conducting of evidentiary hearings; and

(5) Date of final order.

(d) In petitions filed under this article challenging for a second or subsequent time a state court proceeding resulting in a death sentence, the petitioner shall not be entitled to invoke any of the provisions set forth in this Code section to delay the proceedings. To the extent the court deems it necessary to have an evidentiary hearing on any such petition, the court shall expedite the proceedings and the time limits shall not exceed those set for initial petitions.

Section 9-14-48 - Hearing; evidence; depositions; affidavits; determination of compliance with procedural rules; disposition

(a) The court may receive proof by depositions, oral testimony, sworn affidavits, or other evidence. No other forms of discovery shall be allowed except upon leave of court and a showing of exceptional circumstances.

(b) The taking of depositions or depositions upon written questions by either party shall be governed by Code Sections 9-11-26 through 9-11-32 and 9-11-37; provided, however, that the time allowed in Code Section 9-11-31 for service of cross-questions upon all other parties shall be ten days from the date the notice and written questions are served.

(c) If sworn affidavits are intended by either party to be introduced into evidence, the party intending to introduce such an affidavit shall cause it to be served upon the opposing party at least ten days in advance of the date set for a hearing in the case. The affidavit so served shall include the address and telephone number of the affiant, home or business, if known, to provide the opposing party a reasonable opportunity to contact the affiant; failure to include this information in any affidavit shall render the affidavit inadmissible. The affidavit shall also be accompanied by a notice of the party's intention to introduce it into evidence. The superior court judge considering the petition for writ of habeas corpus may resolve disputed issues of fact upon the basis of sworn affidavits standing by themselves.

(d) The court shall review the trial record and transcript of proceedings and consider whether the petitioner made timely motion or objection or otherwise complied with Georgia procedural rules at trial and on appeal and whether, in the event the petitioner had new counsel subsequent to trial, the petitioner raised any claim of ineffective assistance of trial counsel on appeal; and absent a showing of cause for noncompliance with such requirement, and of actual prejudice, habeas corpus relief shall not be granted. In all cases habeas corpus relief shall be granted to avoid a miscarriage of justice. If the court finds in favor of the petitioner, it shall enter an appropriate order with respect to the judgment or sentence challenged in the proceeding and such supplementary orders as to rearraignment, retrial, custody, or discharge as may be necessary and proper.

(e) A petition, other than one challenging a conviction for which a death sentence has been imposed or challenging a sentence of death, may be dismissed if there is a particularized showing that the respondent has been prejudiced in its ability to respond to the petition by delay in its filing unless the petitioner shows by a preponderance of the evidence that it is based on grounds of which he or she could not have had knowledge by the exercise of reasonable diligence before the circumstances prejudicial to the respondent occurred. This subsection shall apply only to convictions had before July 1, 2004.

Amended by 2004 Ga. Laws 661, § 3, eff. 7/1/2004.

Section 9-14-49 - Findings of fact and conclusions of law

After reviewing the pleadings and evidence offered at the trial of the case, the judge of the superior court hearing the case shall make written findings of fact and conclusions of law upon which the judgment is based. The findings of fact and conclusions of law shall be recorded as part of the record of the case.

Section 9-14-50 - Transcription of proceedings

All trials held under this article shall be transcribed by a court reporter designated by the superior court hearing the case.

Section 9-14-51 - Effect of failure to raise grounds for relief in original or amended petition

All grounds for relief claimed by a petitioner for a writ of habeas corpus shall be raised by a petitioner in his original or amended petition. Any grounds not so raised are waived unless the Constitution of the United States or of this state otherwise requires or unless any judge to whom the petition is assigned, on considering a subsequent petition, finds grounds for relief asserted therein which could not reasonably have been raised in the original or amended petition.

Section 9-14-52 - Appeal procedure; application to Supreme Court by petitioner for certificate of probable cause; effect of appeal by respondent

(a) Appeals in habeas corpus cases brought under this article shall be governed by Chapter 6 of Title 5 except that as to final orders of the court which are adverse to the petitioner no appeal shall be allowed unless the Supreme Court of this state issues a certificate of probable cause for the appeal.

(b) If an unsuccessful petitioner desires to appeal, he must file a written application for a certificate of probable cause to appeal with the clerk of the Supreme Court within 30 days from the entry of the order denying him relief. The petitioner shall also file within the same period a notice of appeal with the clerk of the concerned superior court. The Supreme Court shall either grant or deny the application within a reasonable time after filing. In order for the Supreme Court to consider fully the request for a certificate, the clerk of the concerned superior court shall forward, as in any other case, the record and transcript, if designated, to the clerk of the Supreme Court when a notice of appeal is filed. The clerk of the concerned superior court need not prepare and retain and the court reporter need not file a copy of the original record and a copy of the original transcript of proceedings. The clerk of the Supreme Court shall return the original record and transcript to the clerk of the concerned superior court upon completion of the appeal if the certificate is granted. If the Supreme Court denies the application for a certificate of probable cause, the clerk of the Supreme Court shall return the original record and transcript and shall notify the clerk of the concerned superior court and the parties to the proceedings below of the determination that probable cause does not exist for appeal.

(c) If the trial court finds in favor of the petitioner, no certificate of probable cause need be obtained by the respondent as a condition precedent to appeal. A notice of appeal filed by the respondent shall act as a supersedeas and shall stay the judgment of the superior court until there is a final adjudication by the Supreme Court; provided, however, that, while such case is on appeal, the petitioner may be released on bail as is provided in criminal cases except when the petitioner has been convicted of a crime which the Supreme Court has jurisdiction to consider on direct appeal. The right to bail and the amount of bond shall be within the discretion of the judge of the superior court in which the sentence successfully challenged under this article was originally imposed.

Section 9-14-53 - Reimbursement to counties for habeas corpus costs

Each county of this state shall be reimbursed from state funds for court costs both at the trial level and in any appellate court for each writ of habeas corpus sought in the superior court of the county by indigent petitioners when the granting of the writ is denied or when the court costs are cast upon the respondent, but such reimbursement shall not exceed $30,000.00 per annum total for each county. By not later than September 1 of each calendar year, the clerk of the superior court of each county shall send a certified list to The Council of Superior Court Judges of Georgia of each writ of habeas corpus sought in the superior court of the county during the 12 month period immediately preceding July 1 of that calendar year by indigent petitioners for which the granting of the writ was denied or for which the court costs were cast upon the respondent; and such list shall include the court costs both at the trial level and in any appellate court for each such writ of habeas corpus. By not later than December 15 of each calendar year, the council shall pay to the county from funds appropriated or otherwise made available for the operation of the superior courts the reimbursement as set forth in the certified list, subject to the maximum reimbursement provided for in this Code section. The list sent to the council as provided in this Code section shall be certified as correct by the governing authority of the county and by the judge of the superior court of the county. The council is authorized to devise and make available to the counties such forms as may be reasonably necessary to carry out this Code section and to establish such procedures as may be reasonably necessary for such purposes. This Code section shall not be construed to amend or repeal the provisions of Code Section 15-6-28 or any other provision of law for funds for any judicial circuit.

Amended by 2017 Ga. Laws 216,§ 1, eff. 7/1/2017.

Amended by 2011 Ga. Laws 117,§ 1, eff. 5/11/2011.

Chapter 15 - COURT AND LITIGATION COSTS

Section 9-15-1 - Which party liable for costs

In all civil cases in any of the courts of this state, except as otherwise provided, the party who dismisses, loses, or is cast in the action shall be liable for the costs thereof.

Section 9-15-2 - Affidavit of indigence; procedure when filing party not represented by counsel

(a)

(1) When any party, plaintiff or defendant, in any action or proceeding held in any court in this state is unable to pay any deposit, fee, or other cost which is normally required in the court, if the party shall subscribe an affidavit to the effect that because of his indigence he is unable to pay the costs, the party shall be relieved from paying the costs and his rights shall be the same as if he had paid the costs.

(2) Any other party at interest or his agent or attorney may contest the truth of an affidavit of indigence by verifying affirmatively under oath that the same is untrue. The issue thereby formed shall be heard and determined by the court, under the rules of the court. The judgment of the court on all issues of fact concerning the ability of a party to pay costs or give bond shall be final.

(b) In the absence of a traverse affidavit contesting the truth of an affidavit of indigence, the court may inquire into the truth of the affidavit of indigence. After a hearing, the court may order the costs to be paid if it finds that the deposit, fee, or other costs can be paid and, if the costs are not paid within the time permitted in such order, may deny the relief sought.

(c) The adjudication of the issue of indigence shall not affect a decision on the merits of the pending action.

(d) When a civil action is presented for filing under this Code section by a party who is not represented by an attorney, the clerk of court shall not file the matter but shall present the complaint or other initial pleading to a judge of the court. The judge shall review the pleading and, if the judge determines that the pleading shows on its face such a complete absence of any justiciable issue of law or fact that it cannot be reasonably believed that the court could grant any relief against any party named in the pleading, then the judge shall enter an order denying filing of the pleading. If the judge does not so find, then the judge shall enter an order allowing filing and shall return the pleading to the clerk for filing as in other cases. An order denying filing shall be appealable in the same manner as an order dismissing an action.

Section 9-15-3 - When costs may be demanded

The several officers of court are prohibited from demanding the costs in any civil case or any part thereof until after judgment in the same, except as otherwise provided by law.

Section 9-15-4 - Deposit prior to filing by clerk; exception if affidavit of indigence filed; repayment of excess; exemptions

(a) A clerk of the superior court shall not be required to file any civil case or proceeding until the fee required by Code Section 15-6-77, relating to fees of clerks of the superior courts, has been paid to the clerk. The fee shall not be required if the party desiring to file the case or proceeding is unable because of indigence to pay the fee and the party files with the clerk an affidavit to such effect.

(b) The deposit required to be filed by this Code section shall not affect any other law which requires a deposit in excess of or in addition to the deposit of cost required by this Code section.

(c) Nothing contained in this Code section shall be deemed to require a deposit of cost by the state, its agencies, or its political subdivisions; and, without limiting the generality of the foregoing, no clerk of any court shall be authorized to require any deposit of costs in any action or proceeding for the collection of criminal penalties as authorized under Code Section 42-8-34.2.

Amended by 2019 Ga. Laws 231,§ 1, eff. 1/1/2020.

Section 9-15-5 - [Repealed] Deposit by nonresident plaintiff; additional deposit; refund of excess

Amended by 2006 Ga. Laws 453,§ 9, eff. 4/14/2006.

Reserved. Repealed by Ga. L. 1981, p. 1396, § 23, effective July 1, 1981.

Section 9-15-6 - Liability of attorney of nonresident plaintiff for costs; prior payment of costs in action brought by nonresident attorney and plaintiff

(a) When any attorney institutes an action in any of the courts of this state for any person who resides outside this state, the attorney shall be liable to pay all costs of the officers of court in the event that the action is dismissed or the plaintiff is cast in the action.

(b) When the plaintiff and his attorney both reside outside the limits of this state, the proper officers may demand their full costs before they shall be bound to perform any service in any case commenced by the nonresident attorney or plaintiff.

Section 9-15-7 - Liability of attorney guilty of willful neglect or misconduct for costs

If any plaintiff is involuntarily dismissed or cast in the action by reason of the willful neglect or misconduct of his attorney, his attorney shall be liable for the costs which may have accrued in the case. In like manner, if any defendant is cast in the action by reason of the willful neglect or misconduct of his attorney, his attorney shall be liable for the costs thereof.

Section 9-15-8 - Liability for costs of witnesses of adverse party

No party plaintiff or defendant shall be liable for the costs of any witness of the adverse party unless the witness is subpoenaed, sworn, and examined on the trial of the case or unless the plaintiff voluntarily dismisses his case before trial. No party shall be liable for the costs of more than two witnesses to the same point unless the court certifies that the question at issue was of such a character as rendered a greater number of witnesses necessary.

Section 9-15-9 - Costs when recovery on contract is less than $50.00

When any action ex contractu is brought in the superior or state court and the verdict of the jury, unreduced by setoff or payment pending the action, is for a sum under $50.00, the defendant shall not be charged with more costs than would have necessarily accrued if the case had been heard before a magistrate. The remainder of the court costs shall be paid by the plaintiff and may be retained out of the sum recovered by the plaintiff and, if that is insufficient, judgment shall be entered by the court against the plaintiff for the balance.

Section 9-15-10 - Costs in personal actions when damages are less than $10.00

(a) In all actions for slanderous words, in any court having jurisdiction of the same, if the jury renders a verdict under $10.00, the plaintiff shall have and recover no more costs than damages.

(b) In actions of assault and battery and in all other personal actions wherein the jury upon the trial thereof finds the damages to be less than $10.00, the plaintiff shall recover no more costs than damages unless the judge, at the trial thereof, finds and certifies on the record that an aggravated assault and battery was proved.

Section 9-15-11 - Inclusion of costs in judgment; itemization and endorsement on execution

When a case is disposed of, the costs, including fees of witnesses, shall be included in the judgment against the party voluntarily dismissing, being involuntarily dismissed, or cast in the action. It shall be the duty of the clerk of the court, of the magistrate, or of any other officer who may issue an execution to endorse on the execution at the time it is issued the date and amount of the judgment, the items of the bill of cost, written in words, and the amount of each item distinctly stated in figures. No costs or items of costs shall in any case be demanded by any officer unless they are itemized and endorsed as provided in this Code section.

Section 9-15-12 - Liability of plaintiff and attorney for costs when execution returned unsatisfied

If execution issues on a judgment recovered by the plaintiff against the defendant and the executing officer returns the same marked "No property to be found," a fi. fa. may issue against the plaintiff for the purpose of recovering the costs from him; and, if the plaintiff resides outside the state, the fi. fa. shall issue against his attorney also.

Section 9-15-13 - Judgment and execution against attorney for costs

In all cases in which it is made to appear that an attorney is liable for costs, the court shall, on motion, order a judgment and execution against him for the same.

Section 9-15-14 - Litigation costs and attorney's fees assessed for frivolous actions and defenses

(a) In any civil action in any court of record of this state, reasonable and necessary attorney's fees and expenses of litigation shall be awarded to any party against whom another party has asserted a claim, defense, or other position with respect to which there existed such a complete absence of any justiciable issue of law or fact that it could not be reasonably believed that a court would accept the asserted claim, defense, or other position. Attorney's fees and expenses so awarded shall be assessed against the party asserting such claim, defense, or other position, or against that party's attorney, or against both in such manner as is just.

(b) The court may assess reasonable and necessary attorney's fees and expenses of litigation in any civil action in any court of record if, upon the motion of any party or the court itself, it finds that an attorney or party brought or defended an action, or any part thereof, that lacked substantial justification or that the action, or any part thereof, was interposed for delay or harassment, or if it finds that an attorney or party unnecessarily expanded the proceeding by other improper conduct, including, but not limited to, abuses of discovery procedures available under Chapter 11 of this title, the "Georgia Civil Practice Act." As used in this Code section, "lacked substantial justification" means substantially frivolous, substantially groundless, or substantially vexatious.

(c) No attorney or party shall be assessed attorney's fees as to any claim or defense which the court determines was asserted by said attorney or party in a good faith attempt to establish a new theory of law in Georgia if such new theory of law is based on some recognized precedential or persuasive authority.

(d) Attorney's fees and expenses of litigation awarded under this Code section shall not exceed amounts which are reasonable and necessary for defending or asserting the rights of a party. Attorney's fees and expenses of litigation incurred in obtaining an order of court pursuant to this Code section may also be assessed by the court and included in its order.

(e) Attorney's fees and expenses under this Code section may be requested by motion at any time during the course of the action but not later than 45 days after the final disposition of the action.

(f) An award of reasonable and necessary attorney's fees or expenses of litigation under this Code section shall be determined by the court without a jury and shall be made by an order of court which shall constitute and be enforceable as a money judgment.

(g) Attorney's fees and expenses of litigation awarded under this Code section in a prior action between the same parties shall be treated as court costs with regard to the filing of any subsequent action.

(h) This Code section shall not apply to proceedings in magistrate courts. However, when a case is appealed from the magistrate court, the appellee may seek litigation expenses incurred below if the appeal lacks substantial justification.

Amended by 2001 Ga. Laws 297, § 1, eff. 7/1/2001.

Section 9-15-15 - Attorney's fees and expenses assessed in civil actions brought against judicial officers

(a) When any civil action is brought against a judicial officer, other than an action for quo warranto, mandamus, or an action brought under Title 42, Section 1983 of the United States Code, and such action arises out of the performance of the judicial officer's official duties, the plaintiff shall be liable for all attorney's fees and expenses incurred in the defense of the action if the action is concluded in favor of the judicial officer, and the court finds that an attorney or party brought an action that lacked substantial justification or that the action, or any part of the action, was interposed for delay or harassment. As used in this Code section, "lacked substantial justification" means substantially frivolous, substantially groundless, or substantially vexatious. For purposes of this Code section, judicial officers shall include justices and judges of the appellate courts of Georgia and judges of the superior, state, probate, juvenile, magistrate, and municipal courts.

(b) The provisions of subsection (a) of this Code section shall apply both with respect to actions brought against a judicial officer in his or her official capacity and with respect to actions brought against a judicial officer in his or her individual capacity where the action arises out of the performance of the judicial officer's official duties.

(c) Recovery may be had under subsection (a) of this Code section by the state or by a unit of local government with respect to attorney's fees and expenses incurred by the state or by the unit of local government. Where recovery by a governmental unit is so authorized, recovery shall be authorized for attorney's fees paid to outside counsel as well as for compensation paid to counsel employed by the governmental unit. Recovery may also be had under subsection (a) of this Code section with respect to attorney's fees and expenses personally incurred by a judicial officer. Recovery under subsection (a) of this Code section shall include any attorney's fees and expenses incurred in appellate proceedings arising out of an action subject to this Code section.

(d) When a civil action against a judicial officer, other than an action for quo warranto, mandamus, or an action brought under Title 42, Section 1983 of the United States Code, which action arises out of the performance of the judicial officer's official duties is presented for filing, the clerk of court shall file the matter but shall present the complaint or other initial pleading to the district court administrator for the judicial circuit where the action was filed, to assign to a superior court judge of that circuit. If the action is filed against a judge or justice of an appellate court, the chief judge or justice shall assign the matter to a member of that court. The judge shall review the pleading, and, if the judge determines that the pleading shows on its face such a complete absence of any justiciable issue of law or fact that it cannot be reasonably believed that the court could grant any relief against any party named in the pleading, then the judge shall enter an order dismissing the pleading. An order dismissing the pleading shall be appealable in the same manner as an order dismissing an action.

(e) Attorney's fees and expenses under this Code section may be requested by motion at any time during the course of the action but not later than 45 days after the final disposition of the action.

(f) An award of reasonable and necessary attorney's fees or expenses of litigation under this Code section shall be determined by the court without a jury and shall be made by an order of court which shall constitute and be enforceable as a money judgment.

Chapter 16 - GEORGIA UNIFORM CIVIL FORFEITURE PROCEDURE ACT

Section 9-16-1 - Short title

This chapter shall be known and may be cited as the "Georgia Uniform Civil Forfeiture Procedure Act."

Added by 2015 Ga. Laws 98,§ 1-1, eff. 7/1/2015.

Section 9-16-2 - Definitions

As used in this chapter, the term:

(1)

   (A) "Beneficial interest" means either of the following:

   (i) The interest of a person as a beneficiary under any written trust arrangement pursuant to which a trustee holds legal or record title to real property for the benefit of such person; or

   (ii) The interest of a person under any other written form of express fiduciary arrangement pursuant to which any other person holds legal or record title to real property for the benefit of such person.

   (B) Such term shall not include the interest of a stockholder in a corporation, the interest of a partner in either a general partnership or limited partnership, or an equitable interest.

(2) "Civil forfeiture proceeding" means a quasi-judicial forfeiture initiated pursuant to Code Section 9-16-11 or a complaint for forfeiture initiated pursuant to Code Section 9-16-12 or 9-16-13.

(3) "Costs" means, but shall not be limited to:

   (A) All expenses associated with the seizure, towing, storage, maintenance, custody, preservation, operation, or sale of property; and

   (B) Satisfaction of any security interest or lien not subject to forfeiture under this chapter.

(4) "Court costs" means, but shall not be limited to:

   (A) Charges and fees taxed by the court, including filing, transcription, and court reporter fees, and advertisement costs; and

   (B) Payment of receivers, conservators, appraisers, accountants, or trustees appointed by the court pursuant to Code Section 9-16-10 or 9-16-14.

(5) "Financial institution" means a bank, trust company, national banking association, industrial bank, savings institution, or credit union chartered and supervised under state or federal law.

(6) "Governmental agency" means any department, office, council, commission, committee, authority, board, bureau, or division of the executive, judicial, or legislative branch of a state, the United States, or any political subdivision thereof.

(7) "Interest holder" means a secured party within the meaning of Code Section 11-9-102, the claim of a beneficial interest, or a perfected encumbrance pertaining to an interest in property.

(8) "Owner" means a person, other than an interest holder, who has an interest in property and is in compliance with any statute requiring its recordation or reflection in public records in order to perfect the interest against a bona fide purchaser for value.

(9) "Proceeds" means property derived directly or indirectly from, maintained by, or realized through an act or omission relating to criminal conduct and includes any benefit, interest, or property of any kind without reduction for expenses incurred for acquisition, maintenance, or any other purpose.

(10) "Property" means anything of value and includes any interest in anything of value, including real property and any fixtures thereon, and tangible and intangible personal property, including but not limited to currency, instruments, securities, or any other kind of privilege, interest, claim, or right.

(11) "Real property" means any real property situated in this state or any interest in such real property, including, but not limited to, any lease of or mortgage upon such real property.

(12) "State attorney" means a district attorney of this state or his or her designee or, when specifically authorized by law, the Attorney General or his or her designee.

(13)

   (A) "Trustee" means either of the following:

   (i) Any person who holds legal or record title to real property for which any other person has a beneficial interest; or

   (ii) Any successor trustee or trustees to any of the foregoing persons.

   (B) Such term shall not include the following:

   (i) Any person appointed or acting as:

   (I) A guardian, conservator, or personal representative under Title 29 or Chapters 1 through 11 of Title 53, the "Revised Probate Code of 1998"; or

   (II) A personal representative under former Chapter 6 of Title 53 as such existed on December 31, 1997; or

(ii) Any person appointed or acting as a trustee of any testamentary trust or as trustee of any indenture of trust under which any bonds are issued.

(14) "United States" means the United States and its territories and possessions, the 50 states, and the District of Columbia.

Added by 2015 Ga. Laws 98,§ 1-1, eff. 7/1/2015.

Section 9-16-3 - Jurisdiction

(a) A civil forfeiture proceeding shall be filed by a state attorney in the name of the State of Georgia in any superior court of this state and may be brought:

(1) In the case of an in rem action, in the judicial circuit where the property is located;

(2) In the case of an in personam action, in the judicial circuit in which the defendant resides; or

(3) By the state attorney having jurisdiction over any offense which arose out of the same conduct which made the property subject to forfeiture.

(b) If more than one state attorney has jurisdiction to file a civil forfeiture proceeding, the state attorney having primary jurisdiction over the conduct giving rise to the forfeiture shall, in the event of a conflict, have priority over any other state attorney.

(c) A civil forfeiture proceeding may be compromised or settled in the same manner as other civil actions.

Added by 2015 Ga. Laws 98,§ 1-1, eff. 7/1/2015.

Section 9-16-4 - Venue

A complaint for forfeiture pursuant to Code Section 9-16-12 or 9-16-13 shall be tried:

(1) If the complaint for forfeiture is in rem against real property, in the county where the property is located, except where a single tract is divided by a county line, in which case the superior court of either county shall have jurisdiction;

(2) If the complaint for forfeiture is in rem against tangible or intangible personal property, in any county where the property is located or will be located during the pendency of the action; or

(3) If the complaint for forfeiture is in personam, as provided in Article VI, Section II of the Constitution.

Added by 2015 Ga. Laws 98,§ 1-1, eff. 7/1/2015.

Section 9-16-5 - Notice to owner of seizure of vehicle

If a seized vehicle is registered to a person or entity that was not present at the scene of the seizure and whose conduct did not give rise to the seizure, the seizing officer or his or her designee shall make a reasonable effort to determine the name of the registered owner of the seized vehicle and, upon learning such registered owner's telephone number or address, inform such registered owner that the vehicle has been seized.

Added by 2015 Ga. Laws 98,§ 1-1, eff. 7/1/2015.

Section 9-16-6 - Seizure of property

(a) Property subject to forfeiture may be seized by any law enforcement officer of this state or any political subdivision thereof who has power to make arrests or execute process or a search warrant issued by any court having jurisdiction over the property. A court issued warrant authorizing seizure of property subject to forfeiture may be issued on an affidavit demonstrating that probable cause exists for its forfeiture or that the property has been the subject of a previous final judgment of forfeiture in the courts of the United States. The court may order that the property be seized on such terms and conditions as are reasonable.

(b) Property subject to forfeiture may be seized without process if probable cause exists to believe that the property is subject to forfeiture or the seizure is incident to an arrest or search pursuant to a search warrant or to an inspection under an inspection warrant.

(c) The court's jurisdiction over any civil forfeiture proceeding shall not be affected by a seizure in violation of the Constitution of Georgia or the Constitution of the United States made with process or in a good faith belief of probable cause.

Added by 2015 Ga. Laws 98,§ 1-1, eff. 7/1/2015.

Section 9-16-7 - Reporting of seizure; role of state attorney

(a) When property that is intended to be forfeited is taken by any law enforcement officer of this state, within 30 days thereof the seizing officer shall, in writing, report the fact of seizure and conduct an inventory and estimate the value of the property seized and provide such information to the district attorney of the judicial circuit having jurisdiction in the county where the seizure was made.

(b) Within 60 days from the date of seizure, the state attorney shall:

(1) Initiate a quasi-judicial forfeiture as provided for in Code Section 9-16-11; or

(2) File a complaint for forfeiture as provided for in Code Section 9-16-12 or 9-16-13.

(c) If the seizing officer fails to comply with subsection (a) of this Code section or the state attorney fails to comply with subsection (b) of this Code section, the property shall be released on the request of an owner or interest holder, pending a complaint for forfeiture pursuant to Code Section 9-16-12 or 9-16-13, unless the property is being held as evidence. When the court releases property pursuant to this subsection, upon application by the state attorney, it may impose conditions as specified in paragraph (1) of Code Section 9-16-14.

Added by 2015 Ga. Laws 98,§ 1-1, eff. 7/1/2015.

Section 9-16-8 - Forfeiture lien

(a) A state attorney may file, without a filing fee, a forfeiture lien upon the initiation of any civil forfeiture proceeding or criminal proceeding or upon seizure for forfeiture. The forfeiture lien filing shall constitute notice to any person claiming an interest in the property owned by the named person. The forfeiture lien shall include the following information:

(1) The name of each person who has a known interest in the seized property and, in the discretion of the state attorney, any alias and any corporations, partnerships, trusts, or other entities, including nominees, that are either owned entirely or in part or controlled by such persons; and

(2) A description of the property, the value of the property claimed by the state attorney, the name of the court where the civil forfeiture proceeding or criminal proceeding has been brought, and the case number of the civil forfeiture proceeding or criminal proceeding if known at the time of filing the forfeiture lien.

(b) A forfeiture lien filed pursuant to this Code section shall apply to:

(1) The described property;

(2) Each named person and any aliases, fictitious names, or other names, including names of corporations, partnerships, trusts, or other entities that are either owned entirely or in part or controlled by each named person; and

(3) Any interest in real property owned or controlled by each named person.

(c) A forfeiture lien creates, upon filing, a lien in favor of the state as it relates to the seized property or to any named person or related entities with respect to such property. Such forfeiture lien secures the amount of potential liability for civil judgment and, if applicable, the fair market value of seized property relating to any civil forfeiture proceeding enforcing such lien. A forfeiture lien referred to in this Code section shall be filed in accordance with the provisions of the laws in this state pertaining to the type of property that is subject to the forfeiture lien. The state attorney may amend or release, in whole or in part, a forfeiture lien filed under this Code section at any time by filing, without a filing fee, an amended forfeiture lien in accordance with this Code section which identifies the forfeiture lien amended. The state attorney, as soon as practical after filing a forfeiture lien, shall furnish to any person named in the forfeiture lien a notice of the filing of the forfeiture lien. Failure to furnish such notice shall not invalidate or otherwise affect a forfeiture lien filed in accordance with this Code section.

(d) Upon entry of judgment in favor of the state, the state attorney may proceed to execute on the forfeiture lien as in the case of any other judgment.

(e) A trustee, constructive or otherwise, who has notice that a forfeiture lien, a notice of pending forfeiture, or a complaint for forfeiture has been filed against the property or against any person or entity for whom the person holds title or appears as the owner of record shall furnish, within ten days of receiving notice as provided by this subsection, to the state attorney the following information:

(1) The name and address of the person or entity for whom the property is held;

(2) The names and addresses of all beneficiaries for whose benefit legal title to the seized property, or property of the named person or related entity, is held; and

(3) A copy of the applicable trust agreement or other instrument, if any, under which the trustee or other person holds legal title or appears as the owner of record of the property.

(f) A trustee, constructive or otherwise, who fails to comply with subsection (e) of this Code section shall be guilty of a misdemeanor.

Added by 2015 Ga. Laws 98,§ 1-1, eff. 7/1/2015.

Section 9-16-9 - Seized property not subject to replevin, conveyance, sequestration, or attachment; release of property; assignment of complaint for forfeiture; custodian of property

(a) Property attached or seized under this chapter shall not be subject to replevin, conveyance, sequestration, or attachment.

(b) The seizing law enforcement agency or the state attorney may authorize the release of the attached or seized property if the forfeiture or retention is unnecessary or may transfer the civil forfeiture proceeding to another agency or state attorney by discontinuing such proceeding in favor of a civil forfeiture proceeding initiated by another law enforcement agency or state attorney.

(c) A complaint for forfeiture pursuant to Code Section 9-16-12 or 9-16-13 may be assigned to the same judge hearing any other complaint for forfeiture or criminal proceeding involving substantially the same parties or same property in accordance with the Uniform Superior Court Rules.

(d) Property shall be deemed to be in the custody of the State of Georgia subject only to the orders and decrees of the superior court having jurisdiction over the civil forfeiture proceeding.

Added by 2015 Ga. Laws 98,§ 1-1, eff. 7/1/2015.

Section 9-16-10 - Disposition of seized property

(a) If property is seized, the state attorney may:

(1) Remove the property to a place designated by the superior court having jurisdiction over a civil forfeiture proceeding;

(2) Place the property under constructive seizure by giving notice of pending forfeiture to its owners and interest holders and filing notice of seizure in any appropriate public record relating to the property. Notice of a pending forfeiture may be posted in a prominent location in the courthouse for the jurisdiction having venue for the forfeiture if the owners' and interest holders' names are not known;

(3) Remove the property to a storage area within the jurisdiction of the court for safekeeping;

(4) Provide for another governmental agency, a receiver appointed by the court pursuant to Chapter 8 of this title, an owner, or an interest holder to take custody of the property and remove it to an appropriate location within the county where the property was seized; or

(5) Require the sheriff or chief of police of the political subdivision where the property was seized to take custody of the property and remove it to an appropriate location for disposition in accordance with law.

(b)

(1) The court, upon motion of the state attorney, a claimant, or the custodian of the property, may order property or any portion thereof to be sold upon such terms and conditions as may be prescribed by the court if the expense of keeping such property which has been attached or seized is excessive or disproportionate to the value of such property or such property:

(A) Is a depreciating asset;

(B) Is perishable or is liable to perish or waste; or

(C) May be greatly reduced in value by keeping it.

(2) The income from such sale shall be paid into the registry of the court pending final disposition of a civil forfeiture proceeding.

(c)

(1) If the property is currency and is not needed for evidentiary purposes, within 60 days of the seizure the seizing agency, or the state attorney if he or she has possession of such currency, shall deposit the currency into an account:

(A) That is separate from other operating accounts;

(B) That bears interest, if such account is available; and

(C) At a financial institution that has a branch location within the county where the civil forfeiture proceeding is located, and if such financial institution is not available, at a financial institution approved by the chief superior court judge of the circuit in which such county is located.

(2) If the property is a negotiable instrument and is not needed for evidentiary purposes, within 60 days of the seizure the seizing agency, or the state attorney if he or she has possession of such item, shall secure the negotiable instrument in a financial institution that has a branch location within the county where the civil forfeiture proceeding is located, and if such financial institution is not available, at a financial institution approved by the chief superior court judge of the circuit in which such county is located. If such instrument is converted to currency, it shall be deposited in accordance with paragraph (1) of this subsection.

(3) The account holder shall annually pay any interest that accrues under this subsection into the County Drug Abuse Treatment and Education Fund established pursuant to Article 6 of Chapter 21 of Title 15 at the same time the account holder files its annual report in accordance with subsection (g) of Code Section 9-16-19.

Added by 2015 Ga. Laws 98,§ 1-1, eff. 7/1/2015.

Section 9-16-11 - Quasi-judicial forfeiture for property valued at $25,000.00 or less; notice; procedure

(a) If the estimated value of personal property seized is $25,000.00 or less, the state attorney shall post a notice of the seizure of such property in a prominent location in the courthouse of the county in which the property was seized. Such notice shall include:

(1) A description of the property;

(2) The date and place of seizure;

(3) The conduct giving rise to forfeiture;

(4) The alleged violation of law; and

(5) A statement that the owner or interest holder of such property has 30 days within which a claim must be served on the state attorney by certified mail or statutory overnight delivery, return receipt requested, and that such claim shall be signed by the owner or interest holder and shall provide:

(A) The name of the claimant;

(B) The address at which the claimant resides;

(C) A description of the claimant's interest in the property;

(D) A description of the circumstances of the claimant's obtaining an interest in the property and, to the best of the claimant's knowledge, the date the claimant obtained the interest and the name of the person or entity that transferred the interest to the claimant;

(E) The nature of the relationship between the claimant and the person who possessed the property at the time of the seizure;

(F) A copy of any documentation in the claimant's possession supporting his or her claim; and

(G) Any additional facts supporting his or her claim.

(b) The state attorney shall serve a copy of the notice specified in subsection (a) of this Code section upon an owner, interest holder, and person in possession of the property at the time of seizure as follows:

(1) If the name and current address of the person in possession of the property at the time of the seizure, owner, or interest holder are known, provide notice by either personal service or mailing a copy of the notice by certified mail or statutory overnight delivery, return receipt requested, to that address;

(2) If the name and address of the person in possession of the property at the time of seizure, owner, or interest holder are required by law to be on public record with a governmental agency to perfect an interest in the property but the owner's or interest holder's current address is not known, mail a copy of the notice by certified mail or statutory overnight delivery, return receipt requested, to any address on the record; or

(3) If the current address of the person in possession of the property at the time of the seizure, owner, or interest holder is not known and is not on record as provided in paragraph (2) of this subsection or the name of the person in possession of the property at the time of the seizure, owner, or interest holder is not known, publish a copy of the notice of seizure once a week for two consecutive weeks in the legal organ for the county in which the seizure occurs.

(c)

(1) The owner or interest holder may serve a claim to the seized property within 30 days after being served or within 30 days after the second publication of the notice of seizure, whichever occurs last, by sending the claim to the state attorney by certified mail or statutory overnight delivery, return receipt requested.

(2) The claim shall be signed by the owner or interest holder and shall provide:

(A) The name of the claimant;

(B) The address at which the claimant resides;

(C) A description of the claimant's interest in the property;

(D) A description of the circumstances of the claimant's obtaining an interest in the property and, to the best of the claimant's knowledge, the date the claimant obtained the interest and the name of the person or entity that transferred the interest to the claimant;

(E) The nature of the relationship between the claimant and the person who possessed the property at the time of the seizure;

(F) A copy of any documentation in the claimant's possession supporting his or her claim; and

(G) Any additional facts supporting his or her claim.

(3) If any claim is served, even when the state attorney determines that the information provided by the claimant pursuant to paragraph (2) of this subsection is insufficient, the state attorney shall file a complaint for forfeiture as provided in Code Section 9-16-12 or 9-16-13 within 30 days of the actual receipt of the claim. Such complaint shall be filed specifically as to the property claimed and the state attorney shall join as a party any person who serves the state attorney with a claim.

(4) As to any property to which no claim is received within 30 days after service of the notice of seizure or the second publication of the notice of seizure, whichever occurs last, all right, title, and interest in the property shall be forfeited to the state by operation of law and the state attorney shall dispose of the property as provided in Code Section 9-16-19. The state attorney shall serve a copy of the order forfeiting the property by first-class mail upon any person who was served with a notice of seizure.

Added by 2015 Ga. Laws 98,§ 1-1, eff. 7/1/2015.

Section 9-16-12 - In rem forfeiture

(a) In actions in rem, the property which is the subject of the complaint for forfeiture shall be named as the defendant. The complaint shall be verified on oath or affirmation by a duly authorized agent of the state in a manner consistent with Article 5 of Chapter 10 of this title. Such complaint shall describe the property with reasonable particularity; state that it is located within the county or will be located within the county during the pendency of the action; state its present custodian; state the name of the owner or interest holder, if known; allege the essential elements of the criminal violation which is claimed to exist; state the place of seizure, if the property was seized; and conclude with a prayer of due process to enforce the forfeiture.

(b)

(1) A copy of the complaint and summons shall be served on any person known to be an owner or interest holder and any person who is in possession of the property.

(2) Issuance of the summons, form of the summons, and service of the complaint and summons shall be as provided in subsections (a), (b), (c), and (e) of Code Section 9-11-4.

(3) If real property is the subject of the complaint for forfeiture or the owner or interest holder is unknown or resides out of this state or departs this state or cannot after due diligence be found within this state or conceals himself or herself so as to avoid service, a copy of the notice of the complaint for forfeiture shall be published once a week for two consecutive weeks in the legal organ of the county in which the complaint for forfeiture is pending. Such publication shall be deemed notice to any and all persons having an interest in or right affected by such complaint for forfeiture and from any sale of the property resulting therefrom, but shall not constitute notice to an interest holder unless that person is unknown or resides out of this state or departs this state or cannot after due diligence be found within this state or conceals himself or herself to avoid service.

(4) If tangible property which has not been seized is the subject of the complaint for forfeiture, the court may order the sheriff or another law enforcement officer to take possession of the property. If the character or situation of the property is such that the taking of actual possession is impracticable, the sheriff shall execute process by affixing a copy of the complaint and summons to the property in a conspicuous place and by leaving another copy of the complaint and summons with the person having possession or his or her agent. In cases involving a vessel or aircraft, the sheriff or other law enforcement officer shall be authorized to make a written request with the appropriate governmental agency not to permit the departure of such vessel or aircraft until notified by the sheriff or the sheriff's deputy that the vessel or aircraft has been released.

(c)

(1) An owner of or interest holder in the property may file an answer asserting a claim against the property in the action in rem. Any such answer shall be filed within 30 days after the service of the summons and complaint. If service is made by publication and personal service has not been made, an owner or interest holder shall file an answer within 30 days of the date of final publication. An answer shall be verified by the owner or interest holder under penalty of perjury. In addition to complying with the general rules applicable to filing an answer in civil actions as set forth in Article 3 of Chapter 11 of this title, the answer shall set forth:

(A) The name of the claimant;

(B) The address at which the claimant resides;

(C) A description of the claimant's interest in the property;

(D) A description of the circumstances of the claimant's obtaining an interest in the property and, to the best of the claimant's knowledge, the date the claimant obtained the interest and the name of the person or entity that transferred the interest to the claimant;

(E) The nature of the relationship between the claimant and the person who possessed the property at the time of the seizure;

(F) A copy of any documentation in the claimant's possession supporting his or her answer; and

(G) Any additional facts supporting the claimant's answer.

(2) If the state attorney determines that an answer is deficient in some manner, he or she may file a motion for a more definite statement. The motion shall point out the defects complained of and the details desired. If the motion is granted and the order of the court is not obeyed within 15 days after notice of the order, or within such other time as the court may fix, the court may strike the pleading to which the motion was directed or make such order as it deems just. If a motion for a more definite statement is filed, the time requirements for a trial set forth in subsection (f) of this Code section shall not commence until a sufficient answer has been filed.

(d) In addition to any injured person's right of intervention pursuant to Code Section 9-16-16, any owner or interest holder or person in possession of the property who suffers a pecuniary loss or physical injury due to a violation of Code Section 16-5-46, Article 4 or 5 of Chapter 8 of Title 16, or Chapter 14 of Title 16 may be permitted to intervene in any civil action brought pursuant to this Code section or Code Section 9-16-13 as provided by Chapter 11 of this title.

(e) If at the expiration of the period set forth in subsection (c) of this Code section no answer has been filed, the state attorney may seek a default judgment as provided in Code Section 9-11-55 and, if granted, the court shall order the disposition of the seized property as provided for in Code Section 9-16-19.

(f) If an answer is filed, a bench trial shall be held within 60 days after the last claimant was served with the complaint; provided, however, that such trial may be continued by the court for good cause shown. Discovery as provided for in Article 5 of Chapter 11 of this title shall not be allowed; however, prior to trial, any party may apply to the court to allow for such discovery, and if discovery is allowed, the court may provide for the scope and duration of discovery and may continue the trial to a date not more than 60 days after the end of the discovery period unless continued by the court for good cause shown.

(g) An action in rem may be brought by the state attorney in addition to or in lieu of any other in rem or in personam action brought pursuant to this chapter.

Added by 2015 Ga. Laws 98,§ 1-1, eff. 7/1/2015.

Section 9-16-13 - In personam forfeiture

(a) In actions in personam, the complaint shall be verified on oath or affirmation by a duly authorized agent of the state in a manner consistent with Article 5 of Chapter 10 of this title. The complaint shall:

(1) Describe with reasonable particularity the property which is sought to be forfeited;

(2) State the property's present custodian;

(3) State the name of the owner or interest holder, if known;

(4) Allege the essential elements of the criminal violation which is claimed to exist;

(5) State the place of seizure, if the property was seized; and

(6) Conclude with a prayer of due process to enforce the forfeiture.

(b) Service of the complaint and summons shall be as follows:

(1) Except as otherwise provided in this Code section, issuance of the summons, form of the summons, and service of the complaint and summons shall be as provided by subsections (a), (b), (c), and (d) of Code Section 9-11-4; and

(2) If the defendant is unknown or resides out of this state or departs this state or cannot after due diligence be found within this state or conceals himself or herself so as to avoid service, notice of the complaint for forfeiture shall be published once a week for two consecutive weeks in the legal organ of the county in which the complaint for forfeiture is pending. Such publication shall be deemed sufficient notice to any such defendant.

(c) A defendant shall file a verified answer within 30 days after the service of the summons and complaint. If service is made by publication and personal service has not been made, a defendant shall file such answer within 30 days of the date of final publication. In addition to complying with the general rules applicable to filing an answer in civil actions as set forth in Article 3 of Chapter 11 of this title, the answer shall contain all of the elements set forth in subsection (c) of Code Section 9-16-12. If the state attorney determines that an answer is deficient in some manner, he or she may file a motion for a more definite statement. The motion shall point out the defects complained of and the details desired. If the motion is granted and the order of the court is not obeyed within 15 days after notice of the order, or within such other time as the court may fix, the court may strike the pleading to which the motion was directed or make such order as it deems just. If a motion for a more definite statement is filed, the time requirements for a trial set forth in subsection (f) of this Code section shall not commence until a sufficient answer has been filed.

(d) In addition to any injured person's right of intervention pursuant to Code Section 9-16-16, any owner or interest holder or person in possession of the property who suffers a pecuniary loss or physical injury due to a violation of Code Section 16-5-46, Article 4 or 5 of Chapter 8 of Title 16, or Chapter 14 of Title 16 may be permitted to intervene in any civil action brought pursuant to this Code section or Code Section 9-16-12 as provided by Chapter 11 of this title.

(e) If at the expiration of the period set forth in subsection (c) of this Code section no answer has been filed, the state attorney may seek a default judgment as provided in Code Section 9-11-55 and, if granted, the court shall order the disposition of the seized property as provided for in Code Section 9-16-19.

(f) If an answer is filed, a bench trial shall be held within 60 days after the last claimant was served with the complaint; provided, however, that such trial may be continued by the court for good cause shown. Discovery as provided for in Article 5 of Chapter 11 of this title shall not be allowed; however, prior to trial any party may apply to the court to allow for such discovery, and if discovery is allowed, the court may provide for the scope and duration of discovery and may continue the trial to a date not more than 60 days after the end of the discovery period unless continued by the court for good cause shown.

(g) On a determination of liability of a person for conduct giving rise to forfeiture, the court shall enter a judgment of forfeiture of the property described in the complaint and shall also authorize the state attorney or his or her agent or any law enforcement officer or peace officer to seize all property ordered to be forfeited which was not previously seized or was not then under seizure. Following the entry of an order declaring the property forfeited, the court, on application of the state attorney, may enter any appropriate order to protect the interest of the state in the property ordered to be forfeited.

Added by 2015 Ga. Laws 98,§ 1-1, eff. 7/1/2015.

Section 9-16-14 - Restraining order, injunction, and other measures to seize, maintain, or preserve property; hearing

In conjunction with any civil forfeiture proceeding or criminal proceeding involving forfeiture:

(1) The court, upon application of the state attorney, may enter any restraining order or injunction; require the execution of satisfactory performance bonds; appoint receivers, conservators, appraisers, accountants, or trustees; or take any action to seize, secure, maintain, or preserve the availability of property subject to forfeiture, including issuing a warrant for its seizure and writ of attachment, whether before or after the filing of a complaint for forfeiture;

(2) A temporary restraining order under this Code section may be entered on application of the state attorney, without notice or an opportunity for a hearing, if the state attorney demonstrates that:

(A) There is probable cause to believe that the property subject to the order, in the event of final judgment or conviction, would be subject to forfeiture; and

(B) Provision of notice would jeopardize the availability of the property for forfeiture;

(3) Notice of the entry of a restraining order and an opportunity for a hearing shall be afforded to persons known to have an interest in the property. The hearing shall be held at the earliest possible date consistent with subsection (b) of Code Section 9-11-65 and shall be limited to the issues of whether:

(A) There is a probability that the state will prevail on the issue of forfeiture and that failure to enter the order will result in the property's being destroyed, conveyed, encumbered, removed from the jurisdiction of the court, concealed, or otherwise made unavailable for forfeiture; and

(B) The need to preserve the availability of the property through the entry of the requested order outweighs the hardship on any owner or interest holder against whom the order is to be entered;

(4) If property is seized for forfeiture or a forfeiture lien is filed without a previous judicial determination of probable cause or order of forfeiture or a hearing under paragraph (2) of this Code section, the court, on an application filed by an owner of or interest holder in the property within 30 days after notice of its seizure or forfeiture lien or actual knowledge of such seizure or lien, whichever is earlier, and complying with the requirements for an answer to an in rem complaint, and after five days' notice to the district attorney of the judicial circuit where the property was seized or, in the case of a forfeiture lien, to the state attorney filing such lien, may issue an order to show cause to the state attorney and seizing law enforcement agency for a hearing on the sole issue of whether probable cause for forfeiture of the property then exists. The hearing shall be held within 30 days unless continued for good cause on motion of either party. If the court finds that there is no probable cause for forfeiture of the property, the property shall be released. In determining probable cause, the court shall apply the rules of evidence; provided, however, that hearsay shall be admissible; and

(5) The court may order property that has been seized for forfeiture to be sold to satisfy a specified interest of any interest holder, on motion of any party, and after notice and a hearing, on the conditions that:

(A) The interest holder has filed a proper claim and has an interest that the state attorney has stipulated is exempt from forfeiture, provided that if the interest holder is a financial institution, it is also authorized to do business in this state and is under the jurisdiction of a governmental agency which regulates financial institutions, securities, insurance, or real estate;

(B) The interest holder shall dispose of the property by commercially reasonable public sale and apply the income first to its interest and then to its reasonable expenses incurred in connection with the sale or disposal; and

(C) The balance of the income, if any, shall be returned to the actual or constructive custody of the court, in an interest bearing account, subject to further proceedings under this chapter.

Added by 2015 Ga. Laws 98,§ 1-1, eff. 7/1/2015.

Section 9-16-15 - Stay of civil forfeiture proceedings during pendency of criminal proceedings; effect of criminal conviction

(a) For good cause shown by the state or the owner or interest holder of the property, the court may stay civil forfeiture proceedings during the pendency of criminal proceedings resulting from a related indictment or accusation until such time as the criminal proceedings result in a plea of guilty, a conviction after trial, or an acquittal after trial or are otherwise concluded before the trial court.

(b) An acquittal or dismissal in a criminal proceeding shall not preclude civil forfeiture proceedings.

(c) A defendant convicted in any criminal proceeding shall be precluded from later denying the essential allegations of the criminal offense of which the defendant was convicted in any civil forfeiture proceeding against such defendant pursuant to this chapter, regardless of the pendency of an appeal from that conviction; provided, however, that the evidence of the pendency of an appeal shall be admissible. For the purposes of this subsection, the term "conviction" means the result from a verdict or plea of guilty, including a plea of nolo contendere.

Added by 2015 Ga. Laws 98,§ 1-1, eff. 7/1/2015.

Section 9-16-16 - Recovery by an injured person

(a) As used in this Code section, the term "injured person" means any person who suffers a pecuniary loss or physical injury due to a violation of Code Section 16-5-46, Article 4 or 5 of Chapter 8 of Title 16, or Chapter 14 of Title 16. In the event that such person is a child or deceased, the provisions of subparagraphs (B) and (C) of paragraph (11) of Code Section 17-17-3 shall apply.

(b) If an injured person has provided contact information pursuant to Chapter 17 of Title 17, a state attorney shall serve every known injured person, if he or she has not previously been served, with a copy of the complaint for forfeiture and a notice of such person's right of intervention at least 30 days prior to the entry of a final judgment.

(c) Notwithstanding the distribution of forfeiture proceeds as set forth in Code Section 9-16-19, any injured person shall have a right or claim to forfeited property or to the proceeds superior to any right or claim the state or local government has in the same property or proceeds other than for costs. To enforce such a claim, the injured person must intervene in the civil forfeiture proceeding prior to the entry of a final judgment.

Added by 2015 Ga. Laws 98,§ 1-1, eff. 7/1/2015.

Section 9-16-17 - Burden of proof and presumptions

(a)

(1) The state's burden of proof shall be to show by a preponderance of the evidence that seized property is subject to forfeiture.

(2) A property interest shall not be subject to forfeiture under this chapter if the owner of the interest or interest holder establishes that the owner or interest holder:

(A) Is not privy to criminal conduct giving rise to its forfeiture;

(B) Did not consent to the conduct giving rise to the forfeiture;

(C) Did not know of the conduct giving rise to the forfeiture;

(D) Did not know the conduct giving rise to the forfeiture was likely to occur;

(E) Should not have reasonably known the conduct giving rise to the forfeiture was likely to occur;

(F) Had not acquired and did not stand to acquire substantial proceeds from the conduct giving rise to its forfeiture other than as an interest holder in an arm's length commercial transaction;

(G) With respect to conveyances for transportation only, did not hold the property jointly, in common, or in community with a person whose conduct gave rise to the forfeiture;

(H) Does not hold the property for the benefit of or as nominee for any person whose conduct gave rise to its forfeiture, and, if the owner or interest holder acquired the interest through any such person, the owner or interest holder acquired it as a bona fide purchaser for value without knowingly taking part in an illegal transaction; and

(I) Acquired the interest:

111

(i) Before the completion of the conduct giving rise to its forfeiture and the person whose conduct gave rise to its forfeiture did not have the authority to convey the interest to a bona fide purchaser for value at the time of the conduct; or

(ii) After the completion of the conduct giving rise to its forfeiture:

(I) As a bona fide purchaser for value without knowingly taking part in an illegal transaction;

(II) Before the filing of a forfeiture lien on it and before the effective date of a notice of pending forfeiture relating to it and without notice of its seizure for forfeiture; and

(III) At the time the interest was acquired, was reasonably without cause to believe that the property was subject to forfeiture or likely to become subject to forfeiture.

(b) There shall be a rebuttable presumption that any property of a person is subject to forfeiture under this chapter if the state attorney establishes by a preponderance of the evidence that:

(1) The person has engaged in conduct giving rise to forfeiture;

(2) The property was acquired by the person during the period of the conduct giving rise to forfeiture or within a reasonable time after such period; and

(3) There was no likely source for the property other than the conduct giving rise to forfeiture.

Added by 2015 Ga. Laws 98,§ 1-1, eff. 7/1/2015.

Section 9-16-18 - Forfeited property vests in state at time conduct giving rise to forfeiture committed; release of property upon entry of judgment in favor of owner

(a) All property declared to be forfeited vests in the state at the time of commission of the conduct giving rise to forfeiture together with the proceeds of the property after that time. Any property or proceeds transferred later to any person remain subject to forfeiture and thereafter shall be ordered to be forfeited unless the transferee claims and establishes in a hearing under this chapter that the transferee is a bona fide purchaser for value and the transferee's interest is exempt under paragraph (2) of subsection (a) of Code Section 9-16-17.

(b) On entry of judgment for a person claiming an interest in the property that is subject to a civil forfeiture proceeding, the court shall order that the property or interest in the property be released or delivered promptly to that person free of liens and encumbrances.

Added by 2015 Ga. Laws 98,§ 1-1, eff. 7/1/2015.

Section 9-16-19 - Disposition of forfeited property; order of distribution; annual report

(a) As used in this Code section, the term:

(1) "Entity" means and includes, but shall not be limited to, a law enforcement agency, multijurisdictional task force, or office, agency, authority, department, commission, board, body, division, instrumentality, or institution of the state or any political subdivision.

(2) "Law enforcement agency" means a governmental unit of one or more persons employed full time or part time by the state, a state agency or department, or a political subdivision for the purposes of preventing and detecting crime and enforcing state laws or local ordinances, employees of which unit are authorized to make arrests for crimes or seize property while acting within the scope of their authority.

(3) "Multijurisdictional task force" means a cooperative law enforcement effort involving personnel from two or more law enforcement agencies who are employed by or acting under the authority of different governmental authorities.

(4) "Official law enforcement purpose" means expenditures associated with investigations; training; travel; the purchase, lease, maintenance, and improvement of equipment, law enforcement facilities, and detention facilities; capital improvements; victim assistance and witness assistance services; the costs of accounting, auditing, and tracking of expenditures for federally shared cash, proceeds, and tangible property; awards, museums, and memorials directly related to law enforcement; drug and gang education and awareness programs; the payment of matching funds for state or federal grant programs that enhance law enforcement services to the community or judicial circuit; and reimbursement to a governing authority for a pro rata share of the indirect costs incurred by the governing authority for a common or joint purpose benefiting the law enforcement agency and other local government agencies which are not readily assignable to any particular agency.

(5) "Official prosecutorial purpose" means expenditures associated with investigations; hearings; trials; appeals; forensic services; language interpreters or interpreters for the hearing impaired; travel expenses that conform to the provisions set forth in Code Sections 15-18-12 and 50-5B-5; training related to the official functions of the district attorney; the purchase, lease, maintenance, and improvement of equipment; victim assistance and witness assistance services; the payment of matching funds for state or federal grant programs that enhance prosecution, victim, or witness services to the community or judicial circuit; reimbursement to a governing authority for a pro rata share of the indirect costs incurred by the governing authority for a common or joint purpose benefiting the district attorney's office and other local government agencies which are not readily assignable to any particular agency; and the payment of salaries and benefits in conformity with subsection (e) of Code Section 15-18-19 and Code Section 15-18-20.1.

(6) "Prosecuting Attorneys' Council" means the Prosecuting Attorneys' Council of the State of Georgia.

(b) Whenever property is forfeited under this chapter, any property which is required by order of the court or by law to be destroyed or which is harmful to the public shall, when no longer needed for evidentiary purposes, be destroyed or forwarded to the Division of Forensic Sciences of the Georgia Bureau of Investigation or any other agency of state or local government for destruction or for any medical or scientific use not prohibited under the laws of this state or of the United States.

(c) When property, other than currency or real property, is forfeited under this chapter, the court may:

(1) Order the property to be sold, with the income from the sale to be distributed as provided in subsection (f) of this Code section; or

(2) Provide for the in-kind distribution of the property as provided for in subsection (f) of this Code section.

(d) When real property is forfeited, the court may appoint a person to act as the receiver of such property for the limited purpose of holding and transferring title and may order that:

(1) The title to the real property be placed in the name of the state;

(2) The title to the real property be placed in the name of the political subdivision which will be taking charge of such property. Such political subdivision shall then:

(A) Sell the property with such conditions as the court deems proper and distribute the income as provided in subsection (f) of this Code section; or

(B) Hold the property for use by one or more law enforcement agencies;

(3) The real property be turned over to an appropriate political subdivision without restrictions;

(4) The real property be deeded to a land bank authority as provided in Article 4 of Chapter 4 of Title 48; or

(5) The real property be disposed of in any commercially reasonable manner as the court deems proper.

(e) When property is to be sold pursuant to this Code section:

(1) The court may direct that such property be sold by:

(A) Judicial sale as provided in Article 7 of Chapter 13 of this title; provided, however, that the court may establish a minimum acceptable price for such property; or

(B) Any commercially feasible means, including, but not limited to, in the case of real property, listing such property with a licensed real estate broker, selected by a state attorney through competitive bids; and

(2) The income from such sale shall be paid into the registry of the court or deposited into an account as specified in paragraph (1) of subsection (c) of Code Section 9-16-10 as directed by the court.

(f)

(1) The state attorney shall submit a proposed order of distribution to the court and the court shall issue an order of distribution. Such order shall specify the time frame for the transfer of forfeited property and the entity responsible for effectuating the transfer of such property. The state attorney shall provide a copy of the order of distribution to any entity responsible for effectuating such transfer. The state attorney shall provide a copy of the order of distribution to the chief executive officer of each political subdivision whose law enforcement agency will receive a distribution pursuant to such order.

(2) All property forfeited in the same civil forfeiture proceeding shall be pooled together and a fair market value shall be assigned to each item of property other than currency in such pool. A total value shall be established for the pool by adding together the fair market value of all such property in the pool, the amount of currency in the pool, and any accrued interest.

(3)

(A) The first distribution from the pool shall be to pay costs and court costs to the entity incurring the costs or court costs.

(B) Except as provided in subparagraph (E) of this paragraph, the second distribution from the pool, upon the request of the district attorney, shall be 10 percent of such pool which shall be paid to the district attorney's office, in recognition of the district attorney's effort in completing the civil forfeiture proceeding, and shall be used by a district attorney for official prosecutorial purposes. Forfeited property and the sums held by a district attorney shall be in addition to the respective budgets of the state and the counties comprising the judicial circuit for a district attorney and shall not supplant such appropriations.

(C) Except as provided in subparagraph (E) of this paragraph, the third distribution from the pool shall be pro rata to law enforcement agencies and multijurisdictional task forces according to the role each law enforcement agency or multijurisdictional task force played in the seizure and forfeiture of the forfeited property up to the limits set forth in division (4)(A)(ii) of this subsection.

(D) If there remains currency in the pool after the distributions set forth in subparagraphs (A) through (C) of this paragraph, it may be distributed as further set forth in division (4)(A)(iii) or (4)(B)(ii) of this subsection, as applicable.

(E) If the civil forfeiture proceeding results from criminal conduct in violation of Article 11 of Chapter 1 of Title 7, Code Section 16-5-46, Article 5 of Chapter 8 of Title 16, or Chapter 14 of Title 16, after satisfaction of the interest of any innocent party, the court may make any division of the pool among the state, political subdivisions, or agencies or departments of the state or political subdivisions commensurate with the assistance each contributed to the underlying criminal prosecution or civil forfeiture proceeding, or both such actions.

(4) Property distribution shall be as follows:

(A) With respect to political subdivisions:

(i) Property distributed in kind to a political subdivision or multijurisdictional task force for use by an agency, department, or officer of a political subdivision for official law enforcement purposes shall be designated in the order of distribution and shall be titled accordingly; provided, however, that property may be distributed for other purposes to any other entity so long as such designation is made in the order of distribution and reported in accordance with subsection (g) of this Code section. If real property is distributed to a political subdivision, the political subdivision may transfer the real property to a land bank authority as provided in Article 4 of Chapter 4 of Title 48. When in-kind property is no longer needed by the recipient, it shall be disposed of in accordance with the political subdivision's policy and procedure;

(ii) Currency distributed to local law enforcement agencies or to multijurisdictional task forces shall be paid or credited to such agencies or task forces as provided in the order of distribution; provided, however, that such agency or task force shall not be eligible to receive more than 33 1/3 percent of the amount of local funds appropriated or otherwise made available to such agency or task force for the fiscal year in which such funds are distributed. Such currency may be used for any official law enforcement purpose at the discretion of the chief officer of the law enforcement agency receiving such distribution, provided that such distribution shall not be used to supplant any other local, state, or federal funds appropriated for staff or operations or to pay salaries or rewards to law enforcement personnel;

(iii) Currency not distributed pursuant to division (ii) of this subparagraph shall be expended for any official law enforcement purpose; for the representation of indigents in criminal cases; for drug treatment, mental health treatment, rehabilitation, prevention, or education or any other program which deters drug or substance abuse or responds to problems created by drug or

113

substance abuse; for use as matching funds for grant programs related to drug treatment or prevention; to fund victim assistance; or for any combination of the foregoing; and

(iv) When a chief officer of a law enforcement agency does not qualify as a candidate for reelection or has been defeated in any election, he or she shall not transfer any currency or property received due to civil forfeiture proceedings to any other entity prior to leaving office; provided, however, that he or she may continue to expend such currency or make use of such property for any official law enforcement purpose within his or her law enforcement agency; and

(B) With respect to the state:

(i) Property distributed in kind to the state for use by a state agency, officer of the state, or district attorney shall be designated in the order of distribution; provided, however, that property may be distributed for other purposes to any other entity so long as such designation is made in the order of distribution and reported in accordance with subsection (g) of this Code section. When a state agency, officer of the state, or district attorney determines that in-kind property is no longer needed by the recipient, it shall be delivered over to the Department of Administrative Services for such use or disposition as may be determined by the commissioner of administrative services;

(ii) Currency distributed to the state for use by a state agency, officer of the state, district attorney, or as further set forth in this division shall be paid as provided in the order of distribution. It is the intent of the General Assembly that the currency otherwise distributed to the state be used, subject to appropriation from the general fund in the manner provided by law, for funding of Article 2 of Chapter 12 of Title 17, the "Georgia Indigent Defense Act of 2003,' for representation of indigents in criminal cases; for funding of the Georgia Crime Victims Emergency Fund; for law enforcement and prosecution agency programs and particularly for funding of advanced drug investigation and prosecution training for law enforcement officers and prosecuting attorneys; for drug treatment, mental health treatment, rehabilitation, prevention, or education or any other program which deters drug or substance abuse or responds to problems created by drug or substance abuse; for use as matching funds for grant programs related to drug treatment or prevention; or for financing the judicial system of the state; and

(iii) When a district attorney does not qualify as a candidate for reelection or has been defeated in any election, he or she shall not transfer any currency or property received due to civil forfeiture proceedings to any other entity prior to leaving office; provided, however, that he or she may continue to expend such currency or make use of such property for any official prosecutorial purpose within his or her office.

(g)

(1) Property and proceeds forfeited pursuant to this chapter and any income resulting from the sale of forfeited property is government property. It is the intent of the General Assembly that there be accountability and transparency applicable to the distribution of forfeited property and income from the sale of forfeited property. The appropriate accounting and auditing standards shall be applicable to such distribution.

(2) Any law enforcement agency, multijurisdictional task force, district attorney, or state agency receiving property and proceeds forfeited pursuant to this chapter and any income resulting from the sale of forfeited property, including property distributed in kind, shall submit an annual report specifying the property and proceeds forfeited pursuant to this chapter and any income resulting from the sale of forfeited property received during its reporting year and shall clearly identify the use of such property, proceeds, and income, including the specifics of all monetary expenditures and funds on deposit with a financial institution. Such report shall not include any information that is likely to disclose the identity of a confidential source, disclose confidential investigative or prosecution material which could endanger the life or physical safety of any person, disclose the existence of a confidential surveillance or investigation, or disclose techniques and procedures for law enforcement investigations or prosecutions. Such annual report shall be appropriately completed and legible. Such report shall be:

(A) With respect to law enforcement agencies, multijurisdictional task forces, and state agencies:

(i) Submitted on a form promulgated by the Prosecuting Attorneys' Council, as provided in subparagraph (A) of paragraph (3) of this subsection;

(ii) Submitted by each local law enforcement agency to the political subdivision governing its jurisdiction;

(iii) Submitted by multijurisdictional task forces to each political subdivision governing the jurisdictions involved;

(iv) Submitted by state agencies to the state auditor;

(v) Submitted by January 31 each year for the previous calendar year; and

(vi) Copied and submitted to the Carl Vinson Institute of Government of the University of Georgia as provided in Code Section 36-80-21; and

(B) With respect to district attorneys:

(i) Submitted on a form promulgated by the Prosecuting Attorneys' Council, as provided in subparagraph (B) of paragraph (3) of this subsection;

(ii) Submitted by district attorneys to the Prosecuting Attorneys' Council according to the rules and regulations adopted by the Prosecuting Attorneys' Council;

(iii) Submitted to the state auditor;

(iv) Submitted by January 31 each year for the previous calendar year; and

(v) Copied and submitted to the Carl Vinson Institute of Government of the University of Georgia as provided in Code Section 36-80-21.

(3)

(A) The Prosecuting Attorneys' Council shall promulgate and from time to time amend as necessary and post on its website an annual reporting form for use by law enforcement agencies, multijurisdictional task forces, and state agencies to report the information required by this subsection. In creating this form, the Prosecuting Attorneys' Council shall consider input from the Georgia Peace Officer Standards and Training Council, the Georgia Sheriffs' Association, and the Georgia Association of Chiefs of Police. Such form shall include, but shall not be limited to, the following information:

(i) As to property, other than currency, an itemization specifying:

(I) The date the property was received by the entity;

(II) The make, model, and serial number, when relevant; provided, however, that such details shall not be required when such details would disclose the identification of property being used in a confidential investigation or would compromise an ongoing investigation;

(III) The statutes upon which the property was subject to forfeiture;

(IV) The estimated value of the property received;

(V) If the property was sold, the date of the sale and the gross and net income received;

(VI) If the property was retained, the purpose for which it was used; provided, however, that such details shall not be required when such details would disclose the identification of property being used in a confidential investigation or would compromise an ongoing investigation; and

(VII) If the property was destroyed, the date of the destruction;

(ii) As to currency, an itemization specifying:

(I) The amount of currency forfeited and the date the currency was received; and

(II) The statutes upon which the currency was subject to forfeiture;

(iii) If property was returned to an owner or interest holder, by the seizing law enforcement agency or in the order of distribution, a description of such property and date of return of such property;

(iv) The total for the reporting year of the amount of currency forfeited and net income from the sale of forfeited property which the entity received;

(v) A description of the use and expenditure of forfeited funds for the reporting year, specifying for each expenditure the amount expended and the purpose for which each expenditure was made; and

(vi) The total amount of forfeited currency held in a financial institution at the end of the reporting year, including the net income from the sale of forfeited property and interest earned.

(B) The Prosecuting Attorneys' Council shall promulgate and from time to time amend as necessary and post on its website an annual reporting form for district attorneys to use to report the information required by this subsection. In creating this form, the Prosecuting Attorneys' Council shall consider input from the District Attorneys' Association of Georgia. Such form shall include, but shall not be limited to, the following information:

(i) As to in-kind property received, an itemization specifying:

(I) The date the property was received;

(II) The make, model, and serial number, when relevant; provided, however, that such details shall not be required when such details would disclose the identification of property being used in a confidential investigation or would compromise an ongoing investigation;

(III) The statutes upon which the property was subject to forfeiture; and

(IV) A description of the purpose to which the property was put;

(ii) As to currency received, an itemization specifying:

(I) The amount of currency and the date the currency was received; and

(II) A description of the use and expenditure of forfeited currency for the reporting year, specifying for each expenditure the amount expended and the purpose for which each expenditure was made; and

(iii) The total amount of currency received by the district attorney during the reporting year and the amount remaining that has not been expended, including any interest earned.

(4) The annual report required by this subsection may be submitted electronically, provided the submission complies with Chapter 12 of Title 10.

(5)

(A) The district attorney having jurisdiction where the local law enforcement agency or multijurisdictional task force is located shall be authorized to conduct an investigation and bring any criminal prosecution or civil action he or she deems necessary to ensure compliance with this subsection. The district attorney shall provide an entity required to comply with the reporting requirements of this subsection and found to have committed a violation of this subsection 60 days to demonstrate to the district attorney that such entity has come into compliance with this subsection. If, after 60 days, the entity has failed to correct all deficiencies, such entity shall be prohibited from being eligible to receive property derived or resulting from civil forfeiture proceedings until such time as the entity demonstrates to the district attorney that such entity has corrected all deficiencies and is in compliance with this subsection; provided, however, that if the chief officer of the entity has resigned or has been removed from office, the prohibition shall not apply so long as his or her successor in office corrects all deficiencies within 180 days of taking office. At any time after the district attorney finds an entity to be in violation of this subsection, such entity may seek administrative relief through the Office of State Administrative Hearings. If an entity seeks administrative relief, the time for correcting deficiencies shall be tolled, and any action to exclude the entity from receiving property derived or resulting from civil forfeiture proceedings shall be suspended until such time as a final ruling upholding the findings of the district attorney is issued.

(B) If the district attorney is disqualified from conducting any investigation under this paragraph, the district attorney shall notify the Attorney General in accordance with Code Section 15-18-5.

(6) If an audit concludes that a district attorney has used property in violation of this Code section and the auditor notifies the district attorney of such violation, he or she shall take appropriate action to remedy the audit's findings and repay or redistribute property improperly used. If the district attorney fails to remedy the audit's findings within 60 days of such notification, the auditor shall notify the Attorney General for further legal action.

(7) Any person who knowingly and willfully makes a false, fictitious, or fraudulent annual report pursuant to this subsection shall be guilty of a violation of Code Section 16-10-20 and, upon conviction, shall be punished as provided in such Code section. Any entity that employed a person convicted of false statements based on a violation of this subsection shall be prohibited from being eligible to receive property derived or resulting from civil forfeiture proceedings for a period of two years commencing from the date of such conviction, unless such entity no longer employs such person.

Added by 2015 Ga. Laws 98,§ 1-1, eff. 7/1/2015.

Section 9-16-20 - Court may order forfeiture of other property under certain circumstances; civil action; enforcement of judgments; persons having interest in property barred from collaterally attacking forfeiture proceedings; limitations

(a) The court shall order the forfeiture of any property of a claimant or defendant up to the value of property found by the court to be subject to forfeiture if any of the forfeited property:

(1) Cannot be located;

(2) Has been transferred or conveyed to, sold to, or deposited with a third party;

(3) Is beyond the jurisdiction of the court;

(4) Has been substantially diminished in value while not in the actual physical custody of the receiver or governmental agency directed to maintain custody of the property; or

(5) Has been commingled with other property that cannot be divided without difficulty.

(b) In addition to any other remedy provided for by law, a state attorney on behalf of the state may institute a civil action in any court of the United States against any person acting with knowledge or any person to whom notice of a forfeiture lien has been provided in accordance with Code Section 9-16-8; to whom notice of seizure has been provided in accordance with Code Section 9-16-11; or to whom notice of a civil forfeiture proceeding has been provided, if property subject to forfeiture is conveyed, alienated, disposed of, or otherwise rendered unavailable for forfeiture after the filing of a forfeiture lien, filing of a complaint for forfeiture pursuant to Code Section 9-16-12 or 9-16-13, or the service of a notice of seizure pursuant to Code Section 9-16-11, as the case may be. The state may recover judgment in an amount equal to the value of the forfeiture lien but not to exceed the fair market value of the property or, if there is no forfeiture lien, in an amount not to exceed the fair market value of the property, together with reasonable investigative expenses and attorney's fees.

(c) A state attorney may file and prosecute in any of the courts of the United States or as may be necessary to enforce any judgment rendered pursuant to this chapter.

(d) No person claiming an interest in property subject to forfeiture may commence or maintain any civil action concerning the validity of the alleged interest other than as provided in this chapter. No person claiming an interest in property subject to forfeiture may file any counterclaim or cross-claim to any action brought pursuant to this chapter. Except as specifically authorized by subsection (d) of Code Section 9-16-12, subsection (d) of Code Section 9-16-13, or Code Section 9-16-16, providing for intervention, no person claiming an interest in such property may intervene in any civil forfeiture proceeding.

(e) A civil forfeiture proceeding shall be commenced within four years after the last conduct giving rise to forfeiture or to the claim for relief became known or should have become known, excluding any time during which either the property or defendant is out of the state or in confinement or during which criminal proceedings relating to the same conduct are in progress.

Added by 2015 Ga. Laws 98,§ 1-1, eff. 7/1/2015.

Section 9-16-21 - Effect of federal law forfeitures; annual report

(a) Property seized or forfeited pursuant to federal law, and such property or proceeds, authorized by such federal law to be transferred to a cooperating law enforcement agency of this state or any political subdivision thereof shall be utilized by the law enforcement agency or political subdivision to which the property or proceeds are so transferred as authorized by such federal law and regulations or guidelines promulgated thereunder. If federal law and regulations or guidelines promulgated thereunder are silent as to the utilization of such property or proceeds, the property and proceeds shall be disposed of and utilized as set forth in Code Section 9-16-19.

(b) Any law enforcement agency receiving property or proceeds pursuant to federal law shall also comply with subsection (g) of Code Section 9-16-19.

Added by 2015 Ga. Laws 98,§ 1-1, eff. 7/1/2015.

Section 9-16-22 - Construction

This chapter shall be liberally construed to effectuate its remedial purposes.

Added by 2015 Ga. Laws 98,§ 1-1, eff. 7/1/2015.

Chapter 17 - GEORGIA UNIFORM MEDIATION ACT

Section 9-17-1 - Definitions

As used in this chapter, the term:

(1) "Mediation" means a process in which a mediator facilitates communication and negotiation between parties to assist them in reaching a voluntary agreement regarding their dispute.

(2) "Mediation communication" means a statement, whether oral or in a record or verbal or nonverbal, that occurs during a mediation or is made for purposes of considering, conducting, participating in, initiating, continuing, terminating, or reconvening a mediation or retaining a mediator.

(3) "Mediation party" means a person that participates in a mediation and whose agreement is necessary to resolve the dispute.

(4) "Mediator" means an individual who conducts a mediation, or if conducting a mediation pursuant to the Supreme Court of Georgia Alternative Dispute Resolution Rules governing the use of alternative dispute resolution mechanisms by the courts of this state, an individual qualified to mediate under such rules.

(5) "Nonparty participant" means a person, other than a mediation party or mediator, that participates in a mediation, including a representative of a party.

(6) "Person" means an individual, corporation, business trust, estate, trust, partnership, limited liability company, association, joint venture, government; governmental subdivision, agency, or instrumentality; public corporation; or any other legal or commercial entity.

(7) "Proceeding" means:

    (A) A judicial, administrative, arbitral, or other adjudicative process, including related pre-hearing and post-hearing motions, conferences, and discovery; or

    (B) A legislative hearing or similar process.

(8) "Record" means information that is inscribed on a tangible medium or that is stored in an electronic or other medium and is retrievable in perceivable form.

(9) "Sign" means:

    (A) To execute or adopt a tangible symbol with the present intent to authenticate a record; or

    (B) To attach or logically associate an electronic symbol, sound, or process to or with a record with the present intent to authenticate a record.

Added by 2021 Ga. Laws 268,§ 2, eff. 7/1/2021.

Section 9-17-2 - Application

(a) Except as otherwise provided in subsection (b) or (c) of this Code section, this chapter applies to a mediation in which:

    (1) The mediation parties are required to mediate by statute or court or administrative agency rule or referred to mediation by a court, administrative agency, or arbitrator;

    (2) The mediation parties and the mediator agree to mediate in a record that demonstrates an expectation that mediation communications will be privileged against disclosure; or

    (3) The mediation parties use as a mediator an individual who holds himself or herself out as a mediator or as a provider of mediation services.

(b) This chapter shall not apply to a mediation:

    (1) Relating to the establishment, negotiation, administration, or termination of a collective bargaining relationship;

    (2) Relating to a dispute that is pending under or is part of the processes established by a collective bargaining agreement, except that this chapter shall apply to a mediation arising out of such a dispute that has been filed with an administrative agency or court;

    (3) Conducted by a judge where that judge acts as a mediator and may still make a ruling on the dispute; or

    (4) Conducted under the auspices of:

        (A) A primary or secondary school if all the mediation parties are students; or

        (B) A correctional institution for persons who are under the age of 18 years if all the mediation parties are residents of that institution.

(c) If the parties agree in advance in a signed record, or a record of proceeding reflects agreement by the parties, that all or part of a mediation is not privileged, the privileges under Code Sections 9-17-3 through 9-17-5 do not apply to the mediation or part agreed upon. However, Code Sections 9-17-3 through 9-17-5 apply to a mediation communication made by a person that has not received actual notice of the agreement before the communication is made.

Added by 2021 Ga. Laws 268,§ 2, eff. 7/1/2021.

Section 9-17-3 - Mediation communication as privileged; use of mediation evidence

(a) Except as otherwise provided in Code Section 9-17-6, a mediation communication is privileged as provided in subsection (b) of this Code section and is not subject to discovery or admissible in evidence in a proceeding unless waived or precluded as provided by Code Section 9-17-4.

(b) In a proceeding, the following privileges apply:

    (1) A mediation party may refuse to disclose and may prevent any other person from disclosing a mediation communication;

    (2) A mediator may refuse to disclose a mediation communication and may prevent any other person from disclosing a mediation communication of the mediator; and

    (3) A nonparty participant may refuse to disclose and may prevent any other person from disclosing a mediation communication of the nonparty participant.

(c) Evidence or information that is otherwise admissible or subject to discovery does not become inadmissible or protected from discovery solely by reason of its disclosure or use in a mediation.

Added by 2021 Ga. Laws 268,§ 2, eff. 7/1/2021.

Section 9-17-4 - Waiver of privilege; criminal activity

(a) A privilege under Code Section 9-17-3 may be waived in a record if it is expressly waived by all mediation parties and:

    (1) In the case of the privilege of a mediator, it is expressly waived by the mediator; and

    (2) In the case of the privilege of a nonparty participant, it is expressly waived by the nonparty participant.

(b) A person that discloses or makes a representation about a mediation communication which prejudices another person in a proceeding is precluded from asserting a privilege under Code Section 9-17-3, but only to the extent necessary for the person prejudiced to respond to the representation or disclosure.

(c) A person that intentionally uses a mediation to plan, attempt to commit or commit a crime, or to conceal an ongoing crime or ongoing criminal activity is precluded from asserting a privilege under Code Section 9-17-3.

Added by 2021 Ga. Laws 268,§ 2, eff. 7/1/2021.

Section 9-17-5 - When communication privilege is inapplicable; use of mediation evidence

(a) There shall be no privilege under Code Section 9-17-3 for a mediation communication that is:

    (1) In an agreement evidenced by a record signed by all parties to the agreement;

    (2) Available to the public under Article 4 of Chapter 18 of Title 50, relating to open records, or made during a session of a mediation which is open, or is required by law to be open, to the public;

    (3) A threat or statement of a plan to inflict bodily injury or commit a criminal act of violence;

(4) Intentionally used to plan a criminal act, to commit or attempt to commit a criminal act, or to conceal an ongoing criminal act or criminal activity;

(5) Sought or offered to prove or disprove a claim or complaint of professional misconduct or malpractice filed against a mediator;

(6) Except as otherwise provided in subsection (c) of this Code section, sought or offered to prove or disprove a claim or complaint of professional misconduct or malpractice filed against a mediation party, nonparty participant, or representative of a party based on conduct occurring during a mediation; or

(7) Sought or offered to prove or disprove abuse, neglect, abandonment, or exploitation in a proceeding in which a child or adult protective services agency is a party, unless the public agency participates in the Division of Family and Children Services mediation.

(b) There shall be no privilege under Code Section 9-17-3 if a court, administrative agency, or arbitrator finds, after a hearing in camera, that the party seeking discovery or the proponent of the evidence has shown that the evidence is not otherwise available, that there is a need for the evidence that substantially outweighs the interest in protecting confidentiality, and that the mediation communication is sought or offered in:

(1) A court proceeding involving a felony; or

(2) Except as otherwise provided in subsection (c) of this Code section, a proceeding to prove a claim to rescind or reform or a defense to avoid liability on a contract arising out of the mediation.

(c) A mediator shall not be compelled to provide evidence of a mediation communication referred to in paragraph (6) of subsection (a) or paragraph (2) of subsection (b) of this Code section.

(d) If a mediation communication is not privileged under subsection (a) or (b) of this Code section, only the portion of the communication necessary for the application of the exception from nondisclosure may be admitted. Admission of evidence under subsection (a) or (b) of this Code section does not render the evidence, or any other mediation communication, discoverable or admissible for any other purpose.

Added by 2021 Ga. Laws 268,§ 2, eff. 7/1/2021.

Section 9-17-6 - Limited disclosures by mediators

(a) Except as provided in subsection (b) of this Code section, a mediator shall not make a report, assessment, evaluation, recommendation, finding, or other communication regarding a mediation to a court, administrative agency, or other authority that may make a ruling on the dispute that is the subject of the mediation.

(b) A mediator may disclose:

(1) Whether the mediation occurred or has terminated, whether a settlement was reached, and attendance;

(2) A mediation communication as permitted under Code Section 9-17-5; or

(3) A mediation communication evidencing abuse, neglect, abandonment, or exploitation of an individual to a public agency responsible for protecting individuals against such mistreatment.

(c) A communication made in violation of subsection (a) of this Code section may not be considered by a court, administrative agency, or arbitrator.

Added by 2021 Ga. Laws 268,§ 2, eff. 7/1/2021.

Section 9-17-7 - Limited disclosures of mediation and mediation communications

Notwithstanding any provision of this chapter to the contrary, mediation and mediation communications, and such related conduct, shall not be admissible or subject to disclosure, except to the extent agreed to by the parties in writing or as provided in Code Section 24-4-408 or other law or court required rule of this state, unless such communications are subject to Article 4 of Chapter 18 of Title 50, relating to open records.

Added by 2021 Ga. Laws 268,§ 2, eff. 7/1/2021.

Section 9-17-8 - Review of mediator's conflict of interest; required disclosures by mediator; exclusion; special qualifications not required

(a) Before accepting a mediation, an individual who is requested to serve as a mediator shall:

(1) Make an inquiry that is reasonable under the circumstances to determine whether there are any known facts that a reasonable individual would consider likely to affect the impartiality of the mediator, including a financial or personal interest in the outcome of the mediation and an existing or past relationship with a mediation party or foreseeable participant in the mediation; and

(2) Disclose any such known fact to the mediation parties as soon as is practical before accepting a mediation.

(b) If a mediator learns any fact described in paragraph (1) of subsection (a) of this Code section after accepting a mediation, the mediator shall disclose it as soon as is practicable.

(c) At the request of a mediation party, an individual who is requested to serve as a mediator shall disclose the mediator's qualifications to mediate a dispute.

(d) A person that violates subsection (a) or (b) of this Code section is precluded by the violation from asserting a privilege under Code Section 9-17-3.

(e) Subsection (a), (b), or (c) of this Code section shall not apply to an individual acting as a judge.

(f) This chapter shall not require that a mediator have a special qualification by background or profession.

Added by 2021 Ga. Laws 268,§ 2, eff. 7/1/2021.

Section 9-17-9 - Participation with attorney or designated representative

An attorney or other individual designated by a party may accompany the party to and participate in a mediation. A waiver of participation given before the mediation may be rescinded.

Added by 2021 Ga. Laws 268,§ 2, eff. 7/1/2021.

Section 9-17-10 - Application of federal Model Law

(a) As used in this Code section, the term "Model Law" means the Model Law on International Commercial Mediation and International Settlement Agreements Resulting from Mediation, as approved at the 51st Session of the United Nations Commission on International Trade Law on June 26, 2018.

(b) Except as otherwise provided in subsections (c) and (d) of this Code section, if a mediation is an international commercial mediation as defined by the Model Law, the mediation is governed by the Model Law.

(c) Unless the parties agree in accordance with subsection (c) of Code Section 9-17-2, that all or part of an international commercial mediation is not privileged, Code Sections 9-17-3, 9-17-4, and 9-17-5 and any applicable definitions in Code Section 9-17-1 also apply to the mediation and nothing in Article 11 of the Model Law derogates from Code Sections 9-17-3, 9-17-4, and 9-17-5.

(d) If the parties to an international commercial mediation agree that the Model Law shall not apply, this chapter shall apply.

Added by 2021 Ga. Laws 268,§ 2, eff. 7/1/2021.

Section 9-17-11 - Application of federal Electronic Signatures in Global and National Commerce Act

This chapter modifies, limits, or supersedes the federal Electronic Signatures in Global and National Commerce Act, 15 U.S.C. Section 7001, et seq., but shall not modify, limit, or supersede Section 101(c) of such act or authorize electronic delivery of any of the notices described in Section 103(b) of such act.

Added by 2021 Ga. Laws 268,§ 2, eff. 7/1/2021.

Section 9-17-12 - Uniformity across jurisdictions

In applying and construing this chapter, consideration should be given to the need to promote uniformity of the law with respect to its subject matter among states that enact it.

Added by 2021 Ga. Laws 268,§ 2, eff. 7/1/2021.

Section 9-17-13 - Severability

If any provision of this chapter or its application to any person or circumstance is held invalid, the invalidity shall not affect other provisions or applications of this chapter which can be given effect without the invalid provision or application, and to this end the provisions of this chapter are severable.

Added by 2021 Ga. Laws 268,§ 2, eff. 7/1/2021.

Section 9-17-14 - Applicability

This chapter shall apply to all mediation agreements and mediation proceedings entered into on or after July 1, 2021.

Added by 2021 Ga. Laws 268,§ 2, eff. 7/1/2021.

Made in United States
Orlando, FL
13 February 2024